Postlingually Acquired Deafness

Trends in Linguistics

Studies and Monographs 62

Editor

Werner Winter

Mouton de Gruyter
Berlin · New York

Postlingually Acquired Deafness

Speech Deterioration
and the Wider Consequences

by
Roddy Cowie
Ellen Douglas-Cowie

Mouton de Gruyter
Berlin · New York 1992

RF
293.4
.C69
1992

Mouton de Gruyter (formerly Mouton, The Hague)
is a Division of Walter de Gruyter & Co., Berlin.

♾ Printed on acid-free paper which falls within the guidelines
of the ANSI to ensure permanence and durability.

Library of Congress Cataloging in Publication Data

Cowie, Roddy, 1950–
    Postlingually acquired deafness : speech deterioration and
the wider consequences / by Roddy Cowie, Ellen Douglas-
Cowie.
        p.   cm. – (Trends in linguistics. Studies and mono-
graphs ; 62)
    Includes bibliographical references and index.
    ISBN 3-11-012575-7 (cloth : alk. paper)
    1. Postlingual deafness. 2. Postlingual deafness – Com-
plications. 3. Speech disorders. I. Douglas-Cowie, Ellen,
1951– II. Title. III. Series.
    [DNLM: 1. Deafness – complications. 2. Speech Disorders.
WV 270 C874p]
RF293.4.069   1992   92-12793
617.8 – dc20   CIP

Die Deutsche Bibliothek — Cataloging in Publication Data

Cowie, Roddy:
Postlingually acquired deafness : speech deterioration and the
wider consequences / by Roddy Cowie ; Ellen Douglas-Cowie.
– Berlin ; New York : Mouton de Gruyter, 1992
    (Trends in linguistics : Studies and monographs ; 62)
    ISBN 3-11-012575-7
NE: Douglas-Cowie, Ellen:; Trends in linguistics / Studies and
monographs

Typesetting: Satzpunkt, Braunschweig. – Printing: Gerike GmbH, Berlin. –
Binding: Lüderitz & Bauer, Berlin. –
Printed in Germany

This book is dedicated to
Dorothy and Christopher

Acknowledgements

Many people have contributed to the work reported here apart from those who are cited as co-authors, but particular acknowledgements are due to the following. Among the deafened people who helped us we have particular debts to Ian Cowie, Wesley Kerr, Christine Kerr, Bob McCullough, Evelyn McCullough, Alice McWilliams, Bernie Smyth, Howard Stone, and representatives of the National Association of Deafened People. The work depended on cooperation from those who provide services to deafened people, especially David Adams, George Grindle, Mary Mitchell, Kathleen Rice and Brian Symington. We re-ceived help of many forms from academic colleagues, notably Lorraine Gailey, Mark Haggard, David Hale, Harlan Lane, Carol McGuinness, Ann Moriarty, Billy Neil, Lindsay Patterson, Joe Perkell, Geoff Plant, Paul Quigley, Carol Sherrard, Gabrielle Semrau, and Karen Trew. Many students did work with us which made significant contribu-tions: Frances Beagon, Linda Boyd, Adrienne Brankin, Colette Davison, Michaela McDade, Sheelagh McKenna, Patricia Nicholl, Clare Sweeney, and John Wonnacott. Last but not least, we acknowledge the financial support provided by the Economic and Social Research Council of Great Britain, the Royal National Institute for the Deaf, the Trustees of Clive and Vera Ramaciotti, the Ulster Institute for the Deaf, The Wellcome Trust, and our employer the Queen's University of Belfast.

Contents

Chapter 1
Acquired deafness: an overview

Deafness is due to a disorder of the ears, but its repercussions spread throughout a person's life. Other people who are closely involved are often affected too.

The central concern of this book is one repercussion of hearing loss: that is, the deterioration of speech which can follow when someone loses his or her hearing. We describe research on that problem which was carried out in Belfast between 1980 and 1990. However our approach is rooted in the belief that hearing loss needs to be seen in its totality. To strip away one aspect of the problem from others is to risk misunderstanding it, because in reality the various repercussions of hearing loss interact. At the very least, it is essential to realise that hearing loss imposes a multitude of difficulties. The combination can be overwhelming even when no one of them on its own would be a major burden. So although we focus on speech deterioration, we want to present it as part of the overall problem that deafened people face. In a nutshell, that problem is being able to interact in a full and satisfying way with other human beings.

This chapter sets the scene by outlining the main ways in which hearing loss affects people, and the characteristics of the loss which are most relevant to the overall outcome. In broad terms, its aim is to set out the basic facts about hearing loss when it is considered as a disruption of social function rather than as a disorder of the ear. We will return to the theme of speech production at the end, when it can be seen in its context.

1.1. The time of hearing loss

The time when hearing loss occurs has a critical bearing on its impact. Above all, it is critical whether the loss becomes serious early enough to affect the acquisition of language. Obviously this is not a precise cut-off, but it is none the less important for that. We will reflect its importance in the terms we use. We will use the term "deaf" for people whose hearing loss occurred early enough to have a major effect on their acquisition of language, and the term "deafened" for people whose hearing loss occurred after language was firmly established. Not everyone accepts that terminology, but there seem to be no terminologies that are acceptable to everyone concerned with deafness – presumably because deafness is too complex to be described in a vocabulary that is both compact and precise.

This book is about deafened people. Their losses are also referred to as "acquired", "adventitious", or "postlingual". They greatly outnumber those we call the deaf, but they receive vastly less public attention, and there is a widespread tendency to assume that they have the same characteristics as the deaf. It is important to counteract that tendency.

The most striking contrast between the groups involves the way they communicate. By definition, deaf people's hearing makes it difficult for them to acquire language via the normal oral/aural channel. As a result, some form of manual language (such as American Sign Language or British Sign Language) is the first and the preferred channel of communication for most deaf people.

Signing has recently become vastly more familiar and acceptable in education and the media, and, as a result, the general public is very likely to assume that signing is the main medium of communication for anyone with a serious hearing loss. We need to counter that assumption at the outset. Growing acceptance of sign language is an important development which is thoroughly welcome to most people connected with deafness. However it is equally important to realise that the development does not affect deafened people to any noticeable extent. Wood – Turner – Pearl (1986: 7) surveyed the membership of the National Association of Deafened People (NADP) and found that only 20% used a manual system of communication. In the sample we studied, the proportion was similar at 17%: however half of the sign users belonged to the minority (one sixth of the sample) who had lost their hearing before the age of six. In sum, deafened people's main means of communication is overwhelmingly the oral/aural channel which is the subject of this book.

It is not surprising that deafened people do not generally sign. They have acquired language via the ordinary oral/aural channel, and that is the channel that they continue to use. Most of them would find it difficult to learn a sign language, and many of them are positively hostile to the idea that they should. This point is developed in chapter 10. It would mark an admission that they are no longer full members of the normal hearing community where they grew up and lived until their hearing deteriorated.

The concept of community is central to another important contrast between the groups. There has been increasing awareness that there is a "deaf community". Deaf people are educated together, and so they tend to know each other. They share a common (manual) language, and common concerns. As a result, they tend to operate as a community. A striking indication of the point comes from Kyle (1985: 139): he notes that 92% of deaf people marry someone who is deaf.

In contrast, deafened people are not likely to become members of a community whose common characteristic is acquired hearing loss. They will probably not know many other people who have hearing losses, and our experience is that most deafened people are reluctant to become socially involved with other deafened people even when they are introduced. In our sample 43% reported that they never attended a social event with other hearing-impaired people, and only 23% reported that they did so often. Another way of making the point is to note that the main organisation for this group in the United Kingdom, the National Association of Deafened People, recently reported a membership of only about 400 (Heath 1987: 168). There is an obvious practical explanation. A hearing loss is a barrier to communication, and two hearing losses make a denser barrier than one. There may also be subtler psychological pressures against becoming involved with other deafened people: it would mean allowing one's social identity to be redefined in terms of a handicap.

Whatever the reasons, the outcome is quite clear: deafened people do not generally affiliate to a distinctive subculture in the way that deaf people do. It follows that the important questions about deafened people's communications are questions about the way they operate in the general community, not about their relations with a distinctive subculture.

Common sense suggests that age at onset will be linked to subtler differences within the category of deafened people. Of particular concern to us, is the fact that there is evidence that speech production is generally sensitive to age at onset (Cowie – Douglas-Cowie 1983: 190–191). To understand what such an effect is likely to mean, it has to be set in context of wider differences that are associated with age at onset. These differences have been summarised in various ways (e.g. Berry 1933: 1599–1601). We have found it useful to recognise three broad groupings. Once again, these are intimately bound up with the way deafened people operate socially, and so they are relevant to understanding what impaired communication means.

First, there are people whose hearing loss originates in their school years. To some extent at least, they can set the course of their lives in the light of their hearing problem. It is in this group that we find most of the deafened who form links with the deaf community. A large part of their interaction is also likely to involve their parents and siblings, and relationships with those family members are likely to be deeply implicated in coping.

Second, there are people whose loss originates at a time during the ordinary span of working life. For them, hearing loss tends to mean either a struggle to maintain a career and a social life which were set on a well defined course, or else an effort to establish manageable alternatives. At this stage spouses and young children are likely to be the family members who are caught up in the process.

Third, there are those whose loss originates at a time around retirement age or after. Hearing loss may not be so surprising for them, and many of their contemporaries will have similar problems. A substantial number of people in this group find new contacts through hard-of-hearing clubs, where the link has as much to do with general age and circumstances as it has with hearing per se. That is particularly true of people whose loss is not unusual for their age group: our experience is that people whose losses are more severe than the ordinary still tend not to fit.

It is well recognised that late hearing loss is a widespread problem, and correspondingly a good deal has been written about this group (relevant books include Oyer – Oyer 1976; Hull 1977; Schow et al. 1978; Maurer – Rupp 1979; Glendinning 1982; Hinchcliffe 1983). People with late losses are also distinct to some extent from those whose loss originates earlier, in that hearing loss tends to be part of a pattern of difficulties associated with the end of a career, with the redefinition of relationships in the family, and with physical decline. For this book, it is a significant consideration that hearing loss appears to have relatively little effect on speech when it originates late in life. For these reasons, people with late onset of deafness are not a central concern here. Our focus is on those whose loss originates between the time of acquiring language and that of retirement.

Suddenness of onset is another aspect of timing which may be important. Most deafened people have suffered a gradual loss of hearing over a period of years. That is the case with losses due to inherited conditions, or noise, or chronic infection, or aging. However some people suffer abrupt losses. These are associated with accidents that damage the inner ear, or acute infections such as mumps or meningitis, or treatment with drugs which save life at the cost of hearing. Breed – van den Horst – Mous (1980) have gathered evidence that sudden onset creates a more acute trauma than gradual onset. However it is difficult to follow the point through because the evidence is limited.

1.2. Levels and forms of loss

It is conventional to describe hearing loss by specifying the quietest sound that a person can hear. That is measured in decibels, but it is often convenient to use a few verbal categories. Table 1.1 shows a conventional set of categories which we will use (from Ries 1985: 10).

Table 1.1 A rough summary of hearing losses

loss in dB	category	description of the loss
25–40 dB	mild	difficulty only with faint speech
41–55 dB	moderate	frequent difficulty with normal speech
56–70 dB	moderate (substantial)	frequent difficulty with loud speech
71–90 dB	severe	understands only shouted or amplified speech
over 90 dB	profound	usually cannot understand even amplified speech by hearing alone.
over 120 dB	total	no useful hearing

Our main concern is with people in the last two categories, though we have also studied people with severe losses (category 4) for the sake of comparison.

It is convenient to describe a hearing loss by a single figure, but that involves two large simplifications. These reflect the fact that most significant sounds are complex. They contain a range of simple components, each corresponding to a sound at a single pitch – that is to say, vibration at a particular frequency in the air which carries the sound. The array of simple components which makes up a sound is called its spectrum. A spectrum shows a peak at frequencies where the sound has a strong simple component, and a trough at frequencies which are absent from the sound (or weak). The shape of the spectrum determines what we perceive as the quality of a sound. The ear contains sophisticated mechanisms for extracting the component frequencies which make up a complex sound such as speech.

Single figure descriptions of hearing losses are achieved by averaging the losses which are recorded at different frequencies (particularly those which are classically regarded as relevant to perceiving speech). This is a large simplification because hearing-impaired people are quite likely to have very different losses at different frequencies. A particularly common pattern is to find that sensitivity to high frequencies is impaired much more than sensitivity to low frequencies. It follows that even people with profound losses may have appreciable sensitivity at low frequencies.

There is a well-known reason why low-frequency residual hearing is important in the context of speech reception. There is a degree of complementarity between the information which it provides and the information provided by lipreading, and so the two sources together can provide much better speech comprehension than either one alone (e.g. Summerfield 1983: 136–138; Bailey 1983). The characteristics of residual hearing are also potentially relevant to speech production, as the last section of this chapter will show.

Even if we use a different number to describe the ear's response to every frequency, we are still oversimplifying. The reason is that it is not a trivial task to separate a complex signal into its components, and the disordered ear tends to be particularly bad at that task. The effect is closely related to blurring in vision. A short-sighted person may know perfectly well that a letter is present, but not be able to tell whether it is a *b* or an *h* because each bit of the pattern activates photosensitive cells in quite a broad patch on the retina. In just the same way, a person with a hearing loss may be able to register that a sound is present, but may not know whether it is [ɪ] as in *bit* or [ɛ] as in *bet*. In both cases, the components which mark the difference are creating activity in a range of cells, and it is hard to tell whether the resulting auditory blurs are different or not.

Reduced frequency resolution has implications which are important for social life. We rely on good frequency resolution to separate out different auditory events which overlap in time – for instance, to hear a voice against a background of other voices or of noise. When frequency resolution is impaired, overlapping sources simply merge into a single meaningless babble. Hence table 1.1 understates the difficulties that people with impaired hearing face listening to anything but a single speaker in a quiet setting. A large part of social life takes place in settings which are far from that description. Most people positively seek out the lively group, with people cutting across each other, or the buzzing shopping centre, or the club with background music, or the disco. Sound adds pep to these places for people with normal hearing, but it makes them a social desert for people with reduced frequency resolution.

Impaired hearing is often accompanied by tinnitus, which consists of sounds (often ringing or buzzing) in the ear. In the population at large, 2.6% report severely annoying tinnitus (Davis 1983: 45–48). In the NADP membership survey, dealing mainly with people whose losses were profound, 74% reported that they had tinnitus and 13% found it very distressing. Tinnitus can be helped both by psychological therapy (Hallam – Rachman – Hinchcliffe 1984) and by masking with an external sound (Hazell et al. 1985), though the latter is not relevant to people with sufficient hearing to register the masker, and even combined therapy fails to help a substantial proportion of sufferers.

1.3. Prevalence

The problem of hearing loss is pressing partly because of its prevalence. The numbers affected are very large. The only way to describe these numbers satisfactorily is in terms of the variables which have been considered above, age and level of loss. Table 1.2 summarises the best data available, which come from the Institute of Hearing Research in the United Kingdom (Davis 1989: 915).

Table 1.2 The prevalence of hearing loss per thousand people in the relevant age group

Loss in the better ear	Age					
	17–30	31–40	41–50	51–60	61–70	71–80
25 dB or more	18	28	82	189	368	602
45 dB or more	2	11	17	40	74	176
65 dB or more	<1	7	3	9	23	40

The higher the numbers, the more confident one can be of the estimates. At the extremes, which are of particular interest to us, there is a good deal of uncertainty. However a study of profound and total losses by Thornton (1986) indicates that they are consistent with the trends suggested by table 1.2: prevalence roughly doubles with a ten-year increase in age, and roughly halves with a ten-decibel increase in the severity criterion.

Another level of uncertainty arises over long term trends. It is natural to assume that medical advances are steadily reducing the incidence of disability, but there is no reason to believe that that applies to profound acquired hearing loss. In fact Heath (1987: 164–165) has pointed out that changes in medicine may be making profound acquired losses commoner. People are more likely to survive accidents or diseases which destroy the inner ear: and drugs have become available which prevent infections that would otherwise kill, but which destroy hearing.

But although details are uncertain, there is no doubt at all about the broad picture. People whose losses are at least severe form a large group, and they will do so for the foreseeable future. The common stereotype is correct to associate hearing loss with old age, but the association is less clear-cut than is commonly supposed. Cowie (1988: 2–3) reports figures based on combining the proportions of table 1.2 with the demography of the Belfast area. On those figures, it is a reasonable estimate that of the people who have acquired losses which are at least severe, a third are under 65, and a quarter are under 60. The proportions for profound acquired losses are similar.

1.4. Augmenting reception

There are several ways in which impaired hearing can be supplemented. They can make an immense difference to deafened people's lives. Nevertheless, it is important to recognise that what they achieve is limited. The limits on our ability to alleviate the underlying problem of hearing loss are part of the reason why it is necessary to confront the secondary problems which flow from hearing loss.

The oldest way of augmenting reception is lipreading. Lipreading is not a special technique for deafened people. Speech reception involves reconstructing the mouth movements which produced particular sounds, and people with normal hearing use both visual and acoustic information to do that (Summerfield 1983). Hearing loss means that the less important visual channel has to carry a disproportionate burden in speech reception.

It is astonishing how much lipreading can achieve, particularly when the residual signals from hearing complement the information that vision provides (Summerfield 1983: 136—138; Bailey 1983). Unfortunately lipreading depends on mental abilities which are very unevenly distributed through the population, so that many people can make very little of visual clues to speech: and contrary to popular mythology, neither training nor practice seems to improve lipreading very much (e.g. Lyxell – Ronnberg 1987). But even at its best, lipreading has multiple limitations. Communication becomes fragile because it is abnormally dependent on viewpoint and lighting; on attention and complex mental processes in the listener; and on co-operation by the speaker. These issues are considered later in this book. A limitation which is very directly relevant is that lipreading can rarely be used to monitor one's own speech.

Hearing aids are the second long established treatment. In essence they amplify the sound that reaches a user's ear, though modern aids can do considerably more than that: they give a selective boost to frequencies which the user has particular difficulty hearing, and they may also shift the speech signal across the spectrum into the range where the user has most hearing.

In one special form of loss, conductive deafness, hearing aids are extremely effective. Conductive loss occurs because of problems in the sequence of bones which transmit sound from the ear drum to the cochlea, where vibration is transformed into neural impulses and sent to the brain. Unfortunately pure conductive loss is not particularly common. Most losses are at least partly sensorineural, i.e. they are due to problems in the cochlea itself, or in the nerves which carry information from the cochlea to the brain. Davis (1983: 51–52) shows that people whose better ear losses are purely sensorineural outnumber those whose better ear losses have a conductive component by four to one, and they outnumber those whose better ear loss is purely conductive by six to one. Sensorineural losses involve reduced frequency resolution, and amplification does not solve that problem any more than turning up the brightness on a TV screen helps someone with short sight. In fact many hearing aid users switch them off when there is background noise: they cannot separate out the sources they want to listen to, and so the aid simply raises the level of a meaningless din.

It is important to see aids in the context of audio-visual speech reception. At one stage it was unusual to prescribe an aid if it could not restore some ability to understand speech by sound alone. This attitude has changed as it has become clear how effectively the brain synthesises sound and sight. It is now clear that an aid can make a substantial difference to lipreading even if its output is unintelligible in itself. In fact powerful modern aids may benefit lipreading in an individual who shows no response in an audiometric test to the loudest sounds that are used there, 120 dB, across almost the entire speech spectrum (Plant, personal communication).

As a rough rule of thumb, a successful hearing aid improves a sensorineural loss by one of the categories in table 1.1 (Haggard 1983: 269). That can mean an immense improvement in the quality of life, but it does not return it to normal. Many hearing aids are not as successful as that. In a substantial survey, Thomas – Gilhome-Herbst (1980: 81–82) found that about a third of their informants used their aids rarely or never. Of the rest, about half derived no appreciable benefit from their aids.

An important adjunct to hearing aids is the loop system. A loop is a wire which runs round an area, often a public hall. It carries signals from a microphone. When a hearing aid is reasonably close to the loop, it can pick up the signals (providing it is correctly set). This provides much clearer reception than amplifying sound per se .

Recently two new ways of augmenting reception have emerged: tactile aids, and cochlear implants.

In tactile aids the skin is used to receive information about the vibrations which constitute speech sounds. The sounds which reach a microphone may be transformed either into vibrations which are applied to the skin (in vibrotactile aids), or into electrical impulses which activate receptors directly (in electrotactile aids). Tactile aids are pre-eminently supplements to lipreading and residual hearing. A study by Kishon-Rabin – Hanin – Boothroyd (1990) gives a fair illustration of their usefulness: a tactile aid improved profoundly deafened subjects' ability to lipread sentences by up to 15%. That is enough to be very valuable, but it does not represent anything like a return to normal functioning.

Cochlear implants transform sound into electrical impulses which are fed into the nerves of the cochlea via electrodes. Some devices have one electrode, some have many. If there is one electrode, the current usually signals the pitch of the voice which the microphone is picking up (or more precisely, its fundamental frequency – the difference does not usually matter). At the other extreme, new multichannel designs carry information about voice pitch; the position of several peaks in the spectrum which are likely to be significant for speech recognition; and high frequency bursts which are associated with sounds like [f], [s] or [ʃ].

At best, cochlear implants can provide more information than tactile aids. (Different individuals derive very different levels of benefit from them, for various reasons.) They can allow a good subject to recognise some words by sound alone, without lipreading: and in combination with lipreading, they can allow "star" users to perform virtually perfectly in simplified test situations. It is difficult to quantify what that means in real interactions, but there is no doubt that implants can be an incalculable benefit to people who previously heard nothing even with an aid. However an implant is not appreciably better than an aid for people who have any useful hearing at all, and it is a drastic remedy because the device needs to be implanted in the skull by major surgery which destroys any prospect of the cochlea working again in a more normal way (at least with the designs which are most widely used at present).

These aids are an important part of the background against which we propose to consider deafened people's speech production. They mark what technology can do for the underlying malfunction in the ears, and their limitations highlight the importance of responding to the problem on a broader basis. However they also bear another relationship to research on hearing loss and speech production. If hearing loss affects speech in ways that are worth addressing, then these devices should be evaluated partly in terms of their ability to improve speech production. For that reason, the advent of cochlear implants has greatly increased the number of papers which discuss speech production in acquired deafness. This will become apparent in chapter 2.

It would be wrong to discuss reception without mentioning electronic media which form a communications network that is central to most people's lives, but that presents deafened people with profound difficulties. This is an area where information technology makes deafened people's disadvantage very considerably worse. Steps have been taken to redress the effect, but they are limited.

It is ironic that when Alexander Graham Bell invented the telephone, one of his aims was to help his hearing-impaired students, but that in fact the telephone made it standard to communicate in a way that is thoroughly unsuitable for deafened people. Telephone communication has one advantage for people with impaired hearing: it tends to provide a single source so that they are not forced to separate what they want to hear from background noise. However it precludes the use of visual channels, from speechreading to the option of writing as a last resort. The greater the loss, the more that disadvantage outweighs the advantages.

There are various ways of alleviating the problem, but none of them is satisfactory. Amplifying receivers help up to a point, but at best they share the limitations of hearing aids. When deafened people live with their families, a hearing member of the household will often act as an intermediary. This can be important, but it makes for very unnatural interactions. It can also strain domestic relationships because translators resent the peculiar role which the situation imposes on them and the demands which it involves. There are various telephones which transmit text, but they seem not to be widely used by deafened people. Various reasons can be suggested. Plain discomfort with technology may be a factor among older people. Experience suggests that these systems lead to very stilted interactions unless people are fluent typists. Problems may also be linked to the observation that deafened people tend not to form a community, and still less do they associate with the deaf community. In that situation it is rather pointless having a telephone analogue which is used almost solely by hearing-impaired people. In any case, a device which cannot reach one per cent of the outlets in the Yellow Pages is not what most people understand as a telephone. An approach which is developing rapidly involves transmitting video signals as a supplement to the audio message – images of the hands for those who use signing, or images of the face for lipreaders (Wilson – Welbank – Usher 1990). This kind of development may end deafened people's exclusion from telecommunications, particularly if it advances to the point where a video link is standard for everyone.

Another medium which largely excludes deafened people is television. Although speakers are usually visible, their faces are rarely shown in a way that permits lipreading. As a result deafened people are at an additional disadvantage in conversations which are about television or about information which is conveyed on television, such as the news. Teletext and subtitling make a large difference here, but they are still on a frustratingly small scale.

They have penetrated still less into the new medium which has developed from television, video. Subtitled videos are a rarity.

1.5. Social and family effects

Speech is the medium which sustains our social existence, and so it is to be expected that deafness will have a withering effect on a person's social world. What might not be foreseen is how pervasive the effect tends to be.

Studies agree that acquired deafness has the effect of reducing a person's circle of contacts (Thomas – Gilhome-Herbst 1980: 80–81; Wood – Kyle 1983: 179). The result is that deafened people spend an unusual amount of time at home, though this is less true of people who become deaf early in life or whose loss is moderate (Cowie – Stewart 1987: 145).

The home is not a safe haven, though. Deafened people face some fairly well documented problems there. Families tend to regroup to exclude the deafened person (Jones – Kyle 1984). He or she often feels left out of discussions and decision-making in the home (Thomas – Gilhome-Herbst 1980: 80–81; Beattie 1981: 297–301). It seems clear that even those who are close to deafened people rarely understand what deafness involves (Thomas – Gilhome-Herbst 1980: 80; Jones 1987: 127–131; Cowie – Stewart 1987: 144). This is frustrating in itself, and it can have destructive consequences. On one hand, it is claimed that relatives can undermine deafened people's independence through overprotectiveness (Beattie 1981: 309–321): on the other, it is claimed that they can impose impossible expectations because they do not understand deafness (Hardick 1976: 60–62).

Deafened people are not the only ones who suffer in this situation. As Kyle (1985: 140) puts it, "the tension arising around someone who continues to talk but cannot adequately respond to others' speech is enormous". In this area the main evidence comes from deafened people's own reports: most of them are acutely aware of imposing a strain on their families (Wood – Kyle 1983: 179), and the feeling that they are stressing others affects their own lives for the worse (Cowie – Stewart 1987: 145). Few studies have asked relatives systematically, but the evidence that there is confirms that deafened people's relatives are likely to feel strained (Oyer – Paolucci 1970) and to need help because of the stress they suffer (Beattie 1981: 302–307).

A positive point is that deafness seems not to promote outright splits in fundamental relationships. Several studies agree that deafened people's marriages are not abnormally likely to end in divorce, or abnormally prone to rows or separations (Cowie – Stewart 1987: 147). It has been claimed that children are likely to reject a parent who suffers a profound hearing loss (Breed – van den Horst – Mous 1980), but a follow-up study did not confirm the claim (Breed – Mous, unpublished data). However this does not mean that these relationships are normal. It is just as likely to mean that the shared difficulty creates strong bonds as well as strong tensions. There is an obvious gap in our knowledge here.

1.6. Practical restrictions

We have considered the way acquired deafness affects people's social interactions. It is more difficult to define the way deafness affects the practical conduct of life. That is partly because the practical conduct of life involves so many issues and because it is normal to tackle them in such a wide range of ways. However there may be another reason. The worst impact of deafness may actually be on people's private and personal worlds rather than in areas which are publicly observable and whose significance everyone would accept. That theme is taken up in chapter 13.

One would assume that acquired deafness has a strongly negative effect on education and training, since in most contexts oral communication plays a key role. Unfortunately the evidence here seems to be scanty. Certainly accounts by individual deafened people leave no doubt that they have been disadvantaged in this respect (e.g. Rice 1988: 23–24). It has to be realised that this is an issue for a far larger group than those who lose their hearing early on, since ongoing training is an increasingly common feature of life. An awkward trap arises because retraining is particularly important when enforced job changes occur. This is a situation where becoming deaf can both precipitate a problem and obstruct a normal response to it. Such evidence as there is confirms that retraining may not work well for deafened people. Wood – Turner – Pearl (1986: 8) asked about retraining when they surveyed the membership of NADP. Two thirds of those who took retraining felt it had not helped them to find a job.

On the other hand, our experience is that formal education is an area where many deafened people find they can shine. There appears to be no formal evidence on the point, but a surprising number of our deafened contacts have taken degree level courses and found it immensely rewarding.

When we look at acquired deafness and employment, we find a picture ather like the one that arose with family relationships. Outright severance is probably not particularly common, but what endures is strained.

There is room for debate about the numbers of people who lose or change their job as a result of acquired deafness. Studies cited by Kyle – Jones – Wood (1985: 133) report proportions ranging from 50% to 4%. What seems a reasonable estimate comes from substantial studies in Britain by Thomas – Lamont – Harris (1982: 40–42) and Wood – Turner – Pearl (1986: 7). They found figures on the order of $^1/_8$ to $^1/_4$: the higher figure is for the sample with the greater average loss. Another large survey makes the useful point that acquired deafness tends to make for early retirement. On average, members of SHHH (Self Help for the Hard of Hearing, the main U.S. organisation for people with acquired hearing impairments) retire about two years early (Orlans – Meadow-Orlans 1985: 6).

What is clear is that a very large proportion of deafened people find their working lives adversely affected. In both of the British studies which have just been cited, around two thirds of the informants reported that their hearing loss had had adverse effects on working life. Thomas – Lamont – Harris (1982) describe the nature of the problem in more depth. The most widespread problems were difficulty with telephones and difficulty in dealing with the public. Also common were difficulty dealing with colleagues and supervisors and feeling left out at work. Over half of those in work reported loss of status due to hearing loss, mostly in the form of loss of promotion or loss of responsibility. A useful summary of difficulties in the wider sphere is due to Wood – Kyle (1983: 179). They asked informants whether they found it easy to communicate in various situations. The table below indicates how many did find it easy to communicate. Situations are arranged from the most problematic to the least.

Table 1.3 Ease of communication in commonplace situations (after Wood – Kyle 1983)

	Percentage who found it easy to communicate
Pubs and restaurants	5%
Conversations at bus stops	10%
Conversation in the street	11%
Paying bus fares	12%
Buying train tickets	13%
Job interviews	17%
Banks and shops	17%
Tea break	19%
Neighbours calling	23%
Telephone	35%
General conversation at home	45%
Buying petrol	66%

Table 1.3 (continued)

	Percentage who found it easy to communicate
With a doctor	76%
Home at mealtimes	78%

The items at the top of the list need little comment. Several of them are related to travel, which makes the point that mobility can be a real problem for deafened people. It may be worth saying more about the later items. Consultations with a doctor, for example, are comparatively well rated. However in absolute terms the figure is still disturbing. It means that a quarter of the sample did not find it easy to communicate with a doctor – and the people in this sample did not generally have profound or even severe losses. Our contacts also make us vividly aware of associated problems which this list does not bring out. For example in medical consultations, and other contacts with officialdom, appointments and receptionists often pose a far bigger problem than the consultation proper.

1.7. Psychiatric effects

The net effect of deafness is summarised very clearly in its effects on mental health.

There is a literature based on patients who have reached psychiatrists, much of it linked to the servicemen who were deafened in the Second World War. It suggests that hearing loss tends to produce paranoia and psychosis (see Thomas 1981 for a review). That literature is mentioned in order to be set aside. It contains interesting ideas, particularly those of Ramsdell (1978), but it suffers from a number of fundamental flaws. Some authors fail to distinguish pre- and postlingual deafness. Denmark, a psychiatrist who specialises in cases which involve hearing loss, has made it clear that the two groups tend to suffer different psychological problems (Denmark 1969). In many cases, such as soldiers deafened by a shell explosion or whose deafness seems to be emotional rather than physical in origin, there are clearly massive confounding factors. And generally, the fact that the patients have reached a psychiatric consultation builds in a sampling bias which there is no way to recoup. A sample of that kind cannot possibly lead to conclusions about the general effects of hearing loss.

More recently, reliable studies have provided a clearer picture. Thomas – Gilhome-Herbst (1980) dealt with hearing impaired people of employment age. In a large sample, they found no evidence that hearing loss produced paranoia or psychosis. However they did find clear evidence that two less dramatic problems commonly reached a level which is conventionally accepted as pathological. These were depression and loneliness.

The evidence on depression is particularly striking. It was obtained using a test called SAD (Symptoms of Anxiety and Depression). SAD is standardised to indicate clinical depression in 5% of the general population and 75% of known psychiatric cases (Bedford – Foulds 1978). Thomas – Gilhome-Herbst (1980: 78–79) found clinically significant levels of depression in 19% of their hearing-impaired sample. The implication is that 14% of them suffered depression due to hearing loss. This proportion was surprisingly constant across mild and moderate losses, and even some types of severe loss. However depression rose sharply among those who had pure tone losses of over 70 dB and speech discrimination scores below 70% even with amplification. (Poor speech discrimination tends to reflect reduced frequency resolution). 57% of people in that category suffered from clinical depression.

1.8. Speech production and hearing loss

Logically it is reasonable to suspect that hearing loss might affect a person's speech. If people normally rely on hearing to monitor what they are saying, then hearing impairment may have one of two effects.

First, if hearing loss is partial, then one might expect people to adjust their speech so that it sounds as nearly as possible the same as it always did. The simple prediction is that people will tend to talk loudly as a result. Since hearing loss tends to be selective, with a particular impact on frequency resolution and high frequencies, one might expect some more complex adjustments too.

Second, if hearing loss is total, then it is difficult to foresee what might happen, because different theories suggest different possibilities. At one extreme are "closed loop" theories which suggest that complex skills like speaking are held together by feedback. In the case of speech, this would mean that sound from one element of speech triggered the movements which produce the next. At the other extreme are "open loop" or feedforward theories which suggest that once a skill has been thoroughly mastered it ceases to depend on feedback. As one might expect, modern theory suggests that the truth lies between these extremes (e.g. Schmidt 1988: 141–186) – which means that it gives limited guidance to the likely effects of acquired deafness on speech.

We have argued that in fact at least some deafened people do suffer significant speech deterioration (Cowie – Douglas-Cowie 1983), and chapter 2 will show that a growing body of research supports that view. Nevertheless the opposite view has been expressed repeatedly in the literature, notably in recent years by Goehl – Kaufman (1984). It is clear that the issue ought to be resolved, and that is one of the goals that we have set out to achieve.

A second major goal is more difficult because it is inherently less well defined. It is to establish whether the effect is practically significant. There is very little evidence on the question, and again, conflicting arguments are possible. On one side, it is natural to argue that impairments of speech production must be a minor problem by comparison with the massive primary difficulty that deafened people face in speech reception. But it is equally possible to argue that speech difficulties should be taken particularly seriously when they affect people who already have so many problems to face.

What these arguments show is that questions about speech are inevitably entangled with questions about the whole pattern of deafened people's lives and hearing people's behaviour. The first argument is plausible if one thinks of speech as a channel for transmitting factual information. However, speech also creates impressions and evokes reactions, and it is not so clear that being disadvantaged in these respects is a negligible problem. The ability to transmit a message is of limited value if people are disinclined to take you seriously, or to listen at all. It is important in this context that hearing loss itself is not always apparent in a casual encounter. As a result a deafened person's speech may often be the first or the only thing which gives listeners the impression that he or she is not perfectly normal. It is also true that a good deal of speech is not about transmitting messages, but about establishing and maintaining relationships. Deficits which affect that function ought to be taken seriously, and speech which is offputting could well come in that category. Here the second argument from the previous paragraph is highly relevant. If deafened people already have special difficulty maintaining relationships, then problems which affect links that are already fragile deserve attention. It is also relevant to know about deafened people's own values: how do they weigh the practical business of transmitting information against the social matters of contact and people's opinions?

The core of this book reports a study in which we have assembled empirical evidence relevant to these questions, from the acoustic description of deafened people's speech to its impact on listeners, the other factors which impinge on the way listener react to deafened people, and the way deafened people value social acceptance.

It is difficult to see such a large structure as a whole, and impossible to do more than outline key points in a single study. However these are the issues which are relevant to judgements about deafened people's speech, and if we do not address them empirically we can only judge on the basis of a priori intuitions. Exposing the issues, and assembling the best empirical evidence that we can, gives a considerably better base to work from.

Chapter 2
Review of speech literature

The central concern of this book is deafened people's speech. This chapter sets the scene by summarising what is known about deafened people's speech from sources other than the study which we report in later chapters. It falls into two main parts.

The first part considers ideas which tend to be brought to the topic from other areas. These have a major influence on the questions that people ask about deafened speech and the things they take for granted. That is right and proper, but we will argue that it is necessary to be cautious. Ideas drawn from other areas are a rich source of questions. But although the answers sometimes seem to be obvious from what we already know, looking closely tends to indicate otherwise. There is very little that we can confidently anticipate about deafened speech without actually studying it.

The second part looks at the data which have been gathered on deafened speech. There is now a considerable literature. It does at least make it very hard to doubt that acquired deafness can affect speech, and that its effect is pervasive: deterioration has been reported in most aspects of speech, not just a few. However the literature is highly fragmented, and many of the fragments have weaknesses which leave their interpretation uncertain: and there are major areas where very little is known.

2.1. Ideas brought to the study of acquired deafness

The topic of deafened people's speech is linked to a number of other areas which have been more extensively studied. The result is that many reasonably well developed ideas can be brought to bear on the topic. This section is concerned with assembling some of those ideas.

The framework in which they are drawn together is provided by a negative argument, which is that imported ideas do not tell us in advance how deafened people will speak. It is necessary to make that case because there has been a historical tendency for people to believe that they know what the facts will be without having to study them fully. To make this point clear, consider the following comments from the literature.

After the age of six or so deafening has no effect on the vocal production; at this point it seems that vocal production has become completely independent of supporting auditory feedback. (Bower 1979: 87).

Among adults with well established skills, feedforward and production mechanisms have become automatic and auditory feedback is therefore no longer essential. (Ling 1976: 78).

The onset of deafness among adults does not usually interfere with the ability to speak, except that some will tend to shout. (Espir – Rose 1976: 40).

The routine recommendations for speech conservation training in cases of deafness occurring after the acquisition of the sound system of a language is complete are probably unwarranted. (Goehl – Kaufman 1984: 64).

These comments were all undoubtedly based on some evidence, but it should be apparent by the end of the chapter that its quantity and quality cannot have been great. Nor can the literature have been searched in great depth: all of the quotes long postdate Penn's (1955) study which reported a wide range of abnormalities in deafened speech. The fact that statements like these were made can only reflect the fact that the evidence which was to hand fitted expectations. In three of the four cases it is clear what the expectations were. The first two statements are linked to discussions about theories of feedback which suggest that speech should not be affected by acquired hearing loss. The link is made explicit in the fourth, which invokes theories about the role of linguistic knowledge in speech.

When expectations are strong enough to generate this kind of problem, it is important to counter them directly. That is the first aim of this section. However the section is not simply a negative exercise. The argument provides a vehicle for introducing a variety of ideas which are potentially useful for organising information. Having emphasised how little we know for certain from other areas, we return at the end of the section to the positive issue of what we can reasonably ask and expect.

2.1.1. Knowledge about prelingual deaf speech

On the surface, the most obvious source of ideas about speech in acquired deafness is knowledge about speech in the prelingually deaf. Our experience is that people with relatively little knowledge of the two groups often expect their speech to be similar. If anything the literature tends in the opposite direction, which is to assume that the two types of speech cannot bear more than superficial similarities. In that context it is worth noting that the contrast between pre- and postlingual deafness is in the background of all four quotes that were given earlier in section 2.1. We argue in this section that the only safe course is to keep an open mind on the relationship between the two types of speech, and evaluate it in the light of evidence.

The argument against expecting similarities involves a distinction which is widespread in the speech literature (see e.g. Colley 1989: 238–243). Making an utterance involves both high-level and (comparatively) low-level processes. The high-level processes generate plans which specify the linguistic targets that are to be reached, and the low-level processes translate those plans into commands which move the relevant muscles in the appropriate ways. The similarity between deaf and deafened speakers is that both have to put plans into effect without hearing the end result (or at least without hearing very much of it). The difference is that in the prelingually deaf, the high-level machinery which generates the plans was developed in the absence of hearing. As a result, one would expect deaf children to develop a system of targets which is markedly different from the system that their hearing counterparts develop: and there is good evidence that they do (Oller – Kelly 1974; Dodd 1976). In contrast deafened people begin with a normal system of targets. That contrast provides a strong argument against expecting that pre- and postlingual deafness will result in similar forms of speech abnormality.

It is easy to go further and assume that deafened people's speech must be so different from the speech of the prelingually deaf as to make comparisons pointless. We have leant in that direction ourselves (Douglas-Cowie – Cowie 1979: 54), but we are now more cautious. Our outlook was changed by a preliminary attempt to make the comparison (Cowie – Douglas-Cowie 1983: 201–209). Against our expectations, it showed that patterns of errors in deafened people's speech bore interesting resemblances to patterns of errors in the speech of the deaf. That is not a comfortable conclusion, because it raises questions about the distinction between high- and low-level processes in speech. We will develop that point later in the section. Nevertheless it seems necessary to regard the relationship between the groups as an open question. Neither theory nor intuition provide reliable guidance on the issue, and assumptions in either direction are dangerous.

Contrasting the groups can also promote a different kind of conclusion, and a more directly damaging one. It has to do with the scale of the problem rather than its form. Almost all deafened people speak very well by comparison with most people who were born deaf. An illustrative figure is that in our comparison between the groups, the deaf speakers made of the order of 75 times more consonant errors than the deafened (Cowie – Douglas-Cowie 1983: 205). As a result, people who are used to the speech of the deaf can be tempted to judge that speech is not a problem for the deafened. This is a fallacy. One might as well argue that a shark is too small to worry about because a killer whale is so much bigger.

A subtler form of the problem involves the criteria that are used to measure the quality of speech. With the prelingually deaf, intelligibility is a good criterion of speech quality, because full intelligibility is a difficult target to achieve. Applying the same criterion to deafened people tends to suggest that their speech is not a problem, since very few of them are outright unintelligible for much of the time. However intelligibility does not equal normality, and it misrepresents deafened people's speech not to consider other measures of functional abnormality.

In conclusion, comparison with prelingually deaf people's speech highlights interesting questions. Are there systematic resemblances between the patterns of errors which occur in deafened people's speech and those which occur in the speech of the prelingually deaf? If so, why? If there are differences, what are the intermediate stages as age at onset moves from birth to late in life? How does acquired deafness affect speech intelligibility, and what other ways of measuring the significance of deteriorating speech are appropriate to postlingual deafness? Insofar as the comparison draws attention to questions like these, it is useful. However if it leads people to prejudge issues which are actually open, it is dangerous.

2.1.2. Knowledge about feedback

A similar situation occurs with respect to theoretical research on feedback. Its influence is very clear in the literature. Of the claims cited at the beginning of the section, the first two were made in the context of a discussion of feedback. Certainly there are influential theories in this area which suggest at first glance that acquired deafness should not affect speech production. We want to argue that on closer inspection, general theories about feedback tell us very little about what should happen in acquired deafness, though they provide interesting ways of thinking about it.

Theoretical discussions of feedback have their roots in a suggestion by William James (1890). He proposed that skilled behaviours consisted of stimulus-response chains linked by feedback, in the sense that feedback from one element of the chain provides the triggers which initiate the next, and so on. The theoretical attraction of the idea is its parsimony: it avoids the need to postulate mental plans which specify a whole sequence of movements in advance.

Instead feedback serves as a kind of glue which joins separate elements into a sequence.

That is the view of feedback which has been rebutted beyond reasonable doubt (e.g. Lane – Tranel 1971). Mental plans (sometimes known as motor programs) clearly are involved in well-practised performance in general, and in speech in particular. However there is a world of difference between accepting that and claiming that feedback has no role in activities such as speech. There are at least three other roles that feedback is known to play even in skilled performance.

First, there is control over the magnitude of an effort. Sensory input may be used to give the motor program initial parameters concerned with the starting point for its action. It may be also be used to modulate even a well-practised action while it is in progress. A nice example is Lee's demonstration that expert long jumpers use visual feedback during their run-up to adjust the exact lengths of their strides, so that they take off as close as possible to the end of the board (Lee – Lishman – Thompson 1982).

Second, there is calibration. A good example comes from the case where vision is distorted so that an object which is actually to the observer's left (for example) appears straight ahead. When viewers first reach for the object, they (naturally) reach straight ahead and miss it. However they gradually adjust. They do so by recalibrating the systems which translate raw impulses from sensory nerves into a sense of body position: they are readjusted so that the arm feels as if it is oriented straight ahead when it is directed at an object which looks straight ahead (Harris 1965; Welch 1978: 43–79).

This case appears mildly paradoxical because the recalibration brings a system which was working properly into line with one which was not, but the function of the arrangement is straightforward: it allows the organism to compensate for change or drift in any one of a range of components. The function is achieved by allowing feedback from senses which monitor the external world (in this case vision) to affect performance by an indirect route: it is used to recalibrate mechanisms which interpret raw signals concerned with internal states and positions. We know that drift does occur when feedback is not available to prevent it. Manual tasks which can be performed precisely without feedback for a short time become inaccurate when they have to be sustained (Rothwell et al. 1982).

What we have described is one of a family of operations concerned with translating between internal codes. Other members of the family can achieve functionally similar results – for instance, in the pointing example, adaptation could be achieved by adjusting the translators which transform the general command "point ahead" into directives to individual muscles. It is notoriously difficult to distinguish among members of this family (Welch 1978), and we will simply consider them as variants on the general theme of calibration.

The third role of feedback is closest to what laymen tend to mean by the term. We will call it strategic evaluation. A huge part of human activity aims at goals which are complex, incompletely defined, and impossible to achieve finally and totally. In that sort of case, people often vary the strategies that they have used previously, often in small ways, in the hope of coming closer to their ideal aspirations. Feedback in the everyday sense of the word is a key element in that kind of experimentation: it is information which suggests whether the variations seem to have worked.

These various uses of feedback are known to occur in skilled performance of various sorts, and so it is not inconceivable that they will occur in speech. The evidence from research which is directly concerned with speech is also consistent with that view.

What seems unlikely from general theory is that feedback will be an indispensable glue for speech production. The evidence fits the expectation. Speech does not disintegrate into uncoordinated gestures when auditory feedback is removed either experimentally or in acquired deafness, or when anaesthesia removes oral feedback (feedback concerned with touch and muscular contraction in the mouth). However that is quite separate from the possibility that feedback, particularly auditory feedback, plays the other roles we have mentioned.

The evidence indicates that auditory feedback is relevant to controlling the magnitude of several variables which are relevant to speech – certainly volume (e.g. Siegel – Pick 1974) and probably pitch (e.g. Collins 1979; Simon 1979) and nasality (Garber – Moller 1979: 329). The fact that these are relatively slowly changing variables is no accident. The pathway from the ear to the brain to the mouth is relatively slow, too slow to provide instant-by-instant control over gestures as rapid as articulator movements in speech.

The evidence does not show that auditory feedback is used for calibration, but it leaves the possibility open. It is relevant whether oral feedback is used in speech production, because if it were not there would be no question of calibrating it. It is fast enough to be used in controlling the magnitude of articulator movements, and though there is room for debate, the balance of the evidence suggests that it does play that role (Perkell 1980: 358–359; Kelso et al. 1984; Gracco – Abbs 1985). There is also one indication that auditory feedback affects the calibration of oral feedback: prelingually deaf subjects show deficits in judging the size and shape of objects in their mouths (Bishop – Ringel 1973). The finding could be interpreted in other ways, but it certainly underlines the case for recognising that auditory feedback may be involved in calibration. Lane – Webster (1991: 859) make the point that calibration may be particularly critical for mechanisms which have to co-ordinate with the states and movements of other parts of the vocal tract, so that they have to cope with a multidimensional space of possible initial positions and ongoing movements.

The function that we have called strategic evaluation is not widely recognised in the modern academic literature on speech, but it reflects the oldest literature on the subject. Socratic Athens had its experts on the voice, the phonarchoi, and their function was to improve speech. The function continues in elocution classes to the present (Millar 1987). People cultivate forms of speech which reflect their social ambitions rather than their background (Douglas-Cowie 1978). People incorporate the vocal mannerisms of their favourite stars or singers into their own speech, often with bizarre results. Lecturers strive for a style which is simultaneously relaxed and impressive, friendly but not too friendly, and so on. In short, people cultivate their speech at many levels. It is possible that hearing oneself plays no part in the process, but subjective experience suggests otherwise. The implicit problem is that it may not be possible to immobilise the processes which make for change when people lose their hearing, and with it the ability to detect when changes produce undesirable effects.

The point of these arguments is not to show that auditory feedback does have a pervasive effect on speech, but to show that we do not know beforehand whether it will or not. Like comparisons with prelingual deafness, considering feedback is useful because it helps to articulate ways in which speech might conceivably be affected by acquired deafness. However we should not prejudge the evidence of deafened people's speech on the basis of generalisations about feedback, because what is known about feedback does not warrant it.

2.1.3. High- and low-level processes

Theories concerned with feedback are not the only ones which have seemed to show that acquired deafness could not possibly have more than limited effects on speech. The distinction between high- and low-level processes has already been mentioned in relation to pre- and postlingual deafness. It is a very widespread assumption that there is a profound qualitative contrast between high-level processes which deal with discrete, abstract linguistic symbols, and low-level processes which deal with the realisation of these symbols as continuously varying sound patterns (see e.g. Colley 1989: 238–243). Given that picture, it is natural to assume that loss of hearing could only affect the low-level component. Where is the scope for slippage in a high-level component which deals in discrete abstract symbols?

Once again, the effect of this kind of argument is apparent in the literature. It was explicitly invoked by Goehl – Kaufman (1984) in the article cited in 2.1 and the debate which followed. They argued for a view of speech which stressed the importance of "mental linguistic phenomena, both in perception and production" (Kaufman – Goehl 1985: 223). It seems fair to identify the phenomena they had in mind with the kind of abstract linguistic knowledge that we have referred to. Certainly they assumed that these phenomena would not be affected by loss of hearing. The additional step which they took was to suggest that some aspects of speech "are normally determined by linguistic competence" (Goehl – Kaufman 1986: 186), and so we should not expect them to be affected by deafening. They argued that the features which fix a sound's linguistic identity come in that category.

Kaufman and Goehl's point can be answered in a restricted and in a more general way.

In essence the restricted answer has already been given. Certainly abstract linguistic intentions have a crucial role in speech, but there still have to be processes which translate abstract intention into physical performance. It has already been argued that auditory feedback could contribute in various ways to keeping the process of translation smooth. It follows that acquired deafness could disrupt the process of translating abstract linguistic intentions into vocal gestures.

The more general answer is that the formulation of linguistic intentions may not be impervious to hearing loss. Goehl and Kaufman appear to think of linguistic knowledge as a repertoire of Chomskyan rules. Certainly it is hard to imagine that being affected by acquired hearing loss. However there are many points at which it seems reasonable to assume that linguistic knowledge may take forms which are more obviously susceptible to loss of auditory input. We use the phrase "auditory input" here, not auditory feedback. This is to signal the possibility that hearing other people contributes to maintaining knowledge of the language.

There are three broad areas where one might expect auditory input to affect the process of generating linguistic intentions as well as the process of translating them into movement. To some extent they overlap with each other and with points about feedback, but they seem worth stating separately.

(1). Templates. There is a case for the view that various kinds of linguistic target could be specified in the form of templates which describe the acoustic results that motor activity ought to achieve (MacNeilage – Ladefoged 1976: 104–106). If templates of that kind are used, then one might expect them to de-

cay if they were not refreshed. After all, most memory phenomena are subject
to decay or interference.

(2). Magnitudes. Formulating linguistic intentions involves decisions about
where on a continuum a particular utterance should lie. How fast should
speech be? How much should its pitch and volume be varied? How far should
vowel centralisation, or reduction, or assimilation between neighbouring
sounds be carried? Because these decisions are quantitative, it is not difficult
to imagine that input may be needed to prevent drifts away from acceptable
norms.

(3). Selecting variants. Planning speech involves not only choosing acceptable points on various continua, but also moving through the continua in appropriate ways. It is not acceptable to maintain an unvarying word rate. Nor is
it acceptable to use the same patterns of syntax and intonation, over and over,
sentence after sentence. When we speak to different people, we are expected
to choose different subsets of our linguistic repertoire in a pattern of variation
that affects everything from phonology to stylistic register. These kinds of
planning do not obviously reduce to discrete, qualitative rules, and so it is not
hard to believe that hearing could play a large part in negotiating the various
adjustments and balances involved.

Another assumption can be encouraged by the distinction between high-
level processes which form linguistic intentions, and low-level processes
which translate the intentions into action. It is that the effects of acquired deafness are likely to consist of simple disruptions – mainly increased scatter
around the target, or perhaps a tendency to undershoot or overshoot some targets systematically. We should not expect ordered, systematic adjustment. The
assumption follows from two natural extensions of the high-level/low-level
distinction. One is that only the high-level processes carry out planning of any
sophistication: the low-level processes are mere mechanical slaves and do not
have the ability to adjust constructively to altered circumstances. The other is
that high-level processes do not concern themselves with planning to accommodate low-level problems.

Once again, it may be so: but the evidence from other fields does not suggest that it must be. When outside factors impair performance, people can and
do change their pattern of behaviour to circumvent the problem or compensate
for it. Compensation can apparently occur at various levels in the system. For
example impairments produced by alcohol lead drivers to steer towards the
middle of the road, probably to compensate for their variability (Drew –
Colquhoun – Long 1958: 996). This may well be a conscious adjustment, i.e.
high-level processes change behaviour patterns to offset the effects of impaired perception and motor control. Drugs which inhibit cortical function (ni-

tous oxide, alcohol) do not simply lead to deterioration of handwriting: they make it bigger, perhaps to reduce the impact of loss in the accuracy of sensory input (Holding 1989: 285–286). This is presumably not a conscious adjustment. Even low-level processes in speech which one would tend to assume must be mechanical can adjust spontaneously to solve a novel problem. When lip-rounding is prevented by an obstruction, speakers generate an [u] sound by dropping the larynx. That produces the acoustically important effect of lip-rounding, lengthening of the vocal tract, in an unconventional way (Riordan 1977).

We have already mentioned our preliminary comparison of speech errors in pre- and postlingual deafness (Cowie – Douglas-Cowie 1983: 201–205). It suggested that patterns of errors in the two kinds of speech bore non-trivial resemblances. Since speech in prelingual deafness is clearly adapted to functioning without auditory feedback, the resemblance suggests that speech may also adapt itself to the reduction in auditory feedback which occurs in acquired deafness. In the context of evidence from other areas, that does not seem impossible.

If systematic adjustment does take place, then there are four obvious factors which might direct it.

The first factor is residual hearing. It is reasonable to expect that people may modify speech production so that what they say sounds right to them. For instance if they have a greater loss in the high frequencies than in the low frequencies, one might expect them to boost high-frequency components of their speech.

The second factor is risk reduction. The tendency to drive in the middle of the road is an example: it involves adjusting behaviour so that loss of fine control is less likely to have drastic and unacceptable consequences (such as running off the road).

The third factor is least effort. It is widely regarded as a fundamental principle in biology that organisms will tend to minimise energy expended relative to return gained (e.g. Krebs – McCleery 1984). In the particular context of skilled performance, modifications which increase efficiency appear to continue indefinitely (Salmoni 1989) and one of the mechanisms is "alteration of movement control so that the motor system can take advantage of (or exploit) the built-in mechanical-inertial properties of the limbs" (Schmidt 1988: 475). It is reasonable to hypothesise that these tendencies may lead to problems when people lose their ability to monitor whether reducing effort is producing an unacceptable degradation in results.

The fourth factor is more controversial. We have called it "most sensation". We have proposed that deafened speakers may tend to speak so as ensure an amount of feedback that they are comfortable with. Particularly when deafness is profound, this is likely to mean finding ways to increase oral feedback. This is an extrapolation from findings which are well documented and clear, that people find sensory deprivation distressing (Myers 1969) and that people and animals will make efforts to provide themselves with sensory stimulation (Jones 1969). The extrapolation is not unreasonable, but it is most definitely speculative.

2.1.4. Ideas from sociolinguistics

The areas that we have considered so far are traditionally linked to clinical speech research. It is probably apparent that our own thinking is influenced by at least one other. That is sociolinguistics, or more broadly the collection of approaches which stress the complexities of speech as an instrument of communication. Sociolinguistics underlines three points which are important for work on deafened people's speech.

(1). Speech is dynamic, being constantly adjusted to social context in the short term, and evolving over the long term as new influences are absorbed, self image changes, and so on. That emphasis counters the tendency to assume that speech production is a mechanical matter of reproducing highly practised patterns, and helps to indicate why the mechanisms which control speech might need auditory input.

(2). The function of speech is not simply to impart a string of lexical items. It is also fundamentally concerned with conveying an appropriate impression of the speaker and evoking appropriate feelings and dispositions in the listener. Hence the evaluation of speech cannot be confined to the question of intelligibility. If speech is impaired in those respects, then it is a problem to be reckoned with.

(3). Consequently, it is a mistake to assume that only those aspects of speech which have a linguistic function are practically important. Goehl and Kaufman, for instance, lean in that direction in arguing that speech-conservation training is unnecessary because their evidence does not show abnormal articulation of speech sounds. Speech is a social phenomenon, and so the practical question is whether socially significant aspects of the signal are abnormal. We know that voice quality, prosody, paralinguistic features, and so on have a major bearing on the way speakers are received (Knapp 1978: 330–353; Frick 1985; Scherer 1986), and it is misguided purism to ignore them because they are not technically part of speech proper.

2.1.5. Natural expectations

It is important to make the case that evidence from other fields gives no certain guidance on what might happen to speech in acquired deafness. However, it seems fair to say that some possibilities fit more easily with general contemporary assumptions about speech than others. We end this section by outlining what seem to be natural expectations, and what would be more surprising. This provides a framework for discussion of the evidence which follows.

It would be somewhat surprising if acquired deafness affected the way linguistic intentions were formulated, though it is by no means impossible. However it is quite natural to anticipate that their realisation could be affected.

It is natural to expect that acquired deafness may affect aspects of speech which are relatively slow-changing since they logically could be under moment to moment auditory control (and some apparently are). It would be more surprising if it affected aspects which depend on movements too fast for on-line auditory control, notably most aspects of speech sound articulation.

It would be natural to expect speech deterioration in acquired deafness to be essentially random, in the sense that movements simply became less accurate rather than undergoing a systematic shift; and to expect that any trends which did occur would be idiosyncratic. It would be more surprising to find systematic trends across speakers (other than simple loss of precision).

As a consequence of these points, it is natural to expect that there will be very limited resemblances between the speech of the prelingually deaf and speech in acquired deafness.

Different hypotheses give rise to different expectations about the cut-off point between the groups. Goehl and Kaufman's emphasis on linguistic factors leads them to propose that the crux is the achievement of a mature phonology, suggesting a cut-off point in childhood. Emphasis on motor factors suggests a cut-off in adolescence after the relevant muscular and skeletal structures have stabilised. A social perspective suggests that the key may be the establishment of a stable, adult self-image with a correspondingly stable linguistic repertoire. That would suggest a later cut-off in general, with a wide range of individual differences. The first suggestion (i.e. a cut-off point in childhood) is probably what would be most widely expected.

A similar situation holds with rate of decay. If feedback is used directly, then its loss should lead to immediate deterioration. Other options suggest that deterioration should be slower to develop.

As regards practical issues, the natural expectation is that intelligibility will be a problem with early onsets that give rise to speech which is akin to speech in prelingual deafness. With later ages of onset, the issue is likely to be whether speech is socially acceptable. It is widely expected that limited intelligibility will cause practical problems where it occurs, less so that other types of deterioration will cause substantial problems.

2.2. The nature of speech deterioration in acquired deafness

There is now a considerable literature which describes deafened people's speech (see Doster [unpublished manuscript], Sherrard and Still [unpublished manuscript] for earlier reviews of the literature). However it seems fair to say that it lacks focus. The previous section provides a useful way of making the point. It raises a range of questions about deafened speech which are theoretically interesting or practically important: but few can be answered from the literature.

The most basic question is whether acquired deafness does result in speech deterioration. Even this question is difficult to answer with great conviction from the literature.

A very large part of the literature could be written off by a determined sceptic because of three recurring problems. First, speech abnormalities are often described in highly subjective and evaluative terms. Second, very few studies use normal hearing controls. As a result it is possible to dispute whether the features that are highlighted really are abnormal. Third, most studies use very small numbers of speakers. As a result, it is impossible to know for certain whether any abnormality that exists is due to the individual's deafness, or to some other problem or idiosyncracy.

A few larger studies are difficult to write off on these counts, but they too have qualifications attached. Penn (1955) studied speech errors in two large groups of war-deafened veterans, one with conductive and one with sensorineural losses. These were mostly moderate. A wide range of statistically significant differences emerged. It takes considerable ingenuity to escape the conclusion that the errors must have been hearing-related, but the effect could in principle be confined to less than profound losses. In an early study of ours (Cowie – Douglas-Cowie 1983: 186–191), all twelve deafened speakers scored below the single control in intelligibility: applying a Mann-Whitney U test (one-tailed) to that distribution shows a difference on the verge of statistical significance (p = 0.0504). However with a single control one can fairly argue that he or she might have been unrepresentative. Leder – Spitzer (1990) report a study in which 25 deafened speakers were judged significantly different from controls on seven attributes of speech. It is exceedingly difficult to argue that this does not show a difference, but the mean scores could be used to argue that it is very small: the average deafened speaker in the study is rated only mildly disordered in intonation, and not even mildly disordered in other aspects. In sum, it could still be argued that profound acquired losses cause no more than a minimal abnormality – though it would take a very determined sceptic to do so.

A second clear question is whether speech deterioration in acquired deafness shows consistent trends across speakers, or whether it is essentially random. Again, the use of small samples and the lack of controls precludes a clear answer to the question.

A third and different kind of problem arises over the question of whether change within a speaker is chaotic or ordered. Very few studies obtain enough data to reveal any order that exists, either because they describe small fragments of speech in relative isolation, or because they summarise larger chunks of speech in ways that are only able to express rudimentary forms of order (e.g. the mean or the variance of a measure over time).

Despite these limitations, the literature provides a broad sense of the problem. It may still be logically possible to dispute that acquired deafness has more than a minimal effect on speech, but the balance of evidence very clearly suggests that it does. It is also difficult to maintain that the effects of acquired deafness are limited to variables which are known to be directly controlled by auditory feedback: most aspects of speech have been reported to suffer.

The last point provides a broad framework for our review of speech abnormalities per se. We begin from those aspects of speech which it is easiest to anticipate will be affected, those which involve slow-changing processes which are not fully linguistic: and we work towards articulatory aspects of speech, which are both fast changing and quintessentially linguistic. The evidence is considered under three broad headings. First we consider abnormalities which are logically quite distinct from linguistic issues. Next we consider abnormalities in suprasegmental features of language. Then we consider abnormalities of articulation. A major part of the data is from studies that are concerned with the effect of cochlear implantation on speech. The data cited below concern pre-implant conditions only unless otherwise stated.

Apart from evidence on the nature of speech deterioration, the literature raises a number of associated issues. What influences the severity of the disorder? How does it respond to treatment? How serious is it? These are considered after we have looked at the evidence on the nature of speech deterioration.

2.2.1. Non-linguistic abnormalities

2.2.1.1. Breathing problems

Several sources claim that deafened speakers have difficulty with the control of breathing, and note the implications for speech. Luchsinger – Arnold (1965: 635) talk of breathing problems leading to general phonation problems. Parker (1983: 238) talks of inadequate intake of breath leading to disruptive pauses, general voice production problems and increased rate of speech towards the end of a sentence. One subject of Waters (1986: 38) is said to have problems with breath control. Lane – Webster (1991: 860) suggest that "Improper management of the breath stream may also contribute to anomalies in the production of fricative and stop consonants whose spectra depend on part on air volume velocities supplied to the supraglottal constriction."

Objective evidence on breathing problems comes from Lane et al. (1991). In an instrumental study of three deafened subjects, they found two types of problem. Subjects either expended too much air or too little.

A broadly related error relates to the insertion of meaningless phonation. Waters (1986: 38) describes excessive voicing for final voiced sounds leading to the auditory impression of an additional final syllable. Bergmann (1952: 343) talks of "meaningless phonation before and after words, grunts". This error is also mentioned in Penn (1955: 57).

2.2.1.2. Intensity

There is a widespread impression that controlling volume is a central problem for deafened speakers. It is reflected in the quotation from Espir – Rose (1976) which we cited early in the chapter. Many sources informally report problems in this area. Abberton et al. (1985: 533) talk of loudness control being adversely affected; Parker (1983: 239) and Read (1989: 46) indicate some kind of general problem. The nature of the problem is less widely agreed upon. The usual claim is that the speech is too loud (Luchsinger – Arnold 1965: 635; Engelmann – Waterfall – Hough 1981: 1829; Binnie – Daniloff – Buckingham 1982: 186). But there are also claims that speech can be too loud or too soft (Bergmann 1952: 340, 341, 343; Penn 1955: 21; House 1978: 206). Some writers associate over-soft speech with conductive deafness, and over-loud speech with sensorineural deafness (Penn 1955: 21–23; Silverman – Calvert 1978: 395). There are also accounts of "uncontrolled" volume (Penn 1955: 21). Waters (1986: 38) is perhaps referring to the same phenomenon when she talks of "difficulty controlling loudness".

Two formal studies consider volume. They mirror the conflicts among informal reports. Leder et. al. (1987a) studied 19 male deafened subjects and 10 male controls. They found significantly greater mean-intensity values for the deafened group than for the control group in all linguistic contexts tested. They also found that standard deviations were two to three times greater for the deaf, indicating greater intensity fluctuations in deaf speech than in normal. The other study, by Kirk – Edgerton (1983: 286–288), found no significant difference between controls and deafened speakers either in the range or in the standard deviation of intensity. However is not directly comparable with the Leder et al. study in that it studied people who had received cochlear implants speaking with the device switched off.

2.2.1.3. Pitch

In the perceptual study by Leder – Spitzer (1990: 171), pitch disorder was listed as number two in order of severity among seven abnormalities in deafened speech. Two problems with pitch are widely discussed: abnormal average pitch height, and abnormal variation in pitch.

Two types of pitch height disorder are reported. The first is that average pitch is too high overall. Informal reports of this are found in Penn (1955: 25), Luchsinger – Arnold (1965: 635), Engelmann – Waterfall – Hough (1981: 1829), and Parker (1983: 239). Objective evidence comes from studies by Binnie – Daniloff – Buckingham (1982: 184), Kirk – Edgerton (1983: 290), Leder – Spitzer – Kirchner (1987: 323), and Oster (1987: 84). Ball – Faulkner (1989: 29) make essentially the same point, showing that some speakers have high F0 modes. The second type of pitch-height disorder reported is that the pitch is too low. This is much less widely reported. There are a few informal reports (Bergmann 1952: 340), and some formal evidence from Tartter – Chute – Hellman (1989: 2116) and from Ball – Faulkner – Fourcin (1990: 400, 404). Kirk – Edgerton (1983: 285–286) show that pitch is too high in males and too low in females. There are also studies which show that for some subjects pitch height is not affected. Ball – Faulkner – Fourcin (1990: 400) describe some speakers whose average F0 is normal.

The study by Leder – Spitzer – Kirchner (1987) carries particular weight because of its size. It used 21 deafened subjects. It therefore has to be taken seriously as evidence of a trend in the direction of heightened pitch. An important qualification is that it is based on an all-male sample. We do not know whether deafened females show the same trend. It is interesting that there is a trend for the studies which report lowered F0 to do so for female subjects (Kirk – Edgerton 1983; Tartter – Chute – Hellman 1989).

We now turn to pitch spread. Monotonous intonation is associated with deafened speech about as often as problems with volume (e.g. Bergmann 1952: 340; Penn 1955: 27; Luchsinger – Arnold 1965: 635; Binnie – Daniloff – Buckingham 1982: 185; Plant–Hammarberg 1983: 103; Plant 1983: 25, 31). The term "monotonous" seems to be used to indicate monotone pitch, although this is not always clear. Binnie – Daniloff – Buckingham (1982: 185), for example, talk of an "increasingly monotonous, less inflected voice", which tends to suggest that the problem is comparable to the classically monotone pitch of prelingual deaf speech (see e.g. Hood – Dixon 1969; Horii 1982). An alternative interpretation considers monotony as an aspect of intonation, and it is discussed as such under section 2.2.2 below.

Some formal studies do suggest a trend towards monotone pitch. Plant (1983: 25–26) provides F0 traces from a deafened speaker which clearly are monotone by comparison with those from his control subjects. Plant – Hammarberg (1983: 91–92) found a considerably restricted F0 range in two out of three deafened subjects in comparison to normal hearing controls. In a longitudinal study of one subject, Binnie – Daniloff – Buckingham (1982: 185) found that the F0 range became increasingly narrowed as time went on. Other reports of restricted F0 range for some subjects appear in Ball – Ison (1984: 251), Abberton et al. (1985: 533), Waters (1986: 38), Ball – Faulkner (1989: 29).

However intonation, for at least some deafened people, is not simply monotone. Kirk – Edgerton (1983: 285) and Oster (1987: 83–84), for example, measured the standard deviation of F0 in deafened subjects (in the former case cochlear implant users speaking with the device switched off) and found it too high in some subjects. They interpret their results as indicating an erratic and uncontrolled distribution of pitch. Cowie and Douglas-Cowie (1983: 200) talk of "abrupt switches from low to high pitches in adjacent words or syllables". Other studies indicate too wide a pitch range for some subjects (Ball – Ison 1984: 251; Waters 1986: 38; Ball – Faulkner 1989: 29; Ball – Faulkner – Fourcin 1990: 405).

2.2.1.4. Voice quality

Voice quality is frequently commented on as abnormal. However a wealth of terms may be used to describe the abnormality, and it is not always clear what they mean or whether different people mean the same things by the same term.

Laver's phonetic description of voice quality (1980) provides a framework in which to try to set the evidence.

The voice qualities on which the literature appears to be clearest both fall into Laver's category of phonatory settings. Two qualities are described. The first is creak. This is mentioned by, for example, Ball – Ison (1984: 251), Waters (1986: 38), Ball – Faulkner (1989: 29), Read (1989: 46), Ball – Faulkner – Fourcin (1990: 400, 405). Objective data are provided in the studies by Ball – Ison (1984), Ball – Faulkner (1989), Read (1989), Ball – Faulkner – Fourcin (1990). The abnormalities take the form of excessive low-frequency irregularity which corresponds to the auditory impression of creak. Breathy-voice quality is also the product of a phonatory setting, and relates to inefficient vibration of the vocal folds. Several studies talk of deafened speech as being too breathy (Penn 1955: 28; Plant – Hammarberg 1983: 103; Cowie – Douglas-Cowie 1983: 198; Tartter – Chute – Hellman 1989: 2116), but none provides objective measures.

Deafened speakers also show problems at the level of supralaryngeal settings. One group of supralaryngeal settings described by Laver is the velopharyngeal group with which the deafened show problems. There are two sides to the picture. One is that their speech is too nasal (Bergmann 1952: 341; Penn 1955: 29; Binnie – Daniloff – Buckingham 1982: 185; Cowie – Douglas-Cowie 1983: 198; Plant – Hammarberg 1983: 103; Leder – Spitzer 1990: 171). The other is that it is denasal (Penn 1955: 30). There are, however, no objective measures of these qualities in deafened speech.

Beyond these voice qualities, the picture is less clear. A number of terms seem to be linked. These are "vocal harshness" (Engelmann – Waterfall – Hough 1981: 1829), "vocal strain" (House 1978: 206), "strident quality" (Bergmann 1952: 343; Penn 1955: 31–32), "tense quality" (Waters 1986: 38), "rigid quality" (Silverman – Calvert 1978: 389).

2.2.1.5. Rate of speech

Some studies indicate a problem of some sort, but are not specific (Goehl – Kaufman 1984: 63; Leder – Spitzer 1990: 171). In the perceptual study by Leder – Spitzer (1990: 171), abnormalities of rate ranked third in in a list of seven abnormalities whose severity listeners assessed.

The majority opinion is that speech is too slow. This is backed by precise measures from Binnie – Daniloff – Buckingham (1982: 183), Plant (1983: 28), Plant (1984: 40), Leder et al. (1987b: 845), Lane – Webster (1991: 865). Leder et al. (1987b) use the largest sample, consisting of 25 speakers. They found that the mean rate for reading a paragraph was significantly longer for the deafened, and the mean rate for each of the six sentences making up the paragraph was significantly longer.

Several aspects of speech appear to contribute to the general slowness.

(1). Pausing can be longer in deafened speech (Plant – Hammarberg 1983: 95; Lane – Webster 1991: 865). There can also be too many pauses (Plant – Hammarberg 1983: 95).

(2). Even when pausing abnormalities are excluded, speech is still too slow. Binnie – Daniloff – Buckingham (1982: 183) found an increase in mean word duration.

(3). There are informal observations of vowel elongation (Waters 1986: 38). Objective confirmation is provided by Plant (1983: 28) and Lane – Webster (1991: 865). Lane – Webster, for example, found that average vowel duration for the deafened was 98 msec, while it was 86 msec for the deafened. A related point is made by Parker (1983: 244) and Tartter – Chute – Hellman (1989: 2116): they found that stressed syllables were too long in deafened speakers.

(4). Binnie – Daniloff – Buckingham (1982: 183, 185) report syllabic extension of monosyllabic words. There is no suggestion of this in the rest of the literature, and it is not clear whether this is a unique property of their one subject or whether it is a more general trend. Their subject was deafened relatively early (at five years of age).

(5). A study by Zimmermann – Rettaliata (1981: 178) showed abnormally long movement transition times for the articulators during closing gestures.

Almost inevitably, there are also reports that deafened people speak too fast. Penn (1955: 32–33) and Waters (1986: 38) both observe this phenomenon informally. Tartter – Chute – Hellman (1989: 2114) report listener judgements of a deafened teenager prior to implant as showing an accelerated speech rate in connected speech. Oster (1987: 86) made some objective measures of duration time for two deafened subjects, pre- and post-implant. One showed noticeably short duration times. These data on abnormally fast speech are not related to control data.

To complete the picture, there are reports which suggest abnormal variability in rate. Zimmermann – Rettaliata (1981: 170) make the informal observation of "intermittent increased rate of speech", and Waters (1986: 38) observes increased rate towards the ends of phrases. There are no systematic data to back up these observations.

2.2.2. Suprasegmentals

2.2.2.1. The communicative variation of rate

Although rate is often discussed, very little is said about the kind of variation in rate which has a communicative function in normal speech – for example, one of the cues to turn-taking in conversation is slowed rate of articulation. Waters (1986: 38) suggests that this kind of pattern may be taken to excess when she talks of slow rate of speech with particularly lengthened final syllables and sounds.

2.2.2.2. Intonation

Problems with intonation are widely reported. Silverman – Calvert (1978: 389), Tartter – Chute – Hellman (1989: 2116), Read (1989: 46), Leder – Spitzer (1990: 171), all make general observations about intonation. Leder – Spitzer (1990) asked 15 speech-language pathologists to rate the speech of a large sample of deafened speakers (25) and a matched control group (10) on a number of attributes including intonation. Results showed that intonation was first in order of severity of abnormality among the seven speech attributes measured.

Some comments about abnormal intonation presumably refer to the kinds of low-order abnormalities that we have considered under the heading "pitch" in section 2.2.1. Our concern here is with abnormalities which are inherently related to the higher-order units which carry linguistic functions, i.e. tone groups and their component parts. There is relatively little work at this level, but four issues have received some attention.

(1). Monotony. In informal comments the term which is most often linked with deafened intonation is monotony. This may be meant to imply a low-order problem, reduction in the spread of F0. That reading has already been considered (see under 2.2.1). Given the very mixed evidence for reduced F0 range, it may well not be the main reason for perceived monotony. An alternative is that monotony could arise because the same pattern is repeated too unvaryingly. A study by Cowie – Douglas-Cowie – Rahilly (1988) suggests that possibility.

(2). Sentence-final tone groups. Declination in sentence-final intonation tone groups has been proposed as a universal of intonation (see e.g. Lieberman 1967: 23 ff.). It makes sense to suppose that deafness might lead people to revert to a default pattern of declination too much. Plant (personal communication) has described cases where this appears to happen. However three separate studies report lack of declination. Bergmann (1952: 343) and Plant (1983: 25) report pitch going up rather than down at the end of a sentence. Cowie – Douglas-Cowie (1983: 200) talk of sentences "ending on a mid level note, giving impression of being left hanging in mid-air".

(3). The nucleus. In normal intonation the nucleus of the tone group is associated with pitch prominence. There is some evidence to suggest that pitch is not the distinguishing characteristic of the nucleus in deafened speech. Waters (1986: 38) talks of shallow pitch movements on the nucleus and abnormal use of loudness for nuclear emphasis instead.

(4). The grammatical and attitudinal functions of intonation. Normally particular intonation patterns are associated with particular grammatical or attitudinal functions. Two articles suggest a breakdown in this respect. Plant (1983: 25) and Plant – Hammarberg (1983: 92–104) noted that subjects were unable to use intonation properly to mark emphatic stress or a question in the way that the controls did (cf. also Abberton et al. 1985: 534–535).

With few exceptions, these studies are either informal or based on the speech of very few subjects. They are also difficult to interpret because the norms of intonation are very incompletely understood. However they indicate that there is a case for considering that deafened speech may show abnormalities in the linguistic use of intonation rather than just poor pitch control.

2.2.2.3. Stress

Various studies report abnormalities of stress. Problems are reported in two main areas. The first relates to the global distribution of stress. The second relates to stress as a linguistic marker which directs attention to specific items or relationships.

(1). Global patterns. Several studies report global tendencies towards overstressing (Parker 1983: 244; Plant 1984: 40; Cowie – Douglas-Cowie 1983: 200). Luchsinger – Arnold (1965: 635) and Plant – Hammarberg (1983: 103) seem to be describing the same phenomenon when they talk of stress being excessively increased. Similarly (Plant 1984: 40) mentions a lack of distinction between stressed and unstressed syllables. Parker (1983: 244) gives a sense of the problem when she talks of "word-by-word pronunciation" in which words appear to be in their "citation" forms. The general impression is of a tendency for deafened speakers to equalise the distribution of stress among all syllables. This runs counter to a basic feature of English. English is classified as a stress-timed language because some syllables receive more stress than others.

There is some suggestion of a contrary trend. Parker (1983: 244) suggests a tendency to overstress the stressed syllables and almost lose the unstressed syllables. Tartter – Chute – Hellman (1989: 2117) also report that unstressed syllables are too short. In polysyllabic words this can lead to the omission or distortion of whole segments (Parker 1983: 244).

If overstressing occurs, then it compounds problems with intonation. The nucleus is normally said to fall on a stressed syllable with pitch prominence.

There is evidence (see section 2.2.2.2) that nuclear syllables receive too little pitch prominence in deafened speech. If there is also an equalisation of stress, nuclear syllables may be difficult to identify (see section 6.3.3). This will have implications for the recovery of intonation structure in deafened people's speech.

(2). The directive function of stress. A few studies indicate that deafened speakers have problems with the use of stress for emphasis (Plant – Hammarberg 1983: 90–94) and for contrast (Leder et al. 1986), although there appears to be variation from person to person. In the study by Plant and Hammarberg, only one of three deafened subjects appears to be totally unable to signal emphatic stress. The study by Leder et al. (1986: 1970–1971) used two deafened subjects. In pre-cochlear-implant state, one of these was judged by listeners to place contrastive stress correctly only 50% of the time; the other was judged correct 96% of the time.

The problem is documented acoustically by both Plant (1983: 22–25) and Leder et al. (1986: 1970). Leder et al. show that the acoustic correlates of normally-produced contrastive stress are higher F0, longer duration and greater intensity. The deafened subject with poor control had problems with all three acoustic parameters. He was also inconsistent about the parameters he tried to use for contrast. Plant – Hammarberg (1983: 92) focus on the use of higher F0 for normal emphatic stress and show that their two worst subjects fail to use this feature. They also show that one of the subjects appears to compensate for lack of F0 movement by using duration, and by pausing after the appropriate word instead.

The study by Leder et al. (1986: 1971) has a further dimension. It examines contrastive stress prior to, and after, cochlear implant. One parameter of contrastive stress, F0, was quickly rectified after single channel cochlear implant. Duration and intensity parameters improved more slowly. However the improvement in F0 led to a listener judgement of 100% correctness even without appropriate duration and intensity cues.

2.2.3. Articulation

Articulatory disorders are reported in deafened speech, but not often regarded as a major problem. Silverman – Calvert (1978: 389) report deterioration in the "sharpness and precision of enunciation". However Goehl – Kaufman (1984; 1986) and Kaufman – Goehl (1985) argued strongly that this kind of disorder is minor. Certainly, by comparison with prelingual deaf speech it is slight. Cowie – Douglas-Cowie (1983: 205) estimated that consonant errors were 75 times commoner in the prelingual deaf sample studied by Smith

(1972) than in their 1983 sample. The perceptual study by Leder – Spitzer (1990: 171) suggests an intermediate position. Articulatory disorder was rated only sixth in order of severity out of a group of seven disorders in deafened speech. Nevertheless, ratings of deafened speakers' articulation were very significantly worse than ratings of controls.

2.2.3.1. Consonant errors

Errors can be discussed under five headings: (1) omissions, (2) distortions, (3) substitutions, (4) voiced/voiceless distinctions, (5) intrusions.

(1). Omissions. Two main categories of omission are mentioned – (a) omission of consonants in final position and (b) other omissions.

(a) Omission of consonants in final position

Leder – Spitzer (1990: 173) mention final consonant deletion in the report of their perceptual study. Auditory impressionistic transcription in three other studies (Zimmermann – Rettaliata 1981: 170; Plant 1984: 40; Tartter – Chute – Hellman 1989: 2114) backs this up, although each is based on the speech of only one deafened subject. Particular consonants are mentioned. By far the most commonly mentioned group is the alveolar group, in particular [s], [z], [t] and [d] (see Zimmermann – Rettaliata 1981: 170; Cowie – Douglas-Cowie 1983: 206–209; Plant 1984: 40; Tartter – Chute – Hellman 1989: 2114, 2119). Both Cowie – Douglas-Cowie (1983) and Plant (1984) provide information on the frequency of omissions, although with the exception of these two studies, such quantitative information is generally not given. Plant (1984) provides evidence that the alveolar group is most affected. Of a total of 69 consonant omissions in his data, 64 were in the alveolar group. Plant (1984: 40) suggests that the frequency of alveolar omissions may relate to the fact that "these consonants may have weak tactile cues to their production and rely upon audition for maintenance or else a decline in velopharyngeal control may result in imperfect final stop production".

(b) Other omissions

Omissions in other contexts appears not to be as frequent. Taken in terms of the numbers provided by Cowie – Douglas-Cowie (1983: 206), these are in order of frequency:

the semivowels [r] and [l];

the velars [k] and [g] and the dentals [θ] and [ð] and the nasal [n];

[m], [f], [v], [ə], [j], [h].

The omission of consonants as part of cluster reduction is also mentioned, although no specific data are provided (Binnie – Daniloff – Buckingham 1982: 185; Plant – Hammarberg 1983: 103).

(2). Distortions. When the evidence from the various studies and comments is pooled, there is mention of distortion of almost every item in the English consonantal system. There are, however, distortions that appear to stand out.

Most frequently mentioned is the fricative and affricate group, in particular the sibilants [s], [z], [ʃ] and [ʒ]. This group is picked out as salient by the listeners in the perceptual study by Leder – Spitzer (1990: 173). An auditory impression of what might be wrong is supplied by Luchsinger – Arnold (1965: 635) who talk of deafened articulation of these consonants as producing "dulled, diffused or slushy lisping". Other studies which draw attention to fricative and/or affricate distortion are Bergmann (1952: 342), Penn (1955: 34), House (1978: 206), Cowie – Douglas-Cowie (1983: 206–208), Engelmann – Waterfall – Hough (1981: 1829), Goehl – Kaufman (1984: 63), Abberton et al.(1985: 533), Waters (1986: 38), Lane – Webster (1991: 863–864). Most of these studies provide informal comment rather than systematic descriptions. Two exceptions are the studies by Lane – Webster (1991: 863–864) and Cowie – Douglas-Cowie (1983). Lane – Webster give more precise measures of the nature of the error. They use an acoustic measure to show that there is less differentiation between [s] and [ʃ] in the speech of three deafened subjects than there is in three control subjects. Cowie – Douglas-Cowie (1983: 206) provide quantitative information. They show that sibilant distortion is a common error by comparison with the other articulatory errors in deafened speech, although the actual figures mentioned are very small.

A second group of consonants that is frequently mentioned is that of [r] and [l] (see Bergmann 1952: 343; Penn 1955: 34; Zimmermann – Rettaliata 1981: 170; Cowie – Douglas-Cowie 1983: 206–209; Abberton et al. 1985: 533). There is no direct information on the precise nature of the distortion, although two pieces of evidence may bear on it. Cowie – Douglas-Cowie note omission of these consonants as well as substitution of [w] for [r]. Distortion may well be a form of [r] or [l] that is neither fully omitted or fully substituted. The second piece of evidence comes from a study by Tartter – Chute – Hellman (1989: 2118). They use a measure of second formant transition length to show slight acoustic blurring of the stop-semivowel distinction at the alveolar place of articulation.

More general patterns of consonantal distortion have also been proposed. The main source is Tartter – Chute – Hellman (1989). With regard to place of articulation they measured the positive and negative transition slopes of formants and suggest that there may be some fronting of alveolar and velar consonants in deafened speech. With regard to manner of articulation, they use acoustic measures to show slight problems with the distinction between fricatives and voiceless stops and between stops and semivowels.

(3). Substitutions. Reports of various substitutions appear in Bergmann (1952), Luchsinger – Arnold (1965: 635), Cowie – Douglas-Cowie (1983: 206–211). Apart from that by Cowie and Douglas-Cowie, these studies give very little sense of any kind of patterning. Almost anything seems possible. Cowie and Douglas-Cowie provide a diagram showing substitutions and the actual numbers that occur. The study suggests some major substitution trends. They divide consonants into two groups: a labial group comprising [f, v, b, m, w, r] and a postlabial group containing all other consonants. The major substitution trend is for consonants in the labial group to shift forward and for consonants in the postlabial group to shift backwards. There is one major exception, however, to the trend for backward shift. That is provided by a trend in the postlabial group for sibilants and affricates to shift to [ʃ] or something closer to [ʃ] than the target is.

(4). The distinction between voiced and voiceless consonants. Carney (1988: 281) reports changes in voice onset time; Tartter – Chute – Hellman (1989: 2117) report voicing problems related to voice onset time; Zimmermann – Rettaliata (1981: 178) show longer voicing durations and longer voice termination times relative to movement onset in closing gestures in deafened speech. Numerous other studies report a general lack of control over the voiced/voiceless distinction (Bergmann 1952: 340; Luchsinger – Arnold 1965: 635; Cowie – Douglas-Cowie 1983: 208; Parker 1983: 245–246).

(5). Intrusions. Cowie – Douglas-Cowie (1983: 206) report that consonant intrusions take place. The main intrusions involve the consonants [t] and [d], and there is infrequent intrusion of [w], [s] and [θ]. No further information is available on intrusions.

Two problems stand out in the general area of articulation. One is the shortage of evidence about the magnitudes of effects, either in terms of frequency or in terms of acoustic properties. The other is the lack of integration. Not many studies attempt to present an overall picture of articulatory disorders. Exceptions are the studies by Cowie – Douglas-Cowie (1983) and Penn (1955). The sheer number of apparently unrelated observations makes it difficult to grasp what is going on, and perhaps easy to assume that nothing very much is.

2.2.3.2. Vowel errors

Very little has been written about vowel errors in deafened speech. This may indicate the absence of such errors. There is certainly some reason to believe this. Data from the two studies which use the largest samples (Penn 1955; Cowie – Douglas-Cowie 1983), for example, suggest very much lower proportions of vowel than of consonant errors. However more actual studies are needed.

Two main categories of error are described. These are (1) restriction of vowel differentiation and (2) diphthongisation.

(1). Restriction of vowel differentiation. Bergmann (1952: 343) makes the informal observation that vowel sounds are undistinguished from each other. Both physiological measures in Zimmermann – Rettaliata (1981) and acoustic measures in Plant (1983) offer some corroboration. Zimmermann – Rettaliata (1981: 178) found that tongue positions relative to a mandibular reference plane varied abnormally little in the vowels of a single deafened speaker. Plant (1983: 28) showed a restricted range of second-formant values in two out of three deafened subjects. Monsen (1981: 25) found a sharp reduction in second formant movement in one of the two deafened subjects studied. Various studies suggest that the direction of the restriction is towards the central vowel space. This is indicated in impressionistic phonetic transcription by Cowie – Douglas-Cowie (1983: 213–215) and Waters (1986: 38) and receives some back up from acoustic measures by Plant (1984) and by Tartter – Chute – Hellman (1989: 2119). Plant (1984: 40) shows that the average spectra of his one deaf subject peak in spontaneous speech around the Hertz values corresponding to the average formants for the central vowel [ˊ]. Plant shows, however, that this does not happen in the more formal style of reading. Another anomaly in differentiation between vowels was reported by Lane–Webster (1991: 862). They showed that deafened speakers lacked a pattern of differentiation in pitch height which was present in controls. It is not clear from their data how this relates to other reports of anomalies involving vowel identity and pitch: Plant (1984: 41) indicated that his subjects may have been using excess pitch height to distinguish vowels.

(2). Diphthongisation. Either monophthongs become diphthongs (Binnie – Daniloff – Buckingham 1982: 185), especially in final position (Waters 1986: 38), or diphthongs become monophthongs (Plant – Hammarberg 1983: 95; Plant 1984: 45). Data from Cowie – Douglas-Cowie (1983: 211) suggest that both trends occur, and that they are about equally common. Plant – Hammarberg (1983: 100) suggest that diphthongisation problems may relate to feedback strategies.

Finally there are studies which give an assortment of individual vowel errors (Penn 1955: 44; Luchsinger – Arnold 1965: 635; Cowie – Douglas-Cowie 1983: 211–216). But as with consonants, it is difficult to make much of the rather patchy data available.

This completes our survey of the literature on the form speech deterioration takes. It is apparent that although there is a good deal of material, it is difficult to draw firm conclusions in many areas. The discussion section at the end of the chapter returns to the question of where the evidence leaves us.

2.3. Associated issues

This section considers a number of issues which are raised in the literature, but remain outside the framework of the previous section with its emphasis on the form of speech deterioration.

2.3.1. The extent of the problem

This section considers what is known about the functional significance of speech deterioration in acquired deafness.

There is disagreement in the literature as to whether speech deterioration causes a real problem or not. One extreme is represented by Goehl – Kaufman (1984: 63), who quote the assessment of one of their clinical judges¡ "It is all perfectly functional speech." This viewpoint was contested by Zimmermann– Collins (1985) and by Cowie – Douglas-Cowie – Stewart (1986). The disagreement reflects the fact that relatively little research has been done on the topic. Two types of study are potentially relevant. The first concerns intelligibility: the second, social acceptability.

2.3.1.1. Intelligibility

In the case of prelingual deaf speech, functional impairment is examined through experiments on how intelligible the speech is to listeners (e.g. John – Howarth 1965; Osberger – Levitt 1979; Monsen 1983). In postlingual deaf speech, however, hardly any studies of intelligibility have been reported. This may be because researchers simply do not believe that there is an intelligibility problem worth examining. Cooper et al. (1989: 30), for example, state that "a significant loss of intelligibility is not generally found in deafened adults". Various other passing references to intelligibility, however, suggest that there are problems. Ramsden (1981: 54), for example, states that "speech intelligibility may suffer". The problems are often implicit in discussions of cochlear implants: intelligibility is said to improve with implantation, which presupposes that there was something wrong with it in the first place. Abberton et al. (1985: 533), for example, talk of laryngeal difficulties affecting intelligibility, and of an improvement with implantation. Morgon et al. (1984: 203) suggest an important improvement in the intelligibility of the implanted patient. Waters (1986: 37) in a cochlear implant study, draws attention to the importance of obtaining conversational samples of deafened speech as that is where intelligibility starts to suffer. But none of these comments is backed up by objective measures of intelligibility.

The studies which do offer some objective measurement are those by Bilger (1977: 130), Binnie – Daniloff – Buckingham (1982: 185), Cowie – Douglas-Cowie (1983: 186-191) and Plant (1984: 41–42). There are problems with all these studies of intelligibility. None is on a large scale; Bilger (1977), Binnie – Daniloff – Buckingham (1982) and Plant (1984) measure intelligibility on word lists or reading rather than on more informal speech where Cowie – Douglas-Cowie (1983) suggest the problem is likely to be greater; Bilger (1977) uses a rather subjective measure of intelligibility when he asks normal hearing listeners simply to rate intelligibility on a scale from 0% to 100%; and none of the sources offers good control data with detailed information on the spread of intelligibility in the controls. Nonetheless, all of the studies indicate that intelligibility suffers. The studies also concur that there are big inter-subject differences in intelligibility. Cowie – Douglas-Cowie (1983: 186–191) find intelligibility ranging from near zero to near perfect. Bilger (1977) shows a range of intelligibility over twelve subjects from 94% mean intelligibility to 1% mean intelligibility. The single subject in the study by Binnie – Daniloff – Buckingham (1982: 185) shows substantial loss of intelligibility (only 30% – 35% of the words correctly perceived by listeners), whereas Plant's subject showed a much smaller loss (between approximately 81% and 84% of the words were correctly perceived).

2.3.1.2. Acceptability

Intelligibility is not the only index of speech deterioration. It is also relevant to ask how socially acceptable speech is. As sociolinguists have shown, various regional or socially-marked forms of speech are stigmatised, and regardless of their functionality, provoke negative reactions among listeners (see e.g. Giles – Powesland 1975: 24–89). It would hardly be surprising if stigmatisation also held for abnormal varieties of speech. Some evidence to suggest this comes from Silverman (1976: 550), Blood–Blood–Danhauer (1974) and Turnbaugh–Guitar–Hoffman (1981: 290). One pilot group of studies on deafened speech examines this issue (Nicholl 1981; Cowie – Douglas-Cowie – Kerr 1982; Cowie – Douglas-Cowie 1983: 192-196). This is an area where systematic research is clearly needed.

2.3.2. Variables relating to speech deterioration

The literature provides very little information on the factors which affect the extent of speech deterioration. However four main variables seem to be relevant. They are set out below. A few others have been mentioned. For instance Cowie – Douglas-Cowie (1983: 191) mention that differences in motor ability may be relevant, but there is no evidence on the matter.

2.3.2.1. Age at onset of deafness

Profound deafness occurring in childhood seems much more likely to lead to a substantial problem of speech deterioration than deafness acquired later. This was what Kinney (1948: 307) had in mind as far back as 1948 when he wrote, "When 'a person with normal hearing and normal speech becomes totally deaf, he tends to lose his speech to an extent directly proportional to the length of time that he had speech." The strongest evidence for this comes from Cowie – Douglas-Cowie (1983: 190–191) who show that intelligibility is badly impaired in childhood deafened subjects, but much less so in deafness acquired in adulthood. Plant – Hammarberg (1983) looked at three deafened subjects, one deafened at eight, one at nine and one at fifty nine. They concluded (1983: 105) that "the speech of the subjects deafened prior to puberty does appear to have been far more adversely affected than that of the speaker deafened during middle-age". Evidence from cases where age at onset is given fits this broad picture. Waldstein (1989: 39) notes that speakers in his study who were postlingually deafened before puberty display deviations in speech patterning which "compromise phonological integrity", whereas speakers who were deafened after puberty display primarily phonetic deviations. Binnie – Daniloff – Buckingham (1982: 185) studied one subject deafened at five. This subject had badly impaired intelligibility (only around 30% of the words correctly perceived by listeners). Conversely Goehl – Kaufman (1984) using five subjects deafened in mid life, reported no clinically significant deterioration of speech production. Other studies either provide no information on age at onset of deafness (e.g. House 1978; Engelmann – Waterfall – Hough 1981; Waters 1986; Read 1989), or provide none on how it relates to their data (e.g. Leder et al. 1987 [a and b]).

2.3.2.2. Level of loss

It seems highly likely that level of hearing loss relates to level of speech deterioration. However the literature does not allow much examination of this assumption. A central reason is that most of it is concerned with speakers whose loss is profound. It is less clear whether deterioration occurs with lesser hearing losses, but two studies suggest that it may. Penn (1955) showed abnormalities in a sample where the average loss was 45 dB. In a sample of five, three of whom had severe rather than profound deafness, Goehl – Kaufman (1984) found deterioration in some respects. They do not regard it as clinically significant, but Penn (1955: 63) talks of "significant voice and speech deviations".

2.3.2.3. Length of time deaf

From informal comments, it seems that many people expect speech deterioration to be critically related to length of time since onset of deafness. However information on the point is slight. Two issues can be separated.

The first concerns speech in the first couple of years after the onset of deafness. Both Binnie – Daniloff – Buckingham (1982) and Plant (1984) provide some evidence that there is a gradual deterioration of speech. Binnie – Daniloff – Buckingham studied a five-year old deafened subject from six weeks to nine months post onset. Plant compared listeners' reactions to speech produced by one subject, deafened at eleven years old, two months after onset and again at thirty months after onset. Both studies indicate that speech deteriorates gradually over this kind of period. A more informal comment to this effect comes from Kirchner – Suzuki (1968: 98) who say that "an adult who suffers a complete or severe loss of hearing is still able to produce his usual voice for a short period of time before it degenerates into the characteristic voice of the deaf'".

The second issue is what happens in the longer term. The only evidence on this comes from Leder – Spitzer – Kirchner (1987: 323) and Leder et al. (1987a: 225–226). These studies compared subjects with profound hearing loss of less than ten years with those of more than ten years. No difference was found with respect to either mean F0 or mean intensity values. Subjects deafened less than ten years demonstrated less variablity of F0 than those deafened more than ten years, but it is not clear whether this finding is statistically robust or not.

2.3.2.4. Speech and context

A few comments indicate that context is a relevant variable. A study of intelligibility by Cowie–Douglas-Cowie (1983: 189–190) showed that deafened speakers were more intelligible when they confined their speech to the commonplace. Waters (1986: 41) made the informal observation about one subject that the speech was more intelligible in reading than in conversation. There is, however, little formal evidence in this area.

2.3.3. Speech production and cochlear implants

The past decade has seen a growing number of studies on the effects of cochlear implants on speech production. These are mainly concerned with the post-lingually deafened, but some are concerned with speech production in children with prelingual onset of deafness (see e.g. Osberger 1988). These studies consistently report that implantation leads to improvement. The literature is summarised under two headings: the nature of improvement and the extent of improvement.

2.3.3.1. The nature of improvement

The most frequently researched improvements relate to pitch and its role in intonation. Improvements are reported in pitch height, pitch spread and higher-order intonation patterns. There are reports of pitch height being lowered where it was previously too high (Engelmann – Waterfall – Hough 1981: 1829; Kirk – Edgerton 1983: 285), or being raised where it was inappropriately low (Kirk – Edgerton 1983: 286; Tartter – Chute – Hellman 1989: 2116). There are also reports of improved pitch range (Ball – Ison 1984: 251; Abberton et al. 1985: 535) and pitch distribution (Kirk – Edgerton 1983: 285; Oster 1987: 84). These improvements too can be bi-directional e.g. too wide a range improves to an appropriately narrower range and too narrow a range improves to an appropriately wider range. Plant – Oster (1986: 71–74) have reported higher-order improvements in intonation in the form of more appropriate declination patterns at the ends of sentences, and Leder et al. (1986: 1971) have shown that the use of pitch to signal contrast improves with implantation.

Improvements in rate also receive fairly frequent mention. Oster (1987: 86) reports that speech that is too fast becomes more appropriately paced, and Plant – Oster (1986: 74) report an improvement with speech that is too slow. More specifically abnormal pausing times have been shown to improve as has vowel duration (Plant – Oster 1986: 74).

Improvements have also been reported in all the general categories considered in the previous sections. Evidence that breathing improves with implantation is provided by Lane et al. (1991: 529–531). One subject's speech showed reduction in previously excessive volume of air per syllable and average airflow, and two others showed increases from a low rate of average air-flow. Voice quality also improves (Norton 1975: 20). In particular there is im-provement in problems with creak (Ball – Ison 1984: 251; Read 1989: 47–48), and vocal strain and vocal harshness are also said to improve.There are reports of improved articulation, especially in the study by Tartter – Chute – Hellman (1989: 2118–2119) who show improved distinctions among places of articula-tion and among manners of articulation. Norton (1975: 20) talks of improved consonant production. Plant – Oster (1986: 74–76) have shown a normal-isation of formant values in vowels. Braud et al. (1987) report improvement in vowel production. Finally, there is some informal observation of improvement in intensity control (House 1978: 206; Engelmann – Waterfall – Hough 1981: 1829; East – Cooper 1986: 56).

To date most speech production work has been done with single channel implants. These would be expected to bring most improvement to prosody, and in particular to pitch control. A pilot study by Tartter – Chute – Hellman (1989) supports the expectation that multichannel implants may be more rel-evant to articulatory control.

2.3.3.2. The extent of improvement

A superficial reading of these studies tends to suggest that cochlear implants bring major improvements in speech production. In fact a more cautious inter-pretation is in order. Three points are worth drawing attention to. Firstly, not all the subjects studied show improvement at the levels investigated. In a study by Kirk – Edgerton (1983: 287), not all subjects show a convincing improve-ment in sentence duration. Cooper et al.(1989: 33) received a pessimistic re-sponse when they asked relatives whether patients' speech had improved or not. Banfai et al. (1984: 193) showed that relatives and colleagues of im-plantees thought that 73% showed no change in their speech production. They do not, however, tell us whether they had speech problems to start with. Sec-ondly, although there is a degree of improvement, speech is often still outside normal bounds. Kirk – Edgerton (1983: 284–286), for example, show that val-ues for F0 become more normal when speakers use their implant. Nev-ertheless, three out of their four subjects still have a mean F0 outside the range shown by the relevant controls. Thirdly, the speech of some implantees ap-pears to get worse in some respects. Engelmann – Waterfall – Hough (1981: 1829), for example, report that intensity control improves for some but de-teriorates in others who did not have problems in the first place. Oster (1987: 89) showed that new problems of creak arose for one implantee. Plant – Oster (1986: 74–76) reported that their subject's entire vowel space was shown to shift in the post- implant condition. This had both positive and negative effects on perceived vowel quality.

The only study that examines effects on intelligibility is that by Bilger (1977: 130), who found that although some implanted speakers' intelligibility improved, others did not. Basically those who had bad speech to start with did not show improved intelligibility. Other studies mention improved intelligibility (Morgon et al. 1984: 203; Owens 1989) but provide no objective measures. There is no mention of how implantation affects the acceptability of the speech.

There is also rather little information on the inter-subject differences which relate to extent of improvement. Three observations relate to the matter. Waters (1986: 41) observes that the subject who showed least improvement had the best speech to start with, and Read (1989: 47) says that those who had only slight problems to start with did not improve. Conversely Bilger (1977: 130) found that those who had bad speech to start with were rated as showing no improvement. Boothroyd – Medwetsky – Hanin (1988) indicate that improvements in speech production are greatest in those subjects who demonstrate the best receptive performance with the implant.

Two other variables may relate to the extent of improvement. The first variable is time. Oster (1987) and Leder et al. (1986: 1973), for example, show that improvement is very gradual. However Thomas (personal communication) has noted very rapid improvement post-implantation in some respects. The second variable is speech therapy. Therapy can improve deafened people's speech on its own (Waters 1986: 39–41). The effects of speech therapy and the effects of implantation are often confounded in studies, a point also made by Oster (1987: 82). The recent study of breathing in three implanted subjects by Lane et al. (1991) provides a useful disentanglement by showing that speech improves when no therapy is given. However there is no comparable information for other variables.

2.4. Summary

Reviewing the literature gives a strong impression that acquired deafness does affect speech, and that few aspects of speech, if any, can be assumed to be immune from its effects. Unfortunately it is difficult to be a great deal more specific.

Many studies lack controls, and so it is difficult to be sure whether reported effects genuinely lie outside the normal range. In addition many studies use very few subjects. That makes it impossible to know whether a reported abnormality is characteristic of deafness, and difficult to be sure whether it is actually due to deafness – particularly if studies single out speakers who have a noticeable speech problem rather than at least roughly sampling deafened speakers. After all, any population will contain some people with speech abnormalities. The sheer bulk of the data makes it unreasonable to write it all off in these ways, but without large, controlled studies it is impossible to be sure just which observations represent general trends, which are idiosyncratic but deafness-related abnormalities, and which are inevitable accidents. To say this is not to dismiss small-scale case studies in general. They can add invaluable depth if there is a broad framework which indicates how they relate to the general pattern. The difficulty arises when that framework is absent, as it is with acquired deafness.

More large-scale studies have begun to appear, and this is a useful trend. However they have brought limited resolution. As yet there appears to be no case in which a large, well controlled study has demonstrated a specific abnormality and is not contradicted by some other study.

One explanation for this situation is that deterioration is truly idiosyncratic, which we have suggested is probably the most natural expectation. However that conclusion sits uncomfortably with the data. When substantial studies have been carried out, they have tended to show trends which run across subjects: the problem is that different studies show different trends. Cases in point are intensity, pitch height, pitch range, rate, and stress. Under such circumstances, the natural hypothesis is that there are situational variables at work which have not been recognised, i.e. deafened people tend to behave similarly, but that includes shifting according to situation; or deafened people with certain characteristics behave in one way, deafened people with other characteristics behave in another. Sex is the characteristic which stands as out a candidate in this context.

The observation that situational variables or sex may be critical has implications for both methodology and theory. Methodologically, it suggests that these variables should be studied systematically. Theoretically, it directs attention to a possibility which was raised in the first section of this chapter but not claimed as a natural expectation: that is, that auditory feedback may be particularly important for controlling socially significant variation in speech.

Another theoretically interesting issue is whether certain aspects of speech are particularly vulnerable to loss of feedback. Lack of consistency obviously complicates the issue, but it is worth observing that there is no clear pattern where one might have been expected. For example if anything, one would expect articulation to be less vulnerable to acquired deafness than any other aspect of speech. But if one had to identify agreed trends in the data, then trends in consonant production would be among the best candidates – notably omission of final alveolars and distortion of [s] and [ʃ].

In general, a good deal of the evidence is at least not obviously consistent with the expectations that we singled out as natural. Abnormalities may occur in what appear to be high-order abilities such as style-shifting. Articulation probably does suffer. Deterioration may include idiosyncratic effects, but there seem to be common trends across deafened people. Relatively late onsets seem to have an effect. Some aspects of decay seem to proceed relatively slowly after hearing is lost, and some aspects of recovery may be slow. All of these points are subject to the general uncertainty which has been noted, but they indicate that clarifying the effects of acquired deafness on speech is theoretically worthwhile. A phenomenon with so many counter-intuitive features should be highly informative.

Turning from theory to practice, strikingly little has been said about whether deafened people's speech abnormalities matter. This is a clear target for research. Nor is it empty of theoretical interest. Assessing the significance of speech defects is an exceedingly interesting problem, and it is an area crying out for convergence between socially-oriented research, which has traditionally dealt with social and geographic varieties of speech, and clinical research.

In sum, the literature marks out deafened speech as a problem which is surrounded by questions which are interesting theoretically and significant practically. The study which we report in this book aims to bring us closer to answering some of those questions.

Chapter 3
The scope and methods of the Belfast study

Chapters 1 and 2 have provided general background information on acquired deafness and on what is known about its effects on speech production. The rest of the book presents the results of our own study on acquired deafness which was carried out in Belfast during the decade 1980–1990. Its primary concern is with speech production, but it considers other issues in order to set speech production in context. The aim of this chapter is to give an overview of the study. It describes the goals of the study, the techniques which were used to collect information, and the deafened people and controls who participated. An important feature of the study is that formal data collection was supplemented by long-term informal contact, and that too is explained.

One of the chapter's goals is to convey a distinctive style which has emerged as the study proceeded. We have attempted to combine experimental rigour with a synthetic outlook which accepts the value of seeing parts in the context of a larger whole. That kind of combination is of interest beyond the domain of acquired deafness, and we believe that the study provides an interesting example of progress towards it.

3.1. General goals and methods

Deafened people's speech could be studied with many different goals in mind and using many methods. We have addressed goals which we believe are worthwhile, using a package of methods which is reasonably cohesive. Undoubtedly there are other worthwhile goals, and there are other methods which it would be useful to apply. However in a finite study, one has to make choices. This section explains the general reasoning behind ours.

On a theoretical level, we have been influenced by two main goals. One, which led us into the area, is to illuminate the mechanisms of speech production, and in particular the role that auditory feedback plays. The second, which was forcibly borne in on us by meeting deafened people, is to clarify what speech deterioration contributes to their communicative difficulties, and how those difficulties impinge on their lives.

On a practical level, two goals have been particularly important.

The first is to document the problems that occur in a way that carries conviction with the relevant professionals and decision-makers. The need for that is epitomised in the article by Goehl – Kaufman (1984) which has been cited in previous chapters. It refused to accept the evidence which was then available (including some of our own) that speech could be affected by acquired deafness. Our experience indicates that this is not an atypical position. Many people have difficulty accepting that speech can be affected by acquired deafness, and still more are reluctant to believe that it matters. Hence our methods have been geared towards convincing sceptics.

The second practical goal is to help people who are involved with acquired deafness (or potentially involved with it) to understand it better. It is an interesting comment that people sometimes have difficulty seeing this as a practical goal. However deafened people are very much concerned that others should understand what deafness means, and they feel the lack of understanding acutely (see chapter 13). In that context, promoting understanding is on a par with advancing treatment in practical terms. Influencing therapeutic practice has not been one of our central goals – not because we are unaware of the issue, but because it is impossible to do everything and unwise to try. However it is reasonable to expect that understanding will have spin-offs for therapy.

These goals are worth stating separately, but they link to a single issue which is at the core of our work. The essence of deafness is that one localised malfunction generates a highly ramified chain of consequences. We have tried to provide clear evidence on parts of this chain which people tend to find surprising for one reason or another, and to show that the consequences we have highlighted make sense when one thinks them through. Practically, we believe this makes it likelier that people in various roles will respond appropriately to acquired deafness. Theoretically, we believe that it illuminates connections between various aspects of communication which tend to be handled separately.

The basic methods that we have used reflect these concerns.

To ensure that our data are not easily dismissed we have used substantial numbers of deafened subjects and compared them with appropriate controls. We have taken quantitative measures and made comparisons statistically wherever it made sense to do so.

We have set speech deterioration in context at several levels. Our research looks not only at the immediate anomalies in the signal, but also at their effects on listeners. The effects we have considered include not only the basic functional question of whether speech can be understood, but also the way it leads listeners to assess and react to the speaker. Seeing these issues in context depends on looking at the context, and so we have considered other aspects of the communicative process, particularly lipreading. The way we have looked at lipreading reflects the theme that deafness generates a chain of consequences beyond the ones which are immediate and obvious. To give a still wider context we have looked at the way deafened people view their lives overall, including the aspects of communicative difficulty that concern them.

We have chosen these levels not just to give a reasonably broad picture, but also to ensure that each part is fairly directly connected to others. One could, for example, bypass questions about the way speech deterioration affects listeners and try to establish direct statistical connections between the quality of a deafened person's speech and the quality of his or her life. We feel that in the long run this would achieve less than clarifying the intermediate effects which create the connection. This reflects our fundamental belief that it is both practically and theoretically important to make the ramifications of deafness intelligible.

Our descriptions of speech also reflect our overall perspective. The context which we have set highlights the fact that reduced feedback could affect much more than the mechanics of encoding phonemic plans into articulatory gestures. A speaker is continuously engaged in setting style, register, accent, intonation, timbre, voice quality and so on in a way that creates appropriate impressions and reactions in the listener. Hearing what one sounds like may be irrelevant to these adjustments, but we see no good reason to assume that it is. Consequently we see no obvious justification for ignoring the possibility that deafened people's speech may show patterns of abnormalities which are associated with breakdowns at relatively high levels in the process of controlling speech. As a result we have used descriptions of speech which give us the option of looking for these patterns rather than using measures designed specifically to monitor the basic mechanics of speech.

The view which we have taken leads to a difficulty which it is probably best to confront early on. It does not allow us to define our subject with a neat boundary line and a clearly marked centre. This can be intellectually frustrating. However, we believe that this is an area where it is worth resisting the urge to compartmentalise. The impact of acquired deafness does not respect intellectual demarcations. We believe that that in itself is a problem for deafened people, because it helps to create the lack of understanding which confronts them. It is for researchers to adjust their boundaries to accommodate the world, because the world will not adjust to accommodate theirs.

3.2. The components of the study

This section summarises the components of the study so that we can refer to them subsequently.

(1). Collection and analysis of speech. We have recorded speech samples from 50 deafened informants and 75 controls. Subjects are described in sections 3.3 and 3.4, and recording methods and materials are described in section 3.5. Speech samples have been subjected to three distinct kinds of analysis: acoustic analysis, using a spectrum analyser and specially-written programs which describe its output statistically (see chapter 5); a general phonetic analysis which was carried out by Dr. E. Douglas-Cowie using traditional methods of transcription supplemented by instrumental measures (see chapter 7); and an analysis of intonation, again using transcription supplemented by instrumental measures, which was carried out by Dr. Douglas-Cowie and Ms. J. Rahilly (see chapter 6).

(2). Listeners' responses to speech. The main study in this area had two components which we will call the shadowing study and the listeners' impression study. The first component provided a measure of speakers' intelligibility. Each listener heard a recording of a single speaker and tried to "shadow" it – that is, to repeat what they heard word for word as they heard it. The percentage of words which was repeated correctly gave our measure of intelligibility (see chapter 4). The second aspect of the study followed immediately after shadowing was finished. At that stage the subject filled out a questionnaire on his or her impressions of and reactions to the speaker (see chapter 8).

As well as considering intelligibility and attitude data in their own right, we have also tried to establish links between these functional properties and the form speech takes. Regression was used to identify speech attributes which appeared to contribute to particular types of functional problem (see chapter 8).

These studies were supplemented by two which presented listeners with more than a disembodied voice. In a video presentation study, observers watched videos of hearing-impaired speakers: and in an interview study, they were interviewed by a deafened speaker. In both cases they then completed a questionnaire similar to the one in the listeners' impression study (see chapter 9).

(3). Other communicative issues. These studies are concerned with the context in which listeners experience deafened people's speech. We report an observational study which analyses video recordings of the ways people deafened behave in interactions (see chapter 10). We also report a series of experiments on the limitations which are imposed by reliance on lipreading (see chapters 11 and 12). Deafened people's communicative difficulties are a large topic, and our formal studies only cover a small part of it. Hence we have supplemented them with informal observations based on first-hand experience and on interviews.

(4). The psychosocial impact of acquired deafness. We have used interviews and questionnaires to establish how our informants themselves perceive the impact of their hearing loss. Our aim has been to understand what are the problems that concern them as against those which strike an outsider, and to use that as a basis for judging the importance of the issues that we have addressed (see chapter 13).

3.3. The deafened participants

The study rests on contact with a substantial number of deafened people, almost all from the Belfast area. In total, 89 deafened people have participated in some aspect of the Belfast study. In the light of the available evidence (see chapter 2) we were particularly concerned to find people with profound to total losses which originated after the acquisition of language. Because aging has its own effects on speech, we were also particularly interested in people who were in mid-life or younger at the time of testing. We will call people who meet both criteria the primary target group. They are neither a large group nor easy to contact, and so it was not practical to rely on contact methods whose first aim is to ensure representativeness. Our strategy was to maximise sample size by using as many ways of contacting people as possible. The main contact routes were as follows.

(1). ENT (Ear, Nose and Throat) services. Local ENT consultants and the regional hearing therapist alerted us to people in our primary target group. They provided the largest single source of contacts. Other methods of contact were needed, though, mainly because people with profound losses may not keep in touch with the health services.

(2). Social Services. Social workers concerned with the deaf helped in a similar way and provided another substantial group of subjects.

(3). Voluntary organisations. A number of people were contacted through existing voluntary organisations for the hearing-impaired, though when the project began none of them was specifically concerned with the particular target group that concerned us. An organisation which is specifically concerned with that group, the National Association for Deafened People (NADP), was formed while the project was in progress. We took part in the formation of a

Northern Ireland branch (and are still closely involved with it), and another set of contacts emerged from that.

(4). Media coverage. Media coverage was provided by the column for hearing-impaired people in the local newspaper, *The Belfast Telegraph,* in the local magazine *Disability Today*, and also by local radio programs. These routes provided another group of contacts.

(5). Personal contact. Northern Ireland is a tightly-knit society. The fact that we were working on deafness became known, and we were introduced to several deafened people via mutual acquaintances.

One can only estimate the effectiveness of these techniques, but they appear to have reached the main target group reasonably well. Using data from Thornton (1986) and local demographic figures, one can estimate that there are about 40 people in the Greater Belfast area who are under the age of 70 and have postlingually-acquired losses of more than 100 dB (Cowie 1988b: 3). Of these 30 participated in our study. The high proportion gives us confidence that the sample is reasonably representative of speakers in the primary target area.

Inevitably this informal procedure brought us into contact with people who were outside our primary target group, either because their losses were less severe or because onset occurred late in life, or early enough to affect language acquisition. These people were included into the study, and a large part of our information about the effect of less than profound losses on speech is due to them. For the psychosocial-impact questionnaire, it was decided to collect data from a larger number of people with early losses or with relatively moderate losses acquired relatively late in life. They were contacted via local organisations for the hearing-impaired. We can be less confident of representativeness here, but there is no obvious reason to anticipate major biases.

3.3.1. The core deafened sample

The core sample is summarised in table 3.1. It describes the hearing impaired people who participated in the studies concerned with speech. Many also filled in the psychosocial questionnaire and this is noted in the table. They are ordered from the most severe losses to the least, and within that from the latest onset to the earliest. Audiological data were provided by the Audiology Department at the Royal Victoria Hospital in Belfast.

The first seven columns provide basic biographic and medical data:

Column 1 – numerical code for each subject.

Column 2 – sex of subject.

Column 3 – hearing loss: the losses cited are average losses in the better ear.

We have entered a nominal figure of 120 dB when loss was simply described as total.

Column 4 – whether subjects experience annoying tinnitus (by their own report).

Column 5 – age at onset of deafness. Where loss is profound, the age at onset column shows the onset of profound loss even if this was preceded by a milder loss: that seems to be the most useful predictor in terms of speech.

Column 6 – age at time of study. Since our contact with some of the subjects often extended over several years, the age at time of study is not fixed. The figures in Column 6 refer to the ages of subjects when we first contacted them.

Column 7 – social status. This column gives a rough status measure which we have considered because speech is known to be strongly linked to social variables. The categories are 1 = professional; 2 = clerical or administrative; 3 = skilled; 4 = unskilled. Deafened people often elude social categorisation for reasons which are discussed in section 3.4, and so there is little sense in trying to give more precise ratings.

The next five columns specify the studies in which speakers participated.

Column S refers to participation in the shadowing and listeners' impression studies which were designed to provide a measure of speech intelligibility and of listeners' reactions to deafened speech. A total of 47 deafened subjects participated in these studies. They represent a wide range of hearing losses: approximately half have profound to total losses and half have moderate to severe losses.

Column A refers to subjects whose speech was examined both in the acoustic study and in the general phonetic study. The latter was mainly concerned with articulatory aspects of speech and so the "A" stands for both "acoustic" and "articulatory". A total of 23 subjects were involved in both studies. 18 have profound to total losses, 3 have severe losses and 2 have moderate losses. Five additional subjects with profound to total losses were involved in the articulatory study. They are denoted by a small "a". The original intention was that they too should be in the acoustic study, but they had to be dropped from that study because they did not give an acceptable analysis. (Chapter 5 explains the main source of difficulty).

Column F refers to subjects whose speech was considered in the analysis of form/function relations (e.g. the relationship between the form of speech and intelligibility or listener judgement). 21 subjects were involved. As can be seen from table 3.1, they are all but one of the subjects who took part in both the shadowing study and the acoustic and articulatory studies.

Column I refers to participation in the study of intonation. 17 subjects were involved. They all have profound to total losses with one exception, no. 29 who had a severe loss.

Column Q refers to participation in the psychosocial questionnaire study. All but two subjects participated, giving a total of 48 subjects with a wide range of hearing losses (see section 3.3.2 below for other subjects who also participated in the psychosocial questionnaire study bringing the total number to 87).

The last three columns provide slightly more sense of the people we are concerned with. They give information on methods of communication. (It is drawn from the questionnaire study: dots indicate where the questionnaire was not completed.) The columns describe whether the subjects use a hearing aid, whether they lipread and whether they sign.

Table 3.1 Hearing-impaired speakers who participated in the speech experiments

code	sex	loss (dB)	tinn-itus	age at onset	age at test	status	S	A	F	I	Q	hearing aid	lip-reads	signs
1	female	120	+	28	80	2	+	+	+	−	+	−	−	−
2	female	120	+	26	62	3	+	+	+	+	+	−	+	−
3	male	120	+	16	34	3	+	+	+	−	+	+	+	−
4	female	120	+	15	54	4	+	+	+	+	+	−	+	−
5	female	120	+	14	24	2	+	a	−	+	+	−	+	+
6	female	120	+	12	52	4	+	a	−	+	+	−	+	+
7	male	120	+	12	56	1	+	+	+	+	+	−	+	+
8	female	120	•	12	14	2	+	−	−	+	−	•	•	•
9	male	120	−	11	58	1	+	+	+	+	+	−	+	+
10	male	120	•	11	16	4	−	a	−	−	−	•	•	•
11	male	120	+	9	45	4	+	+	+	+	+	−	+	−
12	female	120	+	5	48	1	+	+	+	−	+	−	+	+
13	female	120	−	5	60	3	+	+	+	−	+	−	+	+
14	female	120	−	5	53	1	+	+	+	+	+	−	+	+
15	male	113	+	9	28	2	+	+	+	+	+	−	+	−
16	female	112	+	24	50	3	+	+	+	+	+	+	+	−
17	male	108	+	11	49	1	+	+	+	+	+	+	+	−
18	female	106	+	16	50	4	+	+	+	+	+	+	+	−
19	female	104	−	55	60	3	+	a	−	−	+	+	+	−
20	male	100	+	29	33	2	−	+	−	−	+	−	+	−
21	male	99	−	5	37	2	+	+	+	+	+	+	+	+
22	female	96	+	38	65	3	+	a	−	+	+	+	+	−
23	female	94	+	22	56	3	+	+	+	−	+	+	+	−
24	male	94	+	21	35	3	+	+	+	−	+	−	+	−
25	female	87	−	28	54	4	+	+	+	−	+	+	+	−

Table 3.1 (continued)

code	sex	loss (dB)	tinn-itus	age at onset	age at test	status	S	A	F	I	Q	hearing aid	lip-reads	signs
26	male	86	+	65	70	1	−	−	−	+	+	+	−	−
27	female	85	+	48	55	2	+	+	+	−	+	+	+	−
28	female	85	+	37	71	2	+	−	−	−	+	+	+	−
29	male	81	+	13	25	2	+	+	+	+	+	+	+	−
30	female	73	−	50	75	3	+	−	−	−	+	+	−	−
31	female	69	+	4	40	4	+	−	−	−	+	+	+	−
32	male	68	−	65	68	3	+	−	−	−	+	+	+	−
33	female	66	−	2	52	3	+	−	−	−	+	+	−	−
34	male	60	+	52	58	4	+	−	−	−	+	+	−	−
35	female	58	+	14	24	2	+	−	−	−	+	+	+	−
36	female	57	+	50	68	1	+	−	−	−	+	+	+	−
37	female	55	−	65	75	3	+	−	−	−	+	+	−	−
38	female	55	−	55	65	3	+	−	−	−	+	+	−	−
39	female	55	+	50	52	4	+	+	+	−	+	+	−	−
40	female	55	+	20	42	2	+	−	−	−	+	+	+	−
41	female	55	−	4	75	3	+	−	−	−	+	+	−	−
42	female	55	−	1	68	4	+	−	−	−	+	+	+	−
43	female	51	+	5	24	2	+	−	−	−	+	−	+	−
44	female	49	−	55	74	3	+	−	−	−	+	+	+	−
45	female	48	−	12	68	3	+	−	−	−	+	+	−	−
46	male	48	−	5	36	3	+	+	−	−	+	+	+	−
47	female	45	−	70	84	3	+	−	−	−	+	+	−	−
48	male	38	+	21	59	2	+	−	−	−	+	−	−	−
49	male	36	+	63	73	3	+	−	−	−	+	+	+	−
50	female	34	+	50	65	2	+	−	−	−	+	+	−	−

3.3.2. The sample used in the psychosocial study

The remaining hearing-impaired speakers participated only in the psycho-social questionnaire study, and so they are of less central concern. They are summarised more briefly in table 3.2. (The total group who participated in the questionnaire study consists of the 39 in table 3.2 and the 48 already noted in the core sample in table 3.1)

Table 3.2   Hearing-impaired participants who only completed the psychosocial questionnaire

code	sex	dB loss	tinn-itus	age at onset	age at test	lip-reads	signs
1	female	112	+	1	42	+	−
2	female	108	−	29	62	+	−
3	male	102	+	19	55	+	−
4	female	102	+	14	67	+	−
5	male	100	+	76	80	−	+
6	female	100	+	40	68	+	−
7	male	100	+	40	27	+	−
8	female	100	+	37	70	+	−
9	female	100	+	35	38	+	+
10	female	100	−	28	54	+	−
11	female	100	+	22	67	+	−
12	male	100	+	16	54	+	+
13	male	100	−	10	64	−	+
14	male	100	+	7	43	+	−
15	male	90	+	35	46	+	−
16	female	90	−	1	28	+	+
17	male	90	+	1	28	+	+
18	female	89	+	64	64	+	−
19	female	82	−	19	39	−	−
20	female	77	+	40	82	+	−
21	male	75	+	11	82	−	−
22	female	67	+	50	54	+	−
23	male	65	+	5	62	−	−
24	female	60	−	69	79	−	−
25	male	60	−	66	79	+	−
26	male	60	−	40	70	+	−
27	female	60	−	6	75	+	−
28	female	60	−	1	21	+	−
29	female	60	+	1	34	+	+
30	female	58	−	65	78	+	−
31	female	55	−	43	64	+	−
32	female	55	−	35	88	−	−
33	female	55	+	27	54	−	−
34	female	55	−	7	60	+	−
35	female	54	+	56	73	−	−
36	female	50	+	41	49	+	−
37	female	46	+	70	77	+	−
38	male	40	+	52	59	−	−
39	male	35	+	11	39	+	−

3.3.3. Samples used in minor studies

A few of the deafened subjects took part in the smaller studies reported in chapters 9, 10, 11 and 12.

Chapter 9: Two experiments are reported in this chapter. Experiment 1 looked at a live interaction between a deafened subject and a hearing subject. The deafened subject was No. 17 in table 3.1. Experiment 2 involved two partially-hearing schoolgirls in an experiment designed to see whether cues from speech would affect impression formation in the presence of apparently more valid and informative indicators. The subjects involved are outside our sample. Our information about them is limited because the study was arranged in conjunction with a teacher of the deaf who felt unable to release details of their hearing losses. However it is reasonable to conclude that their losses were moderate to severe when we met them, and that they originated early in life and probably prelingually.

Chapter 10: This chapter reports a study of the verbal and non verbal behaviour of three deafened subjects. Those involved have profound losses and are Nos 5, 11 and 17 in table 3.1.

Chapter 11: This chapter on lipreading is written by one of our deafened sample. He is a profoundly-deafened male (No. 17), and features in many of the minor studies, as well as participating in all the major studies. He is also involved in chapter 9, experiment 1(see above) and in chapter 12 (see below).

Chapter 12: This chapter reports a number of studies on lipreading. In all, six profoundly deafened speakers are involved. They are Numbers 4, 5, 7, 9, 12 and 17 in table 3.1.

3.4. Control speakers

There are two basic approaches to choosing controls. One is to try to match individual controls with individual deafened speakers. The other is to aim for representativeness.

We have recorded matched controls in particular cases. Specifically we had the chance to record same sex siblings for three of the deafened males, and we did so. However, in general, matching is an unsatisfying strategy because the basis for matching is thoroughly unclear.

One natural approach is to match accent types. However as we have reported elsewhere (Cowie – Douglas-Cowie 1983: 192–196), social markers tend to be blurred in deafened speech. Attempting to classify many of our deafened speakers sociolinguistically would be highly dubious.

Another approach is to match on social variables. But in that case, with whom should we match the intelligent and intellectual speaker who was deafened in adolescence and became a building contractor: his brother, who became a professor, or other building contractors? Should we match a part-time journalist who works in a canning factory with other journalists or with other workers in the factory? The examples illustrate a general problem. Deafened people often do not follow the usual pattern where a particular cluster of attributes tends to go with a particular social position. Attributes are quite likely to be mixed unconventionally. The result is that in order to match, one would have to make essentially arbitrary decisions to favour one criterion over others. This seems unwise.

Our basic strategy has therefore been to use control samples which are at least roughly representative. We have considered three main variables: age, sex, and accent type. To describe accent type, we have used Milroy's (1981: 98–103) standard classification of Belfast accents. He distinguishes three basic types: vernacular (abbreviated as V), an accent which is strongly localised and associated with working-class speakers; Belfast Standard (abbreviated BS), which is associated with educated speakers and can be understood easily by non-natives even though it is clearly regional; and careful vernacular (abbreviated CV), which has standard features superimposed on a basically vernacular structure.

Our control samples used in the speech studies are summarised in table 3.3. Males are in the left-hand block, females in the right. Within each block speakers are ordered first by accent (in the third column) and then by age at recording (first column). The studies in which controls participated are shown in the fourth column, using the same abbreviations as before. The three who participated in both the shadowing experiment and the acoustic experiment were also used in the form/function comparison. The second column describes status using the scheme which was applied to the deafened speakers.

Table 3.3 Control subjects in the speech studies

male controls				female controls			
age	status	accent	studies	age	status	accent	studies
25	2	BS	A	19	2	BS	S
28	1	BS	S, A	22	S	BS	I
33	3	BS	S	23	1	BS	I
33	1	BS	S	25	2	BS	A
36	1	BS	I	25	1	BS	S, A

Table 3.3 (continued)

	male controls				female controls		
age	status	accent	studies	age	status	accent	studies
39	1	BS	A	30	2	BS	I
45	2	BS	A	50	2	BS	A
50	2	BS	A	51	2	BS	S
51	1	BS	S, A	60	1	BS	S
54	1	BS	I	61	2	BS	I
56	1	BS	I	63	H	BS	I
59	1	BS	I	63	2	BS	S
61	1	BS	I	22	1	BS/CV	I
29	1	BS/CV	I	40	2	BS/CV	I
35	2	BS/CV	I	30	4	CV	A
50	1	BS/CV	A	35	2	CV	A
50	2	BS/CV	A	50	4	CV	A
14	3	CV	S	52	2	CV	I
21	3	CV	I	55	3	CV	A
25	1	CV	A	61	3	CV	I
25	2	CV	A	73	3	CV	S
25	2	CV	S	23	1	CV/V	I
30	3	CV	A	45	2	CV/V	I
35	2	CV	A	60	H	CV/V	I
38	3	CV	A	64	H	CV/V	I
59	3	CV	I	14	4	V	S
65	2	CV	A	26	4	V	S
81	3	CV	I	35	4	V	A
16	4	CV/V	I	35	4	V	I
50	1	CV/V	I	45	4	V	A
60	3	CV/V	S	45	4	V	S
18	4	V	S	50	4	V	A
19	4	V	A	53	4	V	S
25	3	V	A	55	4	V	A
25	4	V	A	55	4	V	I
35	3	V	A	65	4	V	A
40	4	V	S				
44	3	V	I				
55	3	V	A				

It can be seen that the control groups for the three main studies were chosen to contain all three accent types across a range of ages and for both sexes. We did not use a precise factorial design, but, while it would have been neater to do so, the omission is not particularly important. Much larger samples would be needed to support conclusions about aspects of speech which depend in a complex way on inter-speaker variables. If that kind of conclusion is not in question, then the main requirements are that samples should reflect the extremes of normal performance fairly and that they should be reasonably balanced with respect to any one variable which is being investigated. The present groups seem to meet those requirements satisfactorily. They also compare favourably with most control arrangements in clinically related speech research.

3.5. The speech sample

The bulk of the speech which we have studied comes from three sets of recordings. These were associated respectively with the shadowing study, the acoustic and articulatory analyses, and the analysis of intonation.

In making the recordings, a high priority was attached to putting deafened speakers at ease. This was partly because strained encounters risked our prospects of contacting the speakers again for other aspects of the study, and partly because stress would have had confounding effects on speech. With a few exceptions, recordings were made in informants' homes by a research assistant working on the project. It was generally her second visit, after an initial contact to ask permission, and she spent as long as she judged necessary putting them at ease before recording proper began.

Controls were also put at their ease, though this was generally less of a problem with them.

Recording was carried out using a Sony TC-D5M portable cassette recorder and a SONY ECM - 929LT microphone. The microphone was placed on a table at a comfortable distance from the speaker and recording level was adjusted before reading started to give a reasonable level. Again, more formal procedures were avoided because of the priority attached to putting speakers at ease.

3.5.1. The shadowing study

The deafened speakers who took part in the shadowing experiment, designed to provide a measure of intelligibility and to test listeners' reactions to speech, provided three kinds of speech material. First, they read five passages. Next, they used their own words to tell the story in each of three cartoon strips. Finally they provided a more genuinely spontaneous narrative, which consisted of describing a day in their life. The shadowing experiment controls carried out the first two exercises, but not the third.

The reading passages are given below. They were originally used as exercises for phonetics students in the School of English at Queen's University because they are reasonably balanced phonetically and provide a range of phonetic environments. They span a range of styles and contents, from the ornate style and exotic content of passage 1 to the commonplace style and subject matter of passage 5.

The cartoons were copied from a children's book. Each consisted of several panels which told a whimsical story – one about a cat fishing, one about a pig planting corn, and one about a rat trying (unsuccessfully) to fly an aeroplane.

Reading passages used in shadowing study were as follows.

(1). *The English have no respect for their language and will not teach their children to speak it. They cannot spell it because they have nothing to spell it with except an old foreign alphabet of which only the consonants – and not all of them – have any agreed value. Consequently no man can teach himself what it should sound like from reading it; and it is impossible for an Englishman to open his mouth without making some other Englishman despise him.*

(2). *"Come here at once, John." shouted Elizabeth. "Your attitude to church going is a disgrace. It should be a pleasure to hear the Reverend Martin on a Sunday morning."*

(3). *"Surely you don't mean to say that you are leaving, Philip?"*
"I am surely, and I'm not waiting a moment longer. I get no pleasure at all out of listening to a lot of small talk. So long, I'm away and I won't be back in a hurry."

(4). *"It was unfortunate that Uncle Jim had no time for youngsters. It would have been better to have had Aunt Thelma in charge of their party."*
"Yes, I agree, but she regiments them a bit and will not let them play noisy games."

(5). *"Hello, 74669."*
"Hello, can I speak to Siobhan, please?"
"I am sorry, there is no-one of that name here. This is a branch office of Cromie and MacDougall Ltd. You must have dialled the wrong number."
"Yes I must have. Oh, these telephones."

3.5.2. The acoustic and articulatory studies

For the acoustic and articulatory analyses we used reading passage 4 ("It was unfortunate ...") and the sample of speech in which the subject described a day in his or her life. For deafened speakers, the original recordings were used if they were acceptable for the acoustic analysis. However flaws which were unlikely to affect the shadowing experiment would have been unacceptable in acoustic analysis, and so when it was necessary speakers were re-recorded with the emphasis on minimising extraneous sounds and ensuring that the recording level was set to avoid floor or ceiling effects. Since the first controls had not carried out the "day-in-the-life" exercise, control recordings had to be made from scratch. Thirty-one controls were used.

3.5.3. The intonation study

For the intonation study we used six specially-designed reading passages and a 30 minute sample of free conversation between each subject and the interviewer. The reading pasages (given below) were designed so as to probe well-known relationships between intonation and grammar (Halliday 1967). They were also written in a style that was relatively informal and suited to the Belfast idiom.

Reading passages used in intonation study were as follows.

(1). *"Billy's away down to Bangor this morning."*
"I know that. He's looking at a house down there isn't he?"
"Yes, this'll be the second one we've been after. We thought we'd one bought only somebody made a better offer so we lost it. To tell you the truth, I've gone off the idea."
"A girl I used to work with lives in Bangor. She's in that house ten years. Sure Bangor's really lovely when the weather's clear."

(2). *Bobby started jogging two months ago. It was his wife who gave him the idea. She said he spent far too much time working.*
"What you should do is take some exercise. It worries me that you work so hard."
"Yes, if you like. What do you suggest?"
"You know that park at the end of the road?" she asked. "Let's go running there sometime."
So they bought new tracksuits, got themselves ready and headed for the park. Now they go jogging every Friday, Saturday and Sunday.

(3). *John wanted to get the results of the football match, so he asked his father if he could switch the radio on.*
"Who did you say was winning at half time? Was it them or us? Them? It's no wonder we're losing. I'm surprised we ever win any matches at all. How could we whenever the side keeps changing all the time? And that manager one hasn't a clue. They keep renewing his contract and him no good at all. Sure he might as well stay at home."

(4). *"Do you want to go out for a meal tonight?"*

"Okay, if you want to go I'll go with you, but not to the same place as last time. It was a real disaster that place."

"But I thought you liked it."

"Far from it. I didn't think it would be as crowded as that. It was ridiculous the way they kept letting more in."

"But there's always a crowd there on Saturdays. Nobody else seemed to mind."

"Don't get me wrong. I wouldn't mind trying it on a Sunday, but not tonight."

(5). *Since the old woman was a bit frail, she asked her granddaughter if she would do some shopping for her and the young girl said yes.*

"But Gran", she said. "You forgot to put fruit on your list."

"Fruit?" said her grandmother. "Get me some apples, oranges and bananas."

An hour later, the young girl came back.

She said: "Here's the messages you asked me to get you. By the way, would you have the Telegraph? I want to look at the pets' column."

"Listen, you mention dogs again young lady, and I'll swing for you", shouted her grandmother.

"Ah Gran, dogs don't take a lot of looking after."

(6). *"Hello, is that Radio Rentals?"*

"I won't keep you a moment sir. Now what's the problem?"

"My TV's after blowing up on me and I haven't even paid for it yet."

"Try not to worry Sir, we'll send another one round tomorrow."

"Tomorrow? I want one now."

"But you can't really expect us to do it immediately, Sir."

"Tomorrow's the best you can do, is it? Well, we'll just have to see what the manager Mr Smith says about that, won't we?"

"I don't think it's necessary to call in the manager, Sir. I'll see what I can do. Cheerio now."

3.6. Questionnaires

Two main questionnaires were developed – (i) the questionnaire designed to measure reactions to speech in the listeners' impression study which followed up the shadowing task and (ii) the psychosocial-impact questionnaire. Several variants on the latter were used for smaller associated studies.

3.6.1. Listeners' impression study

The listeners'-impression questionnaire was developed using previous sources concerned with reactions to deaf and deafened people's speech (Davison 1979; Nicholl 1981; Cowie – Douglas-Cowie 1983: 192–196), stereotypes of deaf and deafened people (e.g. Bunting 1981), and general sociolinguistic work on reactions to speech (e.g. Giles – Powesland 1975; Scherer – Giles 1979). The items in the main questionnaire are summarised in table 3.4. All questions are followed by five possible answers. For question 9 the alternatives are:

Very good   Good   Average   Poor   Very poor

For all other questions the alternatives are:

Definitely   Probably   Unsure   Probably not   Definitely not

Table 3.4 Listeners' impression questionnaire

---

1. Which of these reactions would you expect to have on first encountering this person?
(a) embarrassment, (b) pity, (c) shock, (d) keep meeting brief, (e) apprehensive,
(f) disturbed.
2. Would you consider that the speaker might be:
(a) lazy, (b) determined, (c) organised, (d) intelligent, (e) self confident, (f) reliable,
(g) sensible?
3. What standards of employment would suit this person's capabilities?
(a) professional employment, (b) skilled employment, (c) clerical employment,
(d) unskilled employment, (e) no normal employment.
4. Which of these personality traits would you consider the person might have?
(a) friendly, (b) cheerful, (c) co-operative, (d) dull, (e) timid, (f) withdrawn.
5. Would you expect the speaker to interact satisfactorily with other people in:
(a) brief, one-off meetings, (b) casual relationships, (c) close friendships, (d) marriage,
(e) working relationships.
6. What educational standards would you expect this person to attain?
(a) university, (b) college, (c) A-Level, (d) secondary at least, (e) primary at least,
(f) below normal primary level.
7. Which of the following problems do you think this person might have?
(a) depression, (b) irrationally suspicious (paranoid), (c) irrationally worried (neurotic),
(d) aggressive, (e) anxiety, (f) immature, (g) no particular problems.
8. Which of these emotions would you expect to feel in a conversation with this person?
(a) frustration, (b) anxiety, (c) sympathy, (d) confusion, (e) amusement, (f) feel as normal.
9. How well would you consider the speaker expressed him or herself?
(a) vocabulary, (b) grammar, (c) description, (d) imagination, (e) organisation of ideas.
10. Which of these speech defects would you say this person had?
(a) bad control of volume, (b) bad control of pitch, (c) bad(slurred) articulation,
(d) hard to understand, (e) strange quality of sound, (f) normal, (g) monotonous.
11. Do you think that the speaker might suffer any of these handicaps?
(a) mentally deficient, (b) emotionally disturbed, (c) deaf, (d) stroke, (e) autistic,
(f) spastic, (g) crippled.

3.6.2. Psychosocial-impact questionnaire

The main themes of the questionnaire are summarised in chapter 13. A full description of the questionnaire will be given in Stewart-Kerr (forthcoming).

3.7. General contact

An important aspect of the study is that contact with the deafened participants was extensive and relatively personal. At the most basic, someone who participated in all studies listed in table 3.1 was contacted at least four and usually five times (depending on whether re-recording was needed for the acoustic study). One of the visits (connected with the psychosocial questionnaire) usually involved an extended interview which was relatively open-ended (see chapter 13). It was necessary to establish good relationships with the contacts both to get their consent for so many visits, and also to retain the confidence of people involved in referring new contacts.

In many cases contact has gone well beyond this baseline. We were introduced to a group of deafened people in the course of pilot work (reported in Cowie – Douglas-Cowie 1983) and most of them went on to participate in the full study. Long-term contact has been maintained with around twenty participants, mainly through collaboration with voluntary organisations relevant to this group (particularly the local branch of NADP, the National Association of Deafened People, and CORD, the Committee of Organisations Representing the Deaf). This has involved interacting at social occasions, at public meetings, and in committees; co-operating in discussions and experiments on lipreading (see chapters 11 and 12); and acting in an unofficial advisory capacity. A number of contacts have evolved into personal friendships or acquaintances irrespective of academic or social roles.

We have drawn explicitly on informal experience in areas where formal data are lacking (e.g. chapters 10 and 11). However the background of contact plays a more important and pervasive role. In general terms, it is the reader's assurance that we are likely to have asked reasonable questions and to have made informed judgements. Our informal experience underpins the study in several ways. The questions that we have posed formally have been guided by experience which suggests that they are appropriate, academically and practically. Our interpretation of formal data is influenced by informal experience in some broad but important senses: for instance, we can set the results of the shadowing study and the listeners' impression study against experience and judge whether they are a fair representation of reality (we think they are).

Chapter 4
The intelligibility of deafened speakers and the variables which affect it

4.1. Introduction

This chapter uses a single simple measure to establish a number of basic points. These are important in their own right, and they also establish a context which is important for later chapters.

The measure is of intelligibility. Loss of intelligibility is the functional problem which is universally recognised as a reason for concern. As chapter 2 indicates, there is research which indicates that acquired deafness can lead to decreased intelligibility. However it is not conclusive. The point is demonstrated very directly by the fact that Kaufman – Goehl (1985) remained unconvinced by what remains the most substantial study on the point, that by Cowie – Douglas-Cowie (1983). That study suffers from a limited sample size and lack of a full control sample. The other substantial study in the area (Bilger 1977), uses wholly subjective ratings and also lacks controls.

The first concern of this chapter is to establish beyond doubt that acquired deafness can affect speech intelligibility. It reports a study which uses methods geared to that aim. It uses substantial samples, both of deafened speakers and of controls. The method is objective, and it is directly linked to the meaning of the term intelligibility. Speakers are recorded. The recordings are played back to naive listeners and they attempt to "shadow" what they hear – that is, to repeat what is being said word for word as they hear it. The result is a measure of intelligibility in the straightforward, literal sense of how easy it is to follow a speaker's words in real time.

The second concern of the chapter is to identify some of the main factors which affect the quality of deafened people's speech. Intelligibility scores provide the best single index of speech quality because they are face valid, quantitative, and reasonably stable. This makes them a natural measure to examine in relation to variables which one might expect to bear on speech deterioration. There may be factors which have no effect on speech intelligibility and yet affect other significant aspects of speech. However identifying factors which affect intelligibility provides a strong foundation for work on other aspects by identifying variables which should be considered automatically.

Previous work suggests that certain variables are particularly likely to affect intelligibility. Level of loss is clearly one. There is strikingly little formal evidence on the relationship between level of loss and speech deterioration, but Zimmermann – Collins (1985: 220) conjecture that substantial deterioration may not occur unless loss is profound or even total. Years since deafness, has also been considered as a potential variable (see chapter 2, section 2.3.2), again without clear evidence. Age, sex and socio-economic status have such a pervasive effect on speech that they clearly should be considered. Our preliminary work suggests that two other factors may have a particularly strong bearing on speech intelligibility (Cowie – Douglas-Cowie 1983: 189–191). One is the content of the speech; the other is age at onset of deafness.

The study was designed to establish clearly which of these variables do affect speech quality as measured by intelligibility. The sample of subjects was balanced and diverse with respect to as many of the relevant variables as possible. The problems of contacting deafened people impose restrictions on the degree of balance that can be achieved, but with appropriate statistical techniques it is possible to allow for imperfect sampling so long as key variables are not too narrowly spread or too strongly intercorrelated. The sample of speech was also varied. At one extreme it included reading passages in a formal style, and at the other it included narratives in the speakers' own words (generated in response to cartoon strips).

4.2. Method

Details of method are given in chapter 3, but this section provides a summary for convenience.

The deafened speakers were chosen to represent a range of postlingually acquired hearing losses in terms of level and age at onset. Table 4.1 shows the main characteristics of the sample. Fuller details are given in chapter 3 (see section 3.3.1, especially table 3.1). The sample is not perfectly balanced, but it keeps confounding to an acceptable level in most respects.

Table 4.1 Deafened subjects in the intelligibility study

Level of loss	Age at onset					
	< 5	6–15	16–35	36–55	>55	total
15–34 dB	0	0	0	0	1	1
35–54 dB	3	2	1	2	3	11
55–74 dB	3	2	0	3	1	9
75–94 dB	1	0	2	2	1	6
95–114 dB	0	1	3	2	0	6
> 114 dB	3	8	3	0	0	14
Totals	10	13	9	9	6	

The basic requirement for controls was that their accents should represent the spread of speech types that occur in the Belfast area (see Milroy 1981: 98–103; Douglas-Cowie 1984: 533). As a result they included a spread of ages and occupations. Table 4.2 summarises the sample in terms of age and the rough scale that we have used to code status (1 = professional, 2 = clerical or administrative, 3 = skilled, 4 = unskilled work). A mean status score of 2.5 indicates that the group is balanced in this respect. All the cells with more than one subject are reasonably close to this. Again, the imbalances which exist are unlikely to matter (see table 3.3 for further details of control subjects).

Table 4.2 Control subjects in the intelligibility study

Age	number		mean status score	
	males	females	males	females
10–29	4	4	2.5	2.5
30–49	3	1	2.7	4
> 50	2	5	2	2.4

Details of the speech provided by each speaker are in chapter 3 (see section 3.5.1). The speech sample consisted of five reading passages and three narrative passages generated by presenting cartoon strips and asking speakers to tell the story of the cartoon in their own words. The listeners were 660 university students from Northern Ireland – i.e. ten per speaker. They had no specialised knowledge of speech or deafness. They did not know that the study was concerned with deafness – in fact they did not even know that the speaker they were listening to might not be perfectly normal. In the first instance they tried to shadow the eight passages, and we recorded them as they did it.

The intelligibility of a particular speaker on a particular passage was measured by counting the words which each listener had failed to repeat correctly when he or she was shadowing that sample. Error scores were calculated by averaging the scores of the ten subjects who had heard the sample, and then dividing by the number of words to give a percentage score.

4.3. Results

Figure 4.1 shows how overall intelligibility varies according to level of loss (using the categorisation of losses introduced in table 4.1).

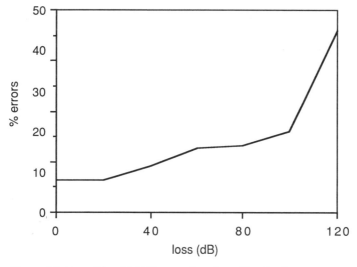

Figure 4.1 Overall intelligibility as a function of hearing loss

If we ignore the single subject with a hearing loss under 30 dB, the remaining data can be put into an analysis of variance with three factors: hearing, sex, and passage. This provides a preliminary way of identifying considerations which need to be taken into account in finer analysis.

As figure 4.1 indicates, the analysis shows a highly significant effect of hearing ($F_{5, 52} = 4.99$, $p < 0.001$). This confirms the most basic point that we wish to establish, that hearing loss does affect intelligibility. There is also a highly significant effect of passage ($F_{7, 364} = 15.0$, $p < 0.0001$). This is not particularly relevant since it shows an effect which applies to hearing and deafened alike. However there is also a significant interaction between hearing and passage (F 35, 364 = 1.66, p = 0.013). This indicates that the effect of hearing varies according to passage.

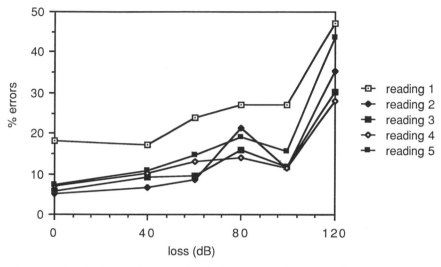

Figure 4.2 Hearing loss and passage in relation to error rate (top panel)

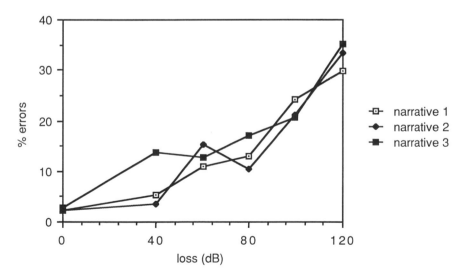

Figure 4.2 Hearing loss and passage in relation to error rate (bottom panel)

Figure 4.2 illustrates the nature of the effects relating to passage. The main effect is due to the raised error rates associated with reading passage 1 ("The English"). It is the most ornate and literary passage, and the fact that it is hardest to follow is not surprising. However it is worth noting how high the error rates associated with it are – they average over 25% for speakers with losses as low as 60 dB. What this means is that even quite moderate losses produce speech deterioration which affects the chances of success in some kinds of communication. In the narrative passages, error rates climb relatively smoothly in relation to hearing loss.

The source of the interaction is a contrast between reading passages and narratives. With reading, there is something like a plateau over a wide range of losses, reaching up to the speakers whose losses are in the range 90–110 dB. Those people, with losses which are profound but not total, are not noticeably different from people with losses of 50–70dB. With narrative, there is a much more even progression of error rate with loss. The most striking single aspect of the contrast is that people with 90–110dB losses have very considerable problems being understood in narrative.

The third variable in the analysis, sex, only participates in one significant effect. It is the interaction between sex, loss, and passage (F 35, 364 = 1.96, p = .001). Figure 4.3 illustrates the basis of the effect. It occurs in the narrative passages. There males with severe to profound losses, (shown with black symbols on the figure) are markedly less intelligible than females (shown with white symbols). The effect does not occur at the extremes (normal hearing or near total loss) or in the reading passages.

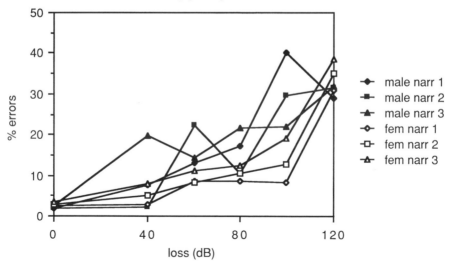

Figure 4.3 Hearing loss and passage in relation to error rate in the narrative

A fourth variable with marked effects is age at onset of deafness. Figure 4.4 summarises the broad pattern that occurs in the data. It separates subjects into three groups – controls, those with losses under 80 dB (called the hard of hearing), and those with losses over 80 dB (called the profound group). A simple mark in the figure represents one speaker's average error rate on one passage. If there are *n* lines radiating from a point, then there are *n* speakers whose scores are at or near the relevant position. This provides a convenient way of conveying where the bulk of observations lie.

Three main patterns stand out from the figure. First, age at onset has a marked effect in the profound group, but not among the hard of hearing. This suggests that the relevant onset variable is age at onset of profound deafness. Second, the relationship between error rate and age at onset is relatively continuous: there is no natural break in the function where one could say that after a certain point becoming deaf has no great effect. Third, age at onset is not linearly related to error rate. A ten year difference in onset tends to makes a large difference to error rate early in life, but relatively little later on. The simplest summary of this non-linearity is to say that error rate is roughly proportional to the inverse of age at onset of profound deafness, assuming that the measure has a value of 0 for those who are not profoundly deaf. We will call this measure inverse age at onset.

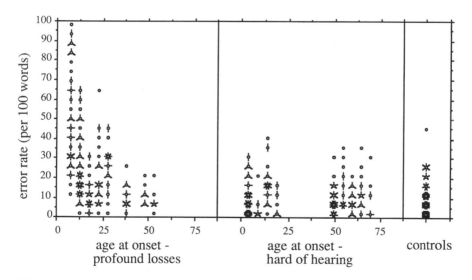

Figure 4.4 Error rate as a function of age at onset and level of loss

The figure suggests that a good predictor of intelligibility based on age at onset would be the inverse of age at onset for people with losses above a certain threshold, and zero for others (that is, it would be the inverse of age at the onset of a certain level of loss). Three thresholds which seem reasonable in the light of the data – 80 dB, 90 dB, and 100 dB – were considered. With a 90 dB cut-off, inverse age at onset correlated significantly with loss in the suprathreshold group: hence it is statistically unsafe to use a 90 dB threshold for this sample. There was relatively little to choose between the other two. The 80 dB cut-off has been preferred here because it gave a lower correlation between inverse age at onset and loss in the suprathreshold group ($r^2 = 0.08$) and a more even division of speakers. In a simple regression, this measure (inverse age at onset thresholded at 80 dB) predicts average error rate per subject with F 1, 64 = 138, p = 0.0001.

Multiple regression was used to examine the combined effects of the variables discussed so far, and a number of others which for one reason or another one might expect to be relevant. Variables in the latter category were age at time of testing, time since onset of deafness, and a rough four-point measure of social status (1 = professional, 2 = clerical or administrative, 3 = skilled, 4 = unskilled work).

Two separate analyses were carried out, one for the reading passages and one for the narratives based on the cartoons. This is the only straightforward way of acknowledging the apparent differences between them given that regression does not easily handle repeated measures from the same subject. The dependent variable in each regression was the average of each subject's scores on a particular type of passage (reading or narration). Seven predictor variables were used. Straightforward variables were status, sex, and age at recording. Hearing loss was reflected in four variables. The first was loss in decibels. The second was inverse age at onset thresholded at 80 dB. The third was the presence of a loss of less than 80 dB. This variable tests for the possibility that less than profound loss will have an effect which is not particularly related to its severity (at least within broad limits). The fourth was years since loss (for all hearing impaired subjects, since there was nothing to indicate a differential relationship).

Table 4.3 summarises the regressions, showing the student listeners' t values used to test the significance of each variable's contribution and the associated probabilities. For both styles, overwhelmingly the most important predictor is the inverse age at onset measure. Both show a weaker effect which relates to the hard-of-hearing group, a significant effect of loss in decibels for the narrative passage and an effect of being hard-of-hearing which comes very close to significance for the reading. The different forms of effect reflects the differences which are apparent in figure 4.2. Status also reaches significance in the reading passage: perhaps surprisingly, higher status speakers were less intelligible. The models account for a substantial proportion of the variance in both cases, with $r^2 = 0.75$ for the reading passage and $r^2 = 0.60$ for the narrative.

Table 4.3 Regressions on mean score for reading passages and mean score for narratives

Predictor variable	reading passages		narrative passages	
	t	p	t	p
inverse age at onset	7.8	0.0001	4.7	0.0001
loss in dB	0.29	0.782	2.2	0.029
having a loss < 80 dB	1.93	0.059	1.53	0.132
status	2.20	0.032	0.57	0.571
sex	0.80	0.428	0.21	0.835
age at test	0.65	0.522	0.25	0.803
years since loss	0.28	0.780	1.19	0.239

Finally, two natural questions are worth answering.

The first question is whether less than profound loss has an effect on speech intelligibility. Insofar as there is a single answer, it is yes. The point is made by an analysis of variance on scores for controls and speakers with losses of less than 80dB. The main effect of hearing is significant ($F_{1,39} = 12.6$, $p = 0.001$). There is also a significant interaction between hearing and passage ($F_{1,39} = 4.93$, $p = 0.032$) which shows that the effect is more marked in the more natural type of speech, the narrative.

The second question is when acquired loss ceases to have an effect on speech. On the data, the best answer is "never". Take the regression equation which was obtained for the narrative passages, and consider somebody with a loss of 120 dB acquired 20 years before. According to the equation, the speaker's error scores remains more than two standard deviations above the controls' mean except in the extreme case which combines all the factors that favour intelligibility – a working-class female deafened at 60 or later. This calculation uses a transform which makes the distribution of control scores reasonably normal: without it matters would look worse.

4.4. Discussion

The data in this chapter establish three basic premises for our study.

The first is that speech deterioration in acquired deafness is a real problem which is worth studying.

Our shadowing measure is not a familiar one, and readers who are used to other measures may feel some uncertainty about interpreting the error scores. However, at base, the shadowing technique is singularly transparent: it is the most direct test available of whether listeners understand speech word for word without having to pause for thought. Its drawback is simply that its relationship with other measures of intelligibility remains to be mapped. This would be worth doing, but the validity of the technique does not depend on it. In fact given the face validity of the shadowing technique, it is arguable that it should be regarded as the standard to which other measures are referred.

When one remembers what the task is, it is reasonably clear that intelligibility is a problem when shadowers miss one word in three. That is the error level for profoundly deafened speakers, and it is common well outside the group whose losses occurred very early in life.

The second basic premise which the data establish is that deafened speech is not a homogeneous phenomenon. Several variables have a substantial effect on the simple measure used here, and to ignore them elsewhere is to court confusion.

Level of loss is clearly one such variable. There is a massive difference between people with profound to total losses and people with moderate or severe losses. The boundary is fuzzy, but it appears to be qualitative: there may be differences within the two groups associated with level of loss, but, if so, they are small compared to the radical difference between the groups.

Age at onset of deafness also emerges as a major variable, confirming our earlier hypothesis (Cowie – Douglas-Cowie 1983: 190–191). Onsets well into adulthood continue to produce marked effects. This is contrary to reasonable hypotheses (see chapter 2), and it directs attention away from the more obvious mechanistic interpretations of the phenomenon. The other time-related variable that we considered, years since deafness, appears to be irrelevant within the range that our subjects spanned. This does not conflict with the general presumption that deterioration occurs over an appreciable time, but it does indicate that the process stabilises after a moderate period. This too constrains theoretical explanations – in fact not many obvious hypotheses fit both of the observations about time course which we have made.

The final set of variables which emerge may be called the sociolinguistic variables. Speech style has a pivotal role among these. Status has an effect in the reading passage. The narratives suggest a continuous effect of loss, and there appears to be a sex difference at intermediate levels of loss. Only the first of these is easy to interpret theoretically, but methodologically they provide a clear warning that ignoring sociolinguistic variables – particularly style – is a potential source of difficulty.

The third basic premise which the data establish is that at least up to a point, deafened people's speech follows orderly laws. There is a great deal of purely individual variation in the sample, as for instance figure 4.4 suggests. Nevertheless the common trends are strong, and the regression models capture a very respectable proportion of the variance. That provides encouragement for later parts of the study which look for order on a more detailed level.

Chapter 5
Automatic acoustic analysis of deafened speech

5.1. Introduction

The previous chapter demonstrated a basic abnormality of function in deafened people's speech. This chapter is the first of three which deal with abnormalities of form.

The particular concern of this chapter is with abnormalities which are relatively gross and which can be measured completely objectively. It is also concerned to show that these abnormalities fall into patterns which are consistent across deafened speakers: although there is idiosyncratic variation, it is superimposed on broad, common trends. Demonstrating these points provides a foundation on which more detailed analysis can be rested.

The approach was prompted by looking at spectrograms. Spectrograms of deafened speakers often look wrong in a broad, intuitive way. However looking at features with an obvious phonetic significance often seems not to clarify what is wrong: in fact one can begin to wonder whether the abnormality is real at all. This led us to look for measures which might reflect the initial, global impression of abnormality in spectrograms. It seemed likely that these abnormalities were related to fairly gross properties of the distribution of energy in speech samples, properties which it is easier at least in the first instance to describe in terms of statistics than in terms of phonetics. These observations led us to develop a package of measures based on a combination of formal considerations relevant to describing any distribution and considerations relevant to speech in particular.

The essence of the package is the systematic combination of a few basic forms of description. Details are described in 5.2., but it is worth giving a sense of the basic concepts here.

The package rests on several types of description which are clearly important for speech, and which lend themselves to statistical treatment. One is a contour showing how the amplitude of the speech signal varies over time. Another is the F0 contour. A third is the spectrum.

The basic spectrum gives rise to several secondary descriptions which are concerned with the way it changes. One key form of change is over time. It can be measured by taking differences between the energy associated with a particular frequency at one time and the energy associated with the same frequency at a previous instant. Taking those differences for every frequency in the spectrum gives a description of change over time. That description has a spectrum-like form in its own right. It is also important for speech whether the energy at a particular frequency is higher than the energies at neighbouring frequencies, since that is the simplest sign of a formant. This is a question about change over frequency. An operation which we call sharpening offers relevant measures. It involves taking the energy at a point in the spectrum, and subtracting from it a proportion of the energy at the next frequency above and the next frequency below. The result is a number which shows (roughly) whether the energy at the central point is greater than the average energies of its neighbours, and if so by how much. There is one of these numbers for each point in the original spectrum, and together they form a new spectrum-like representation which we call the sharpened spectrum.

All of these spectrum-like representations are summarised in the same way. At each frequency the average activity (for want of a better word) is found, giving a basic summary. The elements of that summary are also grouped in a way that reflects their linguistic function. The elements associated with each of four bands are summed to give measures of the activity in these regions. The regions are those where one would expect (according to average data) to find respectively F0, F1, F2, and frication. An additional manipulation is to divide activity in a derived representation by the energy in the relevant part of the basic spectrum. The result is what we have called a level-relative measure. Level-relative measures reveal where high change (for instance) is not just a side effect of high basic energy. That kind of description was only partly incorporated into the basic package, but it proves very useful.

Describing change over time is relevant to the amplitude contour and F0 as well as the spectrum. In each case two different questions arise. One is how much change occurs from instant to instant. Another is how much change there is between key points. In the amplitude contour and F0, the obvious key points are maxima and minima on the contour. In the spectrum, the obvious key points are syllable centres. Simple automatic analysis cannot be expected to find syllable centres, but peaks in the amplitude contour are a reasonable coarse approximation. In principle measures which describe sample-to-sample change can completely mask trends which involve key points, and vice versa. Hence the package systematically considers any question about change on both levels, one dealing with change from sample to sample and the other from one key point to the next.

A similarly systematic approach is taken to obtaining simple numerical summaries for a spectrum or pattern of change or whatever aspect of speech is being examined. Central relationships are expressed as a graph – a histogram or a scattergram. The standard parameters for describing that kind of graph are then obtained – mean, median, and measures related to spread for histograms, correlation and regression coefficients for scattergrams. These parameters are the numbers which are eventually used in comparisons between deafened and control speakers.

The package reflects a philosophy which is unconventional, but reasonable. Descriptors are chosen to form a natural set with its own internal logic, so that they provide something approximating a complete description of speech at a coarse level of resolution. This is different from the ideal which typically drives instrumental analysis of speech, which is to find specialised measures with direct relationships to prespecified characteristics of speech production or perception. However the two types of aim are perfectly compatible. In the long term, they represent different ways of converging on a common goal, in which descriptors that form an orderly and complete set are also precisely related to articulation and perception. In the short term, the two have different applications. The approach which we have developed here offers a useful way of addressing the problem at hand, and showing that deafened people's speech shows substantial and systematic abnormalities.

5.2. Method

The speech samples and the subjects are described in full in chapter 3. The choice reflects variables which the previous chapter found were important. Two passages were used for each speaker, one reading passage ("It was unfortunate...") and the most nearly spontaneous speech sample that we have, which consists of the speaker describing a day in his or her life (see chapter 3, section 3.5.2 for details of the speech sample). Complete sets of data were obtained from 54 subjects, 31 controls and 23 deafened. A few others were rejected in the course of data processing because we were not completely confident of the output of the analysis algorithms. The deafened subjects almost all had losses over 80dB in the better ear, so that the picture was not confused by the less severely affected speech of speakers with milder losses (see chapter 3, section 3.3.1., especially table 3.1 for details of deafened subjects, and section 3.4 for details of control subjects).

Analysis involved two distinct programs.

The signal capture program used an ARIEL RTA 331 spectrum analyser housed in an IBM PC. It contained 31 filters with centre frequencies running from 25 Hz to 16 kHz in 1/3 octave steps, and a 32nd filter which gave the amplitude of the signal. The program sampled the output of these filters at 40 millisecond intervals, and stored the results in files. Maximum sample length was 8 seconds. When a longer passage had to be analysed the experimenter broke it down into stretches which ran between natural breaks. Before capture proper, the whole of a passage was played through a preliminary scanning routine which found the highest output of the amplitude filter and set internal gain so that the amplitude filter's output reached a set maximum value (127) when the passage was replayed and captured. Output was scaled in decibels, but, because of the amplification, absolute values are not significant.

The second program, called FULLSTAT, took files from the first as its input. Multiple files could be analysed together, and so passages which were split at recording were rejoined at this stage. The analysis can be thought of as involving three phases. The first established extended descriptions of the signal. The second obtained graphs which summarised some aspect of an extended description. The third extracted a range of statistical parameters which were associated with each graph. This description does not always capture the sequence of operations in the program, but it summarises the underlying logic fairly.

The first phase provided four descriptions of the signal. These were the basic spectrum obtained by the filter bank, the trace of amplitude provided by the 32nd filter, the sharpened spectrum, and a trace of fundamental frequency.

If $S_{t,f}$ is the entry in the raw spectrum for a time t and for a filter f, then the corresponding entry in the sharpened spectrum $SS_{t,f}$ is given by

$$SS_{t,f} = S_{t,f} - 0.4\,(S_{t,f-1} + S_{t,f+1}) - 0.2\,(S_{t,f-2} + S_{t,f+2})$$
$$+ 0.08\,(S_{t-1,f} + S_{t+1,f})$$

The last term reflects the fact that we are interested in F0, which is a continuous feature (and to a lesser extent other formants): the term raises the entry for a cell whose neighbours suggest that it is part of a structure which extends over time. Fundamental frequency was obtained by an inelegant but robust algorithm which used the sharpened spectrum. The sharpened spectrum was summed over time, and the result used to find the band where F0 was most likely to lie. The first pass decided that a cell (t,f) was part of F0 if (a) the corresponding entry $SS_{t,f}$ in the sharpened spectrum exceeded a conservative threshold, (b) it lay in the target band, and (c) there were no cells below it containing appreciable entries. Subsequent passes attached cells to F0 if (a) they were connected to a cell which had been identified as part of F0, (b) their sharpened spectrum entries exceeded another threshold, and (c) there was not already an F0 entry at that time. The output of the algorithm was always checked by eye against a printout of the spectrum, and passages where its output seemed to be dubious were rejected. The main problem was that occasionally F0 was extended into unvoiced regions. When the basic recovery of F0 had been completed the relevant cells in the basic spectrum were re-examined and interpolation based on values in neighbouring cells was used to estimate pitch to the nearest semitone.

The second phase generated two types of summary, histograms and scatter-grams.

In the largest block of histograms each column was associated with one of the frequency channels in the spectrum analyser. The simplest of these showed the average level at each frequency in the basic spectrum and the sharpened spectrum, and the peak level at each frequency. More complex descriptions dealt with change in the spectrum. The two types of change which were considered have been introduced above. They will be referred to as sample-to-sample and peak-to-peak. The first refers to change measured by comparing spectral values in adjacent samples, and the second to change measured by comparing spectral values at peaks in the amplitude contour. In both cases the measure of change in a channel was the root mean square of the differences between relevant values. For each change histogram a level-relative equivalent was calculated, with one qualification: instead of dividing the mean values in a change histogram by the corresponding mean values for the basic spectrum, FULLSTAT calculated the inverse quantity (average energy upon change). This was because the inverse is statistically more tractable. Two change histograms were also calculated for the sharpened spectrum, one sample-to-sample and one peak-to-peak.

Histograms were also used to summarise the amplitude and F0 traces. Both were again considered on two levels, one based on point by point description and the other based on the identification of higher order structure in the trace.

For amplitude, the point-by-point treatment generated two histograms. In one, each column showed the number of observations at a particular amplitude. For this raw values were divided by 4, giving 32 levels. In the other, it showed the number of observations which differed from their predecessor by a particular amount (signed, not absolute differences were used). For this raw difference values were divided by 8, giving 33 levels (−16 to 16).

Higher order structure was found by picking maxima and minima in the contour, and looking at the properties of segments which ran from a maximum to the next minimum or vice versa. Histograms were formed specifying the distributions of amplitudes at all inflections, at maxima, and at minima; the distribution of rises in amplitude between points of inflection and the distribution of falls in amplitude between all points of inflection; the distribution of the durations of rises in amplitude between points of inflection; and the distribution of the durations of falls in amplitude between all points of inflection.

Again absolute values were on a 32 level scale and differences on a 33 level scale.

For F0, the point by point treatment generated one histogram, showing the number of observations at a particular amplitude.

Higher-order structure involved two types of limit. The contour was divided into continuous stretches, bounded by intervals where F0 was absent. Maxima and minima were then marked on each stretch. Stretches were then assigned to one of six categories: rises, rise/falls, levels, fall-rises, falls, and compound stretches. The last category contains stretches with more than one inflection. A histogram was formed showing the distribution of the six types. A second histogram was formed showing the distribution of stretch durations. A third dealt with pitch change in segments (i.e. the interval from the highest point in the segment to the lowest): again, the distribution of pitch changes was set out as a histogram.

Scattergrams were also generated from the amplitude and F0 contours. In most of them each observation was plotted against its predecessor. The result is a plot which is compact if observations tend to be like their predecessors, diffuse if there tends to be a good deal of difference between them. This kind of plot was constructed for successive samples on the F0 contour and the amplitude contour, and for the changes in amplitude associated with successive segments in the amplitude contour. Another type of histogram was formed by plotting this change in amplitude against the duration of the associated segment.

In the third phase statistical parameters were derived from each graph.

For histograms seven standard parameters were obtained. These were the standard parametric measures of midpoint and spread, mean and variance; and the parameters which are regularly used for corresponding non-parametric descriptions, i.e. minimum, maximum, median, and first and third quartile scores. Most of the histograms which were used were close enough in shape to a normal distribution to make the parametric descriptors reasonably appropriate, but some were clearly not. The non-parametric descriptors were calculated mainly as an insurance against that kind of case. Where it was reasonable to split a distribution into two parts (e.g. for rises and falls in the amplitude contour) separate parameters were calculated for each part.

Histograms whose x axis was frequency were also described in another way, by summing the values associated with four frequency bands. These were chosen to span the usual range of F0, F1, F2, and frication respectively. The boundaries of the bands were defined slightly differently for males and females. They were as follows:

males	50–200 Hz	250–630 Hz	800–2.5kHz	3.15–16kHz
females	63–250 Hz	315–630 Hz	800–2.5kHz	3.15–16kHz

This male/female difference was arrived at in two steps. Initially several sets of alternative boundaries were programmed on the basis of standard tables (Denes – Pinson 1973: 153–155). Then when data were available, analyses were carried out to establish which set of alternatives most nearly equalised the average energy in each band for males and females. A description involving one of these bands is constructed simply by summing the mean activity in the relevant filters for each speaker.

For the scattergrams, two parameters were calculated. These were a correlation coefficient and a regression coefficient. Again, scattergrams were subdivided when it made sense to do so.

The analyses which we have summarised were printed out automatically for each recording. The printout showed the spectrum, amplitude contour, and amplitude contour, followed by the main graphs which have been described, and it finished with a page setting out the relevant parameters of the graphs. These parameters formed the basis of the results which we describe below.

5.3. Results

In broad terms we describe the most global and general findings first, and work towards the more detailed and individual findings.

Perhaps the most important single feature of the data is that there are global and general trends. As chapter 2 suggested, it is natural to expect that the primary effect of acquired deafness may be idiosyncratic breakdown: that is, individual deafened people may lie haphazardly above or below the bounds that the control sample suggests are normal. Trends affecting deafened people as a whole might quite conceivably not be a major feature of the data.

In fact the results are quite different. A large proportion of variables show systematic shifts which are common to deafened speakers as a group. Even where those common effects are absent, many more measures show that hearing has a consistent effect on speakers of one sex, or on one passage, or both. Our description looks first at the general trends, then at the sex- or passage-specific effects, and then finally at the way extreme individuals relate to the trends.

Trends were studied by applying inferential statistics to the measures provided by the FULLSTAT program. Most effects which we report emerged as significant effects or interactions from analyses of variance with two between-variables, sex and hearing level (control or deafened); and one within-variable, passage. When other designs were used they are specified.

Descriptive statistics are given in the tables which accompany the text, using a standard format wherever it makes sense. The standard format provides reasonably full information, and because it is reused it should become easy to read.

5.3.1. The spectrum

Two very global abnormalities occur in the spectrum. The first is that energy is anomalously distributed across it, and the second is it that changes anomalously over time. These are considered in turn.

Table 5.1 summarises the main abnormalities in the distribution of energy across the spectrum. The mean of the spectrum is shifted upwards by about 1/3 octave in the deafened speakers. That is shown in the first block of table 5.1. The numbers refer to positions in the sequence of filters. Filter 15 has a centre frequency of 500 Hz, and centre frequencies are spaced at 1/3 octave intervals. The source of the effect is clarified by measures which consider activity in the formant related frequency bands. The band associated with F2 contains far too much energy in the deafened, as the table shows.

It is worth pointing out that all but one of the measures in the table show a significant interaction between hearing, sex and passage. This kind of context-related effect is pervasive. It will be taken up later when we have summarised the effects which are relatively context free – at least so far as our data shows.

Table 5.1 Indicators of basic abnormalities in energy distribution across the spectrum

	females		males		F	p
	reading	narrative	reading	narrative		
spectrum mean						
control	15.2	15.2	13.9	14.0		
deaf	16.3	15.8	14.4	14.7		
main effect					13.2	.001
hearing*sex*passage interaction					7.11	.010
average level F0						
control	69.8	52.4	74.0	55.9		
deaf	68.4	42.6	50.0	50.5		
main effect of hearing					2.19	.145
hearing*sex*passage interaction					5.77	.020

Table 5.1 (continued)

	females		males		F	p
	reading	narrative	reading	narrative		
average level F1						
control	400	407	468	462		
deaf	407	388	468	478		
main effect of hearing					.013	.909
hearing*sex*passage interaction					3.99	.051
average level F2						
control	47.8	31.5	32.4	24.6		
deaf	90.8	52.6	39.4	37.9		
main effect of hearing					26.4	.001
hearing*sex interaction					7.15	.010
hearing*sex*passage interaction					6.77	.012
average level Fr						
control	24.4	22.3	16.2	11.7		
deaf	34.8	19.3	9.0	17.5		
main effect of hearing					.200	.657
hearing*sex*passage interaction					16.4	.001

The second set of global abnormalities affects change in the spectrum over time. The simplest statement about this is that the deafened change too much. Table 5.2 summarises total change on the four main change measures that FULLSTAT provides. The numbers are produced by summing the mean change associated with each filter, and taking the average of these sums for each speaker. The underlying units are dB, but the number of operations which are superimposed on the dB measurement make it best to regard the measures as numbers on an arbitrary scale.

It is worth pointing out that the different measures of spectral change are neither wholly different nor indistinguishable. All four measures show significant or near significant main effects of hearing and interactions between hearing, sex and passage. But on the other hand, the interaction is much less marked in the measures which deal with the sharpened spectrum than in the measures which deal with the raw spectrum, and the main effect is somewhat clearer in the measures which deal with peak-to-peak change. This pattern in the differences between the measures raises interesting questions about the precise nature of the abnormalities, particularly the context-dependent ones.

We will not pursue these. However we will treat the different measures as at least somewhat distinguishable sources of evidence, and take seriously effects which occur on some but not all of them.

Table 5.2   Total change according to the four main measures concerned with spectral change

	females		males		F	p
	reading	narrative	reading	narrative		
total sample-by-sample change						
control	239	198	224	182		
deaf	272	208	214	222		
main effect					3.26	.077
hearing*sex*passage interaction					8.15	.006
total peak-to-peak change						
control	164	158	146	141		
deaf	196	157	153	171		
main effect					4.83	.033
hearing*sex*passage interaction					7.84	.007
total change in the sharpened spectrum						
control	158	133	146	124		
deaf	177	141	145	149		
main effect					4.56	.038
hearing*sex*passage interaction					6.98	.011
total peak-to-peak change in the sharpened spectrum						
control	121	111	107	100		
deaf	139	114	112	120		
main effect of hearing					5.81	.020
hearing*sex*passage interaction					5.92	.019

Again, we can form a more specific picture of abnormalities in change. The first point is that change is abnormally concentrated in the centre of the spectrum. That is shown by the fact that the variances of the distributions concerned with change tend to be low in deafened speakers, as table 5.3 shows. It is worth reiterating that in this context variance is not being used to measure variation within groups. There is a variance associated with the speech of each subject on each exercise with respect to each measure, and it describes the spread of the associated histogram. The underlying units are positions in the sequence of filters, as in table 5.1.

Table 5.3   Main indications that change is concentrated in mid-spectrum among deafened speakers

	females		males		F	p
	reading	narrative	reading	narrative		
variance of sample-to-sample change:						
controls	30.0	31.7	32.8	33.4		
deaf	26.6	27.0	25.3	29.8		
main effect of hearing					6.36	.015
hearing*sex*passage interaction					5.28	.026
variance of peak-to-peak change:						
control	28.5	30.7	30.2	32.1		
deaf	25.6	25.3	24.1	28.0		
main effect of hearing					5.77	.020
hearing*sex*passage interaction					3.25	.077
variance of sample-to-sample change in sharpened spectrum:						
control	30.1	31.1	31.6	32.4		
deaf	27.2	27.3	26.6	30.7		
main effect of hearing					4.25	.045
hearing*sex*passage interaction					5.54	.023
variance of peak-to-peak change in sharpened spectrum:						
control	27.2	29.9	28.4	29.5		
dcaf	25.6	25.5	24.3	28.6		
main effect of hearing					2.63	.111
hearing*sex*passage interaction					5.66	.021

Closer description needs to take account of the basic skew set out in table 5.1. This can be done by taking measures from the four formant-related bands and dividing them by the relevant speaker's average level in the relevant band. The result is a measure which does not simply reiterate the known shift in average spectral shape. We have called measures like this level-relative measures. Three level-relative measures of temporal change are considered below.

Sample-to-sample and peak-to-peak change are considered relative to level. Less obviously, maximum value is considered relative to level. This is a measure of change because if the maximum value of a measure is close to its average level, its change over time must necessarily be small. Change measures on the sharpened spectrum are not considered because sharpening has its own, different effects, and so compound measures are potentially confusing.

The fricative region behaves differently from the others. Analyses of variance were carried out on the three level-relative change measures associated with the fricative band. Two of the three, the ones which involve sample-to-sample and peak-to-peak change, showed a significant interaction of hearing, sex and passage (respectively $F\ 1,\ 50 = 7.78$, $p = 0.007$ and $F\ 1,\ 50 = 4.33$, $p = 0.043$). The interactions occur because level-relative change in this region is anomalously high for deafened males in the reading passage. The anomaly means that the deafened males reverse a trend which is uniform across the other groups. Elsewhere, level-relative change in the fricative region is considerably higher in the narrative. The deafened males reverse that trend.

The remaining bands were considered together and an analysis of variance was carried out for each of the level-relative change measures. All three analyses showed the same basic result, an interaction between hearing and band. This occurs because the deafened show too much level-relative change in the F0 band and too little in the F2 band. Details are summarised in table 5.4. Simple effects analyses show that the difference associated with F0 is significant for the peak-to-peak measure, the difference associated with F2 is significant for the measure based on maximum value, and both are close to significance for the measure based on sample-to-sample differences. It is reasonably clear that change is abnormal in both, but again we will not dwell on why particular measures show certain abnormalities particularly clearly.

Table 5.4 Level-relative change measures

	sample-sample				peak-peak				maximum			
underlying interaction:	F1,50	p			F1,50	p			F1,50	p		
	7.07	.001			4.95	.009			8.05	.001		
simple effects:												
	means:				means:				means:			
	control	deaf	F2,100	p	control	deaf	F2,100	p	control	deaf	F2,100	p
F0	.778	.893	4.00	.051	.541	.648	4.90	.031	5.10	5.86	1.43	.237
F1	.711	.733	.402	.529	.505	.538	1.16	.287	4.14	3.98	.519	.475
F2	1.49	1.32	3.05	.087	1.20	1.10	1.12	.296	12.1	8.97	6.78	.012

Level-relative measures are relevant to clarifying spectral differentiation as well as temporal differentiation. Values in a particular region of the sharpened spectrum can be considered relative to values in the corresponding region of the basic spectrum. High values show that points in that region tend to stand out relative to their neighbours in the frequency domain.

When we apply analysis of variance to level-relative measures of sharpened spectra, there is a significant interaction between hearing and spectral region (F 3, 150 = 6.5, p < 0.001). Table 5.5 summarises the relevant means. Simple effects analysis confirms what is apparent by eye: the deafened speakers show significantly too much spectral sharpening relative to level in the region of F2 (F 1, 50 = 9.6, p = 0.003), and significantly too little in the fricative region (F 1, 50 = 4.1, p = 0.048).

Table 5.5 Mean level-relative values for the sharpened spectrum

	F0	F1	F2	fricative region
controls	.57	.61	.37	.58
deaf	.58	.61	.43	.53

It is worth drawing together the evidence on formant-related bands. Table 5.6 provides a brief summary which shows up the strong pattern running through the evidence. An 'i' indicates a hearing*sex*passage interaction. It is apparent that not only do deafened speakers show trends on individual measures, but also the trends on individual measures form an orderly whole. This gives a strong suggestion that there are general and lawful pressures underlying the shifts which occur in deafened people's speech.

Table 5.6 Summary of trends involving formant-related bands

	F0	F1	F2	fr
spectral differentiation	*	*	too high	too low
average energy	i	i	too high	i
temporal differentiation	too high	*	too low	i

5.3.2. The amplitude contour

Like the spectrum, the amplitude contour reveals a variety of differences. It is worth reiterating that our measure of amplitude does not correspond simply to problems with volume. Informally it seems most unlikely that absolute amplitude was abnormal in these speech samples. The way our analysis normalised the signal precluded measuring absolute amplitude, and so we cannot demonstrate the point formally. However there were several clear abnormalities which involved relative properties of amplitude.

Beginning with the most global problem again, the average variance of amplitude was too high in the deaf (F 1, 50 = 13.6, p = 0.001), particularly in the reading passage (F 1, 50 = 7.98, p = 0.007). Table 5.7 shows how variance differs between the two groups. The units are based on a decibel scale, but again the operations involved in normalising and obtaining variance mean that they do not have a simple description.

Table 5.7   Variance of amplitude as a function of hearing and passage

	read	spontaneous
controls	67	71
deaf	86	79

Essentially high variance means that the deafened spent too little of their time at amplitudes which were near their average. The statistics concerned with maxima and minima help to give a more specific picture of the way this happened.

One way of spending too much time far from the average is to oscillate between extremes – so that you are either loud or silent. If the deafened did that, then we would expect to find that the mean amplitude at maxima was too great, mean amplitude at minima was low, and variance at both was low. This picture is partially confirmed, though only partially. Table 5.8 illustrates.

For the narrative passage, the mean amplitudes for maxima and minima are generally consistent with the predicted raising of maxima and lowering of minima. Mean variances are higher in the deaf than in the controls, but not nearly so much so as they are in the reading passage. All this fits a tendency to oscillate between extremes in the narrative if not in the reading. There is also a more direct confirmation of that pattern. One of the few significant effects involving scattergram type plots is an interaction between hearing and passage (F 1, 50 = 11.4, p = 0.001) involving the correlation between change in a segment and change in its successor. The interaction rests on the fact that the deafened show more strongly negative correlations than controls do in the narrative passage. A strongly negative measure indicates that a rise tends to be followed by an equal and opposite fall, and vice versa.

This tendency to oscillate between extremes accounts for part of the abnormal variance in deafened speakers. A second factor appears to account for a large part of the remaining abnormality. It is that controls make occasional excursions well beyond their average level, whereas deafened speakers do not. With normalised measurement, the occasional excursions have the effect of shrinking the scale on which the vast bulk of the signal is measured. Hence their absence increases variances across the board, which is what is observed in deafened speakers.

Table 5.8   Distribution of maxima and minima in the amplitude contour for deafened and hearing speakers

	females		males		F	p
	reading	narrative	reading	narrative		
mean amplitude at maxima						
control	24.7	21.6	24.6	21.5		
deaf	24.8	22.4	23.5	22.4		
main effect of hearing					.136	.714
hearing*passage interaction					.390	.054
mean amplitude at minima						
control	15.2	12.5	14.5	12.0		
deaf	14.5	11.9	12.4	12.3		
main effect of hearing					2.31	.135
hearing*passage interaction					3.77	.058
variance of amplitude at maxima						
control	35.1	45.5	35.3	46.9		
deaf	58.8	48.5	54.3	57.7		
main effect					22.4	.000
hearing*passage interaction					10.0	.003
variance of amplitude at minima						
control	50.4	55.1	54.6	56.3		
deaf	69.4	60.4	66.1	64.7		
main effect					13.2	.001
hearing*passage interaction					5.83	.020

In general terms, variance of change per segment fits that pattern of increased variances across the board (a segment being a stretch of contour running between two inflexions, a maximum and a minimum). Variance was too high among the deaf ($F_{1, 50} = 7.22$, $p = 0.010$). This is illustrated in table 5.9.

Table 5.9 Variance of change per segment in the amplitude contour

	reading	narrative
controls	30	24
deaf	34	31

However table 5.9 combines rises and falls in the amplitude contour, and they behaved differently. As table 5.10 shows, rises were abnormal on all counts. Not only did they cover too much of the range of levels, but they were also too protracted. In addition they were too variable on both counts. Fall size had too high a variance, as it should if the deafened show too few excursions to extremes. Falls were not abnormal overall on any other count, but an interaction shows that they were significantly too large in the narrative.

The pattern of exaggerated rises and falls in the narrative fits the tendency to oscillate between extremes which has already been mentioned. The differential exaggeration of rises in the reading passage involves accentuation of a tendency which is present in normal speech. The mean change in a rise is greater than the mean change in a fall, but its duration is actually shorter – i.e. the contour tends towards a sawtooth pattern where amplitude builds up rapidly and declines slowly (and often discontinuously). That pattern is accentuated among deafened speakers.

Table 5.10 Rises and falls in the amplitude contour

	females		males		F	p
	reading	narrative	reading	narrative		
mean change/rise						
control	6.31	5.92	6.26	5.92		
deaf	6.94	6.48	6.81	6.53		
main effect					8.22	.006
variance of change/rise						
control	30.3	28.5	29.4	28.8		
deaf	31.0	29.9	30.6	30.5		
main effect					11.1	.002
mean duration of rise						
control	2.18	2.18	2.12	2.23		
deaf	2.35	2.33	2.27	2.48		
main effect					11.2	.002

Table 5.10   (continued)

	females		males		F	p
	reading	narrative	reading	narrative		
variance of rise duration						
control	1.15	1.25	1.12	1.28		
deaf	1.42	1.58	1.27	1.69		
main effect					12.6	.001
mean change/fall						
control	3.17	2.60	3.33	2.79		
deaf	3.09	3.08	3.35	3.10		
main effect of hearing					1.38	.245
hearing* passage interaction					4.11	.048
variance of change/fall						
control	12.1	10.4	13.4	12.0		
deaf	14.4	14.1	15.7	15.0		
main effect					9.30	.004
mean duration of fall						
control	2.86	3.10	2.89	3.07		
deaf	2.86	3.12	2.96	3.14		
main effect					.347	.559
variance of fall duration						
control	2.40	3.36	2.85	3.36		
deaf	2.38	3.19	2.90	3.60		
main effect					.009	.924

5.3.3. The F0 contour

We now consider measures on the F0 contour. This topic is complicated by problems in the extraction phase. Initially we believed that F0 was showing no large-scale abnormalities, but a different picture has emerged from reanalysis using measures chosen to be insensitive to the typical errors which affected extraction.

The median was taken as a robust index of each subject's central tendency for pitch. Table 5.11 below summarises average values of subjects' medians. Analysis of variance yielded two significant effects, for sex (F1, 49 = 86.1, p< 0.0001) and hearing (F 1, 49 = 4.28, p = 0.044).

Table 5.11   Median pitch of deafened and hearing speakers

	hearing	deafened
females	186 Hz	200 Hz
males	120 Hz	135 Hz

As a robust measure of pitch range we took the distance between the lowest observation and the point below which 75% of the observations lay. Table 5.12 summarises average values for this 75% range measure. There is a relatively consistent pattern of increased range among the deafened, and this is mirrored in an analysis of variance which shows a marginal effect of hearing.

Table 5.12   Pitch range (using 75% measure) for deafened and control speakers

	females		males		F	p
	reading	narrative	reading	narrative		
75% pitch range:						
controls	70.1	54.1	38.0	38.2		
deaf	94.5	79.3	37.0	66.9		
main effect of hearing					2.93	.093

The other abnormalities in F0 involved high-order structure. They appear when some of the less common features in our original categorisation are grouped together. So rise and fall-rise features are grouped together as features which end with a rise (rise end features for short), and fall and rise-fall features are grouped together as features which end with a fall (fall end features for short). Applying analysis of variance to these categories gives a significant interaction between hearing, passage and feature type (F 3, 150 = 4.76, p = 0.003). Table 5.13 shows the relevant means. The controls show a marked increase in compound features in the reading passages – that is, there are more stretches where F0 continues unbroken through more than one inflection. That makes sense if one assumes that reading favours rather elaborate phrases. The deafened do not show that style shift.

Table 5.13 Feature type, hearing and passage in the intonation contour

		fall end	rise end	level	compound
hearing	reading	.0255	.0216	.0116	.1273
	narrative	.0283	.0253	.0184	.0834
deafened	reading	.0335	.0193	.0136	.0958
	narrative	.0332	.0215	.0169	.0857

Looking more closely at the first two categories by taking them into a separate analysis, we find a significant interaction between hearing, sex, and feature type (F 1, 50 = 5.97, p = 0.018). It is illustrated in table 5.14 below. The essential point is that the deafened show different abnormalities according to sex. Compared to control males, deafened males have too few features which end in a rise and too many which end in a fall. It is tempting to link this to the conjecture that declination at phrase ends is a universal default pattern, and to suggest that we are seeing a tendency to revert to it when feedback is lost. However the deafened and control females show very similar ratios of rise end to fall end features, though both are too common in the deafened.

Table 5.14 Feature type, hearing and sex for short non-level features in the intonation contour

	females		males	
	fall end	rise end	fall end	rise end
hearing	.0136	.0108	.0132	.0127
deaf	.0159	.0124	.0175	.0079

5.3.4. Rate

A final point on this level of description concerns rate. The acoustic analysis provides a crude measure, that is the time taken to read the reading passage. Analysis of variance shows that this measure was significantly affected by both sex (F 1, 50 = 9.1, p = 0.004 – females took more time) and hearing (F 1, 50 = 9.3, p = 0.004 – the deafened speakers took about one eighth longer).

Reduced rate is consistent with other reports in the literature (see chapter 2). However it would be misleading to say that that is what our data show. Some of the effect that appears above is due to pauses which are too long or too frequent. Some of it is due to slowing which is context-specific, particularly at the ends of sentences. Particularly in the narrative (which the data above do not cover) some people speak at a fast, relentless pace, and some people's speech rate fluctuates between too fast and too slow. In sum, rate abnormalities are clearly complex, and it is not appropriate to summarise them in a single trend.

5.3.5. Interactions

We now turn to the interactions which have emerged throughout the data. They create a surprisingly consistent picture when they are related to another recurring aspect of the data, which is that on most measures controls show a relatively consistent shift in scores between the two exercises, reading and the narrative. This is not surprising in view of the phenomenon of style shift which is well known in sociolinguistics. Because controls show style shifts on most measures, the sources of most interactions can be described in terms of whether deafened speakers of a particular sex exaggerate a style shift that is found in the controls, or reduce it, or even reverse it.

Table 5.15 shows that this approach reveals a degree of consistency in the interactions involving sex and passage which have been cited. The fact that a letter is present in a cell indicates that the relevant deafened speakers show a shift which (intuitively) appears to be anomalous in the relevant way. If the letter is 'r', then the shift leaves that group with a score for reading which (again intuitively) is markedly abnormal. If the letter is 'n', then the shift leaves the group with a score for the narrative passage which is similarly abnormal. A letter 'o' indicates that neither of the above is clearly true.

Two points are apparent from the table. First, the general trend is for deafened females to exaggerate normal style shifts and for males to underplay or reverse them. Second, inappropriate sex-related style shift is likely to result in abnormal reading more often than abnormal narrative – though note that narrative may be abnormal as a result of other types of change which are not of this kind and so are not shown in the table. The obvious example involves the amplitude contour. It is most clearly abnormal in the narrative, an effect which applies to both sexes.

Table 5.15 Summary of interactions involving hearing, sex and passage for spectral abnormalities

Variable	Females			Males		
	Exaggerate	Reduce	Reverse	Exaggerate	Reduce	Reverse
total change						
sample-by-sample	r				o	
peak-to peak	r					n
in sharpened spectrum	r					o
peak-to peak in						
sharpened spectrum	r					n
variance of change						
sample-by-sample				r		
in sharpened spectrum				r		
peak-to peak in						
sharpened spectrum		o		r		
average level						
F0 band	n				o	
F1 band			n			o
F2 band	r				o	
fricative band	r					r
level relative change						
fricative band						r

The main value of the trends shown in table 5.15 is to reiterate that the effects of acquired deafness show a considerable degree of order. Complex interactions recur in the data, but they are not evidence of random, idiosyncratic complications. They point to a recurrent form of problem which seems to be solved on sex-related lines. The division which occurs fits sociolinguistic findings about style shift. The shift which tends to be associated with reading is a shift towards relatively standard forms. Females are known to shift towards standard forms more readily than males, and there is a tendency for males to assert their maleness by shifting towards non-standard forms in certain contexts – though not generally in reading. Hence the shifts which are observed here have a broad flavour of standard sex role marking carried to excess or applied out of context.

Thus far we have focused on the question of whether deafened speakers as a group differ from controls as a group. That is different from the perspective which speech clinicians tend to adopt, where the key question is whether an individual is outside normal limits. It is worth commenting briefly on our evidence from that perspective. Two main points ought to be made.

The first point is that the trends which we have described mean that many deafened individuals are well outside normal limits, at least according to a simple definition. Table 5.16 summarises the relevant information. It shows that almost all of the deafened lie outside normal limits on at least one measure, and about half of them lie outside normal limits on more than two. The table is constructed using criteria which are simple and reasonably conservative. The definition of "beyond normal limits" is just that the speaker was clearly beyond any control of either sex on either passage with respect to the relevant measure, not just that he or she was beyond the limits associated with same sex speakers on similar material. Also the counts are based on a reduction which groups similar measures together, so that, for instance, only one score is entered whether a speaker is beyond normal limits on one or five of the measures concerned with the F2 band. The effects of sex and style which show in the table are partly due to the factors which were discussed above, but they are also partly due to this method of tabulation: it seems to reflect abnormalities among females better than it reflects abnormalities among males.

Table 5.16 Frequency with which deafened speakers lie outside normal limits on given numbers of indices

number of indices on which the speaker lies beyond normal limits	Reading		Narrative	
	male	female	male	female
0	1	0	3	4
1–2	7	4	7	4
3–4	3	2	1	4
> 4	0	6	0	0

The second point is that the individuals who lie outside normal limits tend to be associated with trends in the group. One can imagine a situation where the main pattern of abnormality in a clinical group was dispersion, with some members above normal limits and others below. As we have already indicated, the natural expectation in the case of acquired deafness is probably that abnormalities will follow that kind of unstructured dispersion from norms. We have argued that that is not what the data show. It is worth establishing that the argument applies to extreme cases as well as to the relatively small shifts which account for most of the group trends.

Table 5.17 summarises the relevant evidence. It considers variables on which four or more individuals lay outside normal limits. Variables such as median pitch and pitch range do not appear because there were not enough extreme individuals (in both of these cases, there were three). The criteria of extremeness were as outlined above. The first six variables are made by grouping similar measures together, again as described above.

Table 5.17 Relationships between extreme cases and trends on variables which give rise to more than four extreme cases

Variable	direction	Reading		Narrative	
		male	female	male	female
energy in	high		10		4
F2 band	low				
variance of	high		1*		
spectral change	low	3		1	1
variance of peak/	high	3	4	2	1
trough position	low				
variance of changes	high	1	4	1	1
in level contour	low		1*		2*
duration of segments	high				
in level contour	low		2	1	1
variance of level	high		2	1	2
segment durations	low			1*	
inverse of level relative	high		5		1
change: mean	low				
inverse of level relative	high		3		
change: total	low		1*		
inverse of level relative	high		1*		
change: F0 band	low	2		1	1
inverse of level relative	high		4		
change: fricative band	low	1*			
sample-to-sample change in	high			1*	
sharpened spectra: variance	low	2	1	1	1
sample-to-sample change in	high		4		
sharpened spectra: total	low				
peak-to-peak change in the	high	3	1	2	
sharpened spectrum: F1 band	low				

The table shows the link between group trends and extreme cases in two ways. First, where a trend in a given direction is expected from the analysis given above, the relevant entry in the second column is underlined. Sixty observations are in the direction of a statistically identified trend, whereas eleven observations are in the opposite direction to one of these trends. Second, where the majority of observations are in one direction, but a few go in the other, the observations which go against the majority are asterisked. Only nine observations are in the latter category. At least some apparent exceptions of both types may well relate to sex effects, with males tending to err in one direction and females in the other. However it is not worth pursuing that idea without considerably more data.

It certainly right to acknowledge that deafened speech may depart from normality in more than one direction. The effect seems to be particularly marked with some variables. The striking example is the duration of segments in the amplitude contour, where the group trend is for segments to last too long, but some speakers make them very markedly too short. However, the exceptions very definitely prove the rule. The overall picture is that most deafened speakers who depart from normality with respect to a particular variable do so in a predictable direction.

What is unpredictable is the collection of variables that will be markedly affected in a particular speaker. One of the criteria for grouping variables for table 5.17 above was that measures which affected essentially the same people should be combined if they were logically connected. The variables which are left, those which are used in the table, do not reduce in that way. Inevitably there is a degree of overlap, but essentially each one is associated with a different subgroup. This suggests an interesting picture of the way acquired deafness affects speech. There are relatively universal pressures, which are reflected in the group trends that are revealed by statistics. However individual factors determine which pressures will be controlled and which (if any) will lead to marked departures from normality.

5.4. Discussion

The findings in this chapter reinforce and develop three general points which have been introduced in previous chapters.

The first point is that the abnormalities in deafened people's speech are substantial. The measures which have been considered in this chapter are essentially simple and gross, made by a rudimentary signal capture system. The fact that they reveal a multitude of abnormalities testifies to the fact that the differences between deafened and normal speech are neither slight nor subtle.

The second point is that the differences between deafened and normal speech are systematic at a finer level than the previous chapter could show. Not only the amount of deterioration that occurs, but also its form, can be seen to follow broad general trends. We have been at pains to acknowledge that there are exceptions to these trends, but they are quite clearly a minority. The unavoidable inference is that there are systematic pressures governing the way speech changes when auditory input is withdrawn.

The third general point is that many of the changes which occur are related to sociolinguistic variables. The effect is very much more marked at this level of description than it is at the coarser level of the previous chapter. This certainly underlines the methodological point that ignoring these variables is a potential source of confusion, and reinforces the view that conflicts in the literature may reflect variability in this respect rather than idiosyncratic between-speaker variation. Theoretically, it reinforces the view that auditory feedback may have a major role in guiding socially significant selections among forms which are linguistically permissible.

On a more detailed level, the data reinforce some existing findings, which helps to consolidate the sense that there is an underlying norm. This applies particularly to findings which involve F0. The finding of an increased median reinforces the data of Leder – Spitzer – Kirchner (1987: 323). The trend towards increased pitch spread reinforces a number of studies which report aberrations in that direction (e.g. Ball – Faulkner – Fourcin 1990 : 404; Oster 1987: 84) and in doing so may help to debunk the idea that deafened intonation is monotone. The tendency to use too many "fall end" features, albeit in particular contexts, offers some generality to Plant's observation (personal communication) that declination may become too prevalent. However it is also worth noting that these trends are not particularly robust. Although they reflect some of the main concerns of previous research, this study does not suggest that they involve particularly salient features of deafened speech. We emphasise that this does not mean intonation is relatively little affected: what it means is that the major abnormalities are not captured by description at this level. The next chapter shows that considering the linguistic function of intonation does reveal major abnormalities.

Abnormality in the amplitude contour is a much more marked feature, and it is less widely considered in the literature. Our findings again reinforce Leder et al. (1987a: 225), who reported increased variability in amplitude. However they go much further, showing that the rise and fall of amplitude – particularly the former – is structurally abnormal. The natural interpretation of the pattern is in terms of breathing and phonatory mechanisms. These have been studied by Lane et al. (1991) in a small number of subjects. It should not be difficult to check whether our acoustic abnormalities are linked to the physiological mechanisms studied by Lane's group. If they are, then it seems that those mechanisms are a source of major and pervasive problems for deafened people.

The least predictable area of abnormality involves the spectrum. Abnormalities in the fricative region are not surprising given the attention that has been paid to distortions of [s] and [ʒ]. However the overwhelming spectral effect is the high energy in the F2 band, which is largely responsible for the raised mean of the spectrum in deafened speakers. Its meaning is not obvious, but there are two reasonable possibilities.

The first relates to vocal effort. It has been shown that various forms of vocal effort increase the energy in the upper part of the spectrum relative to the lower – an effect which is logically related to the raised mean which we found. Raising speech intensity has a particularly marked effect on the upper spectrum (Brandt – Ruder – Schipp 1969: 1547), as has deliberately clear speech (Picheny – Durlach – Braida 1986: 437, 443) and the kind of overtight or strained voice associated with "creak" (Hammarberg et al. 1980: 446–447; Izdebski 1980; Gobl 1989). Hammarberg et al. reported that hyperfunctionality, a disorder where high subglottal air pressure is improperly balanced by high muscle tension in the larynx ands neck, shows both this kind of spectral imbalance and high F0 – which is also a characteristic of our deafened speakers.

It is clearly a possibility that our speakers' spectral abnormalities are related to a vocal-effort phenomenon. This has the attraction of suggesting a link between two major aspects of the data, spectral abnormality and abnormality in the amplitude contour. It also fits with Lane–Webster's (1991: 865) conjecture that phonatory problems may underlie a variety of superficially different problems in deafened speech. However there is a problem with the interpretation. The effects of vocal effort are particularly notable above 2 kHz, as is apparent from the data of Picheny – Durlach – Braida (1986: 437) on clear speech and implicit in the use of a 2–5 kHz band in studies on voice quality. The F2 band in our study is 800–2.5 kHz, so that the overlap is very imperfect.

The second possibility is that high energy in the F2 band has an articulatory significance. Ensuring that F2 is strong and well-defined (as the level-relative sharpening measure shows it is) has an interesting interpretation. F2 is the best single guide to vowel identity, which is why it was selected for presentation in early multi-channel cochlear implants (Dowell – Seligman – Whitford 1990). If deafened speakers overemphasise it, it stands in interesting relation to our earlier conjecture that deafened speakers adjust to ensure that critical features are preserved even if less important ones are not (Cowie – Douglas-Cowie 1983: 209–211 and 220–225). That relationship is clearly speculative. However we will describe evidence in chapter 8 which supports the view that the F2 anomaly is related to articulatory abnormalities. That has the implication that in acoustic terms, abnormalities related to articulation are a relatively substantial part of deafened people's problems.

The previous paragraphs illustrate the character of the approach we have taken to analysis. It is not a stand-alone tool for speech analysis, but it is a useful supplement to other techniques. One major strength is its ability to offer a broad brush picture which deals with a range of issues and gives an indication of their relative salience. Another comes from the fact that it is phonetically atheoretical. Because of that it can show up anomalies which one would be unlikely to look for starting from a conventional viewpoint. If they appear, one can begin to look for explanations in phonetic or articulatory terms. Its simplicity means that it can be applied to large samples, and the quantitative data that it yields can be manipulated in many ways. Chapter 8 illustrates an important use of that property, in which acoustic data are linked to listeners' evaluations of speech. The major limitation at present is the lack of established mapping rules from statistical acoustic descriptors to other ways of describing speech. However if the approach is accepted and standardised, that problem is likely to diminish rapidly as experience accumulates.

Chapter 6
Intonation

6.1. Introduction

Intonation refers to the use of particular patterns of pitch in a linguistically relevant way. Pitch in deafened speech has more often been studied as a straightforward acoustic attribute than as a series of linguistically relevant patterns. This chapter describes the first extensive formal study of deafened intonation.

There are several good reasons to study intonation in acquired deafness. First, it is an area where deafened speech is known to be abnormal. The clearest single indicator is in the study by Leder – Spitzer (1990: 171) in which intonation was rated the most abnormal feature of speech in a sample of deafened speakers. Other relevant sources are reviewed in chapter 2.

The second reason is that abnormal intonation is likely to have substantial implications for the success of deafened people's communication. Intonation conveys important grammatical, semantic, emotional and social information. Anyone who has listened to a speech synthesiser will appreciate what a difference appropriate intonation can make to understanding and acceptability. The chapter reflects the issue of functional significance by indicating, on an intuitive level, how deafened intonation seems likely to impair communication.

The third reason for studying deafened intonation is that this is an area where there is a chance of effective speech therapy. Abberton et al. (1983) have shown that laryngograph displays of intonation can be used to improve abnormal intonation in both prelingually and postlingually deafened subjects.

Finally, intonation is relevant to the issue of feedback in speech. It provides a good case for the study of whether auditory feedback only affects low-level execution of plans or whether in fact it affects higher-order plans. Is the fundamental higher-order structure of intonation affected and if so how, or is all that is wrong low-level aberrations in the realisation of normal linguistic plans?

6.2. Data collection and the model for analysis

6.2.1. Data collection

The study reported here is based on the speech of 17 deafened subjects (9 males and 8 females) and 28 controls (13 male and 15 female). The deafened subjects all had losses over 80 dB in the better ear. Each was recorded in two styles, (1) reading and (2) conversation. The full details of the sample and the speech data collected are described in chapter 3 (see sections 3.3.1. for details of the deafened sample, 3.4. for details of the control sample and 3.5.3. for details of the speech sample).

There are two main principles that direct the approach to data collection and analysis. The first is that intonation should be studied in a way that takes account of its central role in communication and allows one to specify the ways in which poor intonation might impair communication. This has meant that we have designed reading passages which probe deafened people's success in using intonation to convey particular linguistic functions e.g. information focussing, or attitudinal functions. We have also taken a somewhat wider view of communication by examining the intonational markers of style. The second principle is that the data should be statistically reliable.

6.2.2. Model of intonation analysis

The form of intonation analysis used starts with the unit that is commonly recognised as the base unit of intonation – the tone group. The tone group is then analysed following the traditional British School model of head, nucleus, tail analysis (see e.g. Crystal 1969). This section first describes the basic bones of the approach, and then considers problems with its application to the speech data in this study.

In this approach to intonation, speech is divided into tone groups on the basis of external and internal criteria. As far as external criteria are concerned, the crucial marker of tone-group boundaries is the presence of certain phonological features. In particular, there will be a step up or down in pitch between tone groups. These boundaries may coincide with pauses and with limits of grammatical or semantic entities e.g. the clause. External criteria are used in conjunction with internal criteria. The fundamental internal criterion is the presence of a "nucleus". This is usually defined in phonetic terms as a prominent syllable in the tone group which is distinguished by its pitch. This often involves pitch movement on the syllable but may also involve the syllable obtruding in pitch from its neighbours. That is, there may be a marked step up to the nucleus from the pitch of the preceding syllable or a marked step down to the nucleus from the preceding syllable. In semantic and grammatical terms the nucleus tends to mark a word which carries important grammatical and attitudinal information. The rest of the tone group is described in terms which suggest its subservience to the nucleus. Thus the stretch from the first stressed syllable (the onset syllable) to the nuclear syllable is called the "head", suggesting its lead up to the nucleus; and the syllables that follow the nucleus are called the "tail", suggesting that they are an addendum to the nucleus. Each component can be described in terms of its pitch shape. The model usually seems to be applied to speech using auditory analysis of trained phoneticians in the first instance, and acoustic investigation (particularly of the nucleus) may follow.

The model has most commonly been applied to speakers of Received Pronunciation or standard Southern British English, but the control subjects used in this study are from Belfast. Most people can hear that Belfast intonation sounds extremely different from Received Pronunciation intonation. The study has used the basic components of the model described because in broad essence they fit normal Belfast intonation and in the majority of cases can be applied to deafened Belfast intonation. The realisations of the components, however, are very different in Belfast from the usually cited norm of RP. For example rising and level nuclei are far more common in Belfast than in RP where the fall is the default type of nucleus. Quirk et al. (1964: 681) give a figure of around 20% for rising nuclei in RP, whereas we have found a figure of around 70% for rising nuclei in Belfast speech. Unlike RP, Belfast intonation is typified by a high level tail usually following after a rising nucleus.

There are, however, some fundamental problems with the model as applied to Belfast and deafened intonation. These problems relate to the identification of tone groups and to the identification of the nucleus.

In Belfast, phonological criteria do not provide useful signals of tone group boundaries. There usually is no marked pitch jump between the end of one tone group and the beginning of another. Problems with applying phonological criteria to tone group identification have been reported before, particularly in spontaneous speech in non-RP varieties (e.g. Brown – Currie – Kenworthy 1980: 29; Currie 1980). In line with these studies, the present study has found pause to be the most reliable indicator of tone-group boundaries.

The second problem with the model relates to the nucleus. There are two levels of this problem.

First, some tone groups contain more than one prominent syllable, and it is not always possible to identify one of the syllables as nuclear. This is true of Belfast normal intonation and even more so of Belfast deafened intonation. Other work on regional varieties has indicated similar problems (Currie 1980). We have dealt with these anomalous tone groups by separating them from the main data analysis and discussing them as a special case in section 6.3.3.

The second level of the problem relates to the very specific associations that the term "nucleus" has in the literature.While the term is broadly applicable to Belfast, there are features of Belfast intonation that make it desirable to use a term with less specific associations. We have chosen the term "prominent syllable". For example, the term nucleus has associations with large pitch movement on the nuclear syllable. In the context of RP, listeners require a pitch movement of 88 Hz on the nuclear syllable for categorical perception of a rising nucleus (Ainsworth – Lindsay 1984: 380). But in Belfast we have found that pitch movement on the prominent syllable is very considerably less (around 33 Hz) and even less in deafened speech. Pitch obtrusion and syllable duration appear to play much more crucial roles in marking the prominent syllable in Belfast than are normally associated with the term nucleus (see section 6.5 on pitch obtrusion). We have found downward pitch obtrusion culminating in the lowest pitch point in the tone group to be the main marker of the prominent syllable in Belfast. In addition its prominence seems to be associated not just with being the longest syllable but with a progressive build-up of duration towards it. Table 6.1 shows the mean durations of the five stressed syllables in a sentence randomly selected from one of the reading passages. Control and deafened subjects are averaged, since analysis of variance indicated that both showed the same pattern of change across the sentence: the syllable identified auditorily as prominent was much the longest, and duration increased towards it.

Table 6.1 Mean duration of stressed syllables in seconds

syllable 1	.173
syllable 2	.206
syllable 3	.215
syllable 4 (prominent)	.265
syllable 5	.246

The term "prominent syllable" can also be applied to tone groups where there are multiprominence syllables (see above) but where none can legitimately be said to be nuclear in the sense of marking the central focus of the tone group. To complete the terminology we use the term "leading sequence" rather than head and "final sequence" rather than tail. A fuller description can be found in Rahilly (1991).

Finally we have extended the basic model to add more detailed information about the components of the tone group. This has taken the form of looking at the prominent syllables in terms of the pitch of their starting points and the degree of pitch movement involved. The procedure is described in detail in 6.5.3.

The description of the results falls into three sections. These start with intonation structure and work towards realisation.

6.3. Tone-group structure

This section describes differences between normal and deafened intonation for (1) tone group length, (2) structure of tone groups with one prominence and (3) structure of tone groups with multi-prominence syllables.

6.3.1. Tone-group length

The number of words for each tone-group was counted for each subject. This gave a range of 1 to 18 words per tone group in conversation and a range of 1 to 12 words per tone group in reading. The number of tone groups in each of the possible word-length categories (i.e. 1 to 18) was counted for each speaker and expressed for each speaker as a percentage per category. These data were then tabulated in terms of three factors: hearing level, sex and passage. Three analyses of variance were carried out, one for the conversation data and two on the reading passage.

A five-way analysis of variance was carried out on tone-group length in the conversation. The two between-subject variables were hearing with two levels (hearing and deafened) and sex with two levels (male and female). There were three within-subject variables related to tone-group length. These were as follows. The top two length categories (i.e. 17 and 18 words respectively) were ignored because they showed minimal numbers of occurrence, and the remaining 16 categories were divided in 3 ways. First they were considered in two halves (i.e. one-word to eight-word categories versus nine-word to sixteen-word categories). Secondly each half was divided and considered as two groups (i.e. 1 to 4 words, 5 to 8 words, 9 to 12 words and 13 to 16 words).

Thirdly each of these groups of four was halved and considered in pairs of two.

Two effects involving hearing reached significance. The first was an interaction between hearing and tone-group length considered in two basic halves (i.e. one-to eight-word categories and nine- to sixteen-word categories). This effect clearly reached significance at p = .016 (F 1, 40 = 6.37). The deafened have too few tone groups in the 9 to 16 word length categories compared to the controls. Table 6.2 shows the effect.

Table 6.2   Mean frequencies of tone groups of particular lengths in conversation

	length 1 to 8 words	length 9 to 16 words
hearing	9.49	3.09
deafened	10.4	2.08

The second effect showed an interaction between hearing, sex and word length category considered in quarters (F 1, 40 = 5.42, p = 0.025). The deafened males have too many tone groups in the first quarter (i.e. 1–4 words), particularly relative to the number in the second quarter (i.e. 5 to 8 words); whereas the deafened females show a more normal relationship between the first two quarters. Table 6.3 shows the effect.

Table 6.3   Mean frequencies of tone groups of particular length by hearing and sex (for conversation)

	Females		Males	
Number of words	1–4	5–8	1–4	5–8
hearing	7.07	11.88	6.31	12.71
deafened	7.32	13.09	9.84	11.22

Two analyses of variance were carried out on the aggregated scores from all the reading passages. The first, a four-way analysis of variance, parallelled the analysis on conversation. There were two between-subject variables, hearing and sex, and one within-subject variable, tone-group length which had two levels. Tone-group length, which had a maximum of 12 words in reading, was first considered in two halves (1–6 words and 7–12 words) and then each half was divided giving four quarters, 1–3, 4–6, 7–9, and 10–12 words. No significant effects were found.

A second analysis was carried out on a subgroup of word categories which appeared graphically to reveal differences between hearing and deafened. This was a three-way analysis involving sex, hearing and tone-group length confined to nine-, ten- and eleven-word categories. This showed a significant interaction between hearing and tone group (F 10, 58 = 6.73, p = 0.002). The deafened have too many tone groups in the nine-, ten- and eleven-word region, with a particularly large number in the eleven-word category. The effect is seen in table 6.4.

Table 6.4   Mean frequencies of tone groups of particular length in reading (9, 10 and 11 word categories)

	9 words	10 words	11 words	Total mean
hearing	5.17	5.19	0.89	11.26
deafened	5.97	5.60	2.69	14.25

One level of explanation of the data lies in a comparison of the linguistic structures of the tone groups for controls and deafened. In the informal conversation, the deafened break their speech up according to clear short syntactic groups, whereas the controls expand the short groups into longer sequences. This is reflected in the lack of long tone groups in the deafened conversation and the large number of very short groups, at least for the deafened males. The effect is as if the deafened were reading an over-punctuated text rather than engaging in unscripted speech. Examples where deafened tone-group boundaries conform rigidly to short syntactic groups are given in table 6.5. Tone-group boundaries are marked by slashes and the parallel syntactic groups in deafened and control speech are italicised.

An explanation for deafened tone-group structure in the reading passages can also be found in the linguistic structure of the text. The deafened show too many long tone groups here (focussing around 9, 10 and 11 words). Many of the sentences or clauses in the reading passages are 9, 10 or 11 words. What seems to happen is that the deafened adhere to the sentence as their unit of length much more rigidly than the controls who break up sentences according to their own interpretation.

Table 6.5 Tone-group boundaries and syntactic types (conversation)

Syntactic type	Deafened realisation	Control realisation
Direct speech (boundary after reporting verb in deaf)	*and he says* / where was your car first registered	*and she said* dear love them
Comment clauses (i) initial (boundary after in deaf)	but *by jove* / we're not as bad as other parts	*like I mean* right down near the end of the road
(ii) medial (boundary on either side in deaf)	I got over it quite quickly /*in a way* / because	and I'm always more than surprised *you see* because Granny
Co-ordinate clauses	we'll take a tent with us/ *and* *stay the night*	he wasn't off them six months *and he's never been well since*
Adverbials	he always kept a big gun / *up in the bedroom*	that's round *in Nevis Avenue there at the corner*
Tag utterances	he's looking at a house down there / *isn't he*	that was easy *wasn't it*

Deafened tone-group length may not impair the functional side of speech, but it gives rise to inappropriate communication. One can speculate about the effects of this. For example, if the deafened do not have the long fluid tone groups characteristic of informal style, does their informal speech come across as socially stiff and stilted? Or if they read in long tone groups of sentence-length without breaking them up to reflect their interpretation, do they come across as stupid readers? We do not have definite answers to these questions, but they suggest the importance of looking beyond functional impairment in deafened speech to the wider problems that inappropriate communication may cause.

6.3.2. Tone-group structure in tone groups with one prominence

The structure of each tone group for each subject in both styles (reading and conversation) was labelled according to one of four possible types – (1) leading sequence + prominence + final sequence (LPF), (2) leading sequence +

prominence + no final sequence (LP0), (3) no leading sequence + prominence + final sequence (0PF), (4) no leading sequence + prominence + no final sequence (0P0). These data were then expressed as a percentage for each person for each style (scores from individual reading passages were aggregated) and tabulated according to sex and hearing of the subject.

A five-way analysis of variance was carried out to see if there were any significant differences in tone-group structure between deafened and controls. The between-subject variables were sex and hearing, each with two levels, and there were three within-subject variables. These were (1) whether the tone groups had a leading sequence or not, (2) whether the tone groups had a final sequence or not and (3) whether they occurred in reading or in conversation.

The analysis showed that there was a two-way interaction between hearing and the presence or absence of a final sequence (F 1, 37 = 8.91, p = 0.005). The deafened have fewer tunes than the controls with a final sequence and more without. This means that tone groups tend to end on a prominence. A three way interaction shows that the effect is most marked when the leading sequence is present (F 1, 37 = 4.2, p = 0.048). This means that the LP0 category is commoner in deafened speech. Table 6.6 shows the effect. There were no effects of style or sex.

Table 6.6 Tone-group structure: percentage in the four categories

| | with final sequence | | without final sequence | |
	LPF	0PF	LP0	0P0
controls	21.9	10.3	41.1	24.6
deafened	18.4	7.4	47.2	26.0

Table 6.6 shows that the tendency to push the prominence to the end of the tone group, particularly in the LP0 form, is a feature that characterises normal Belfast speech as well as deafened. However the deafened appear to be taking this normal tendency too far. Looking at the linguistic context of this aberration suggests that the statistical distortion of a normal tendency has functional implications. The distortion takes the form of placing the prominence on a final syllable when sense indicates that shifting the prominence leftwards would be more appropriate. Table 6.7 gives some examples of a contextually in-

appropriate final placement of the prominence. The prominent syllables are in italics.

Table 6.7   Contextually inappropriate final placement of the prominence in deafened speech

Normal functional role of prominence placement	Suggested control placement	Actual deafened placement
to focus information	I teach the *older* ones	I teach the older *ones*
	He was always a very *humor*ous man	He was always a very humourous *man*
for conversational repair	We went to a word *proc*essing/ to a *computer* course	We went to a word*proc*essing/ to a computer *course*
to introduce information of a contrastive nature	no... on the *front* of the Knockbreda Road	no... on the front of the Knockbreda *Road*

This table suggests that the final placement of the prominence may have significant implications for how much sense the deafened make. If, as in the examples listed, the prominence is placed on a semantically or grammatically inappropriate word, then there is a danger of misunderstanding or at the very least a suggestion of distinct peculiarity.

6.3.3. Multi-prominence tone groups

Multi-prominence tone groups are those where it is not possible auditorily to identify one syllable as more prominent than the others. Acoustic analysis suggests no easy way of weighting the syllables either in terms of pitch, duration or intensity, and there are none of the usual signals of tone-group boundaries that would allow one to assign them to different tone groups. These multi-prominence groups occur sporadically in normal speech and constitute at most around 10% of a subject's total tone groups. In deafened speech they are more prevalent (around 25%) but only in the speech of a few subjects.

The distribution and function of prominences within these groups differs for deafened and controls. In control speech, multi-prominence groups are used to carry strong affectual overtones and the prominences are distributed over appropriate words. In deafened speech the prominences tend to be more frequent within a multi-prominence group and to carry no affectual connotations. Table

6.8 gives some examples. Tone-group boundaries are marked by slashes, and prominences are in italics.

Table 6.8 A comparison of the function of prominences in multi-prominence groups in deafened and control speech

	example	affect	number of prominences
control	/ I was *nev*er so em*barr*assed in my *life* /	exaggerated embarrassment	3
	/now *that's* to *me* ri*dic*ulous /	exaggerated sense of of the preposterous	3
deafened	/ be*fore* the *post came* /	none	3
	/and *ask*ing the *girl* for *some*thing /	none	3
	/*All Saints' Par*ish *Church* /	none	4

Multi-prominences in deafened speech are not just too common but are clearly inappropriate in the contexts in which they are used. The effect is of heavily stressed speech, more in line with a hectoring style than with everyday discourse. One can speculate about the effects of such inappropriate communication on listeners.

6.3.4. Conclusion

This section has shown that there are significant differences between deafened and controls in tone-group structure. These take the form of differences in tone-group length, differences in the arrangement of the tone-group components of leading sequence, prominence and final sequence, and differences in the fundamental way in which tone groups are structured (i.e. multi-prominence as opposed to single-prominence structure).

There appears to be one common theme running through the data for the deafened. It is that the data are characterised by a lack of flexibility and tendency towards rigidity. Perhaps the most obvious example of this is trend towards putting prominences in final position, regardless of sense. The rigid adherence to particular syntactic groupings in tone-group delineation both in reading and in conversation can also be seen as a manifestation of the same trend. Likewise, the use of multi-prominence tone groups suggests inflexibility and lack of variation.

6.4. The shapes of tone-group components

This section describes differences between deafened and controls in the pitch shapes of prominences, leading sequences and final sequences in single-prominence groups.

6.4.1. Pitch shape of prominences

Speakers used four basic pitch shapes on prominent syllables – rises, falls, levels and rise-falls. Prominent syllables for each subject were classified according to one of these shapes and tabulated according to hearing, sex and style. Each individual's scores for all of the reading passages were aggregated. Proportions of prominences in each shape category were expressed in percentages.

An analysis of variance was carried out on a subset of the data – that for falling and level shapes only. This subset was chosen after exploration of the data showed that the numbers of rise-falls were minimal and very constant across subjects and style and could therefore be eliminated to give a less messy picture. This meant that analysing data for any two of the remaining shapes would be sufficient to provide an overall picture. Falls and levels were chosen as they were where deafened abnormalities appeared to be centered. A four-way analysis of variance was carried out. The two between-subject variables were sex and hearing, each with two levels, and the two within-subject variables were passage with two levels (reading and conversation) and type of shape with two levels (falling shape and level shape).

The analysis showed two interactions. The first was an interaction between hearing and sex (F 1, 36 = 4.23, p = 0.047). Deafened males have too many falling and level prominences. This implies that they have too few rises. Table 6.9 shows the effect.

Table 6.9 Percentages of falling and level prominences in deafened and control speech (combining reading and conversation)

	females	males
hearing	23.3	19.5
deafened	21.5	27.1

The second interaction was between hearing, passage and prominence shape (F 1, 36 = 10.1, p = 0.003). The deafened, regardless of sex, fail to signal style-shift as the controls do. The mark of style-shifting for the controls is a drastic reduction in the number of falling prominences in conversation compared to reading and a corresponding increase in the number of level prominences. Although the deafened make some shift in this direction, they fall far short of the dramatic style-shift of the controls, retaining too high a proportion of falls. Their number of levels, however, is near the control number. This implies that once again that the deafened are short in rises. Table 6.10 shows the effect.

Table 6.10 Prominence shapes and style shifting

	reading		conversation	
	falls	levels	falls	levels
controls	21.7	18.5	5.2	40.1
deafened	18.7	25.8	14.2	38.6

The nature of deafened abnormalities in prominence shape can be further explored by comparing the linguistic distribution of falls in control speech with that of deafened speech. Falls in control speech tend to be related rather closely to particular grammatical contexts. They occur mostly in indicative sentence final position. In deafened speech, however, they occur over a much wider range of environments – in subordinate position and in questions. The functional effect of this, if any, is hard to gauge, but one point should be made. That is, deafened falls are not just too many but are also misplaced. This can only serve to heighten their abnormality.

We have seen that the patterns of prominence shapes in deafened speech create inappropriate stylistic behaviour. It can be argued that the patterns create another type of social innappropriateness. Section 6.2.1. made the point that one of the distinguishing hallmarks of normal Belfast intonation is its small numbers of falling nuclei. This distinguishes it from more standard English where the fall predominates. It is not surprising, therefore, to find that the standard form, the fall, is more prevalent in control speech in the formal reading task than in the more informal conversation. But the deafened retain this feature of standard English in informal contexts. Their behaviour is thus not merely stylistically inappropriate, but is also socially inappropriate in failing to follow the prevailing norms of the community.

6.4.2. The shape of leading sequences

The shapes of leading sequences were classified into one of four types – roughly level, rising, rise-falling and falling. These shapes represent the overall trend in the leading sequence. These were counted for each subject and expressed as percentages of the total number of leading sequences. The data were then tabulated according to sex, hearing level and style. Scores from each individual reading passage were aggregated.

An analysis of variance was carried out on a subset of the data, that for level and rising leading sequences only. This subset was chosen after exploration had shown that falling leading sequences were minimal and constant across subjects and style and could therefore be eliminated from the analysis to give a less messy picture.This meant that any two of the remaining shapes would be sufficient to provide an overall picture of the data. Rises and levels were selected as they appeared to be where the differences in distribution between deafened and controls lay. A four-way analysis of variance was carried out. The two between-subject variables were sex and hearing, each with two levels, and the two within-subject variables were passage (i.e. reading or conversation) and type of leading-sequence shape (i.e. level or rising).

The analysis produced two interactions. There was a three-way interaction between hearing, passage and leading-sequence shape (F 1, 36 = 8.9, p = 0.005). The interaction shows that the deafened basically overdo the style-shift between reading and conversation which is present in control speech. In control speech, reading is characterised by slightly more levels than rises, and in conversation there are massively more rises than levels. The deafened show a similar trend in style-shifting, but they exaggerate it. In reading they have too many levels and too few rises, and in conversation they have too many rises and too few levels. Table 6.11 shows the effect.

Table 6.11 Stylistic distribution of leading sequence types (levels and rises)

	reading		conversation	
	levels	rises	levels	rises
controls	40.2	31.0	17.1	60.7
deafened	55.4	24.9	12.0	67.3

The analysis of variance also showed a less strong four-way interaction with sex (F 1, 36 = 4.7, p = 0.037). This shows that the deafened males particularly overdo the style-shift appropriate to leading sequences. On both levels and rises in both styles they show abnormal patterns of distribution compared to the control males. The deafened females, on the other hand, only show a disproportionate style-shift in respect of levels in the reading style, where they have too many. Table 6.12 shows this effect.

Table 6.12 Stylistic distribution of leading sequences by sex (percentages of levels and rises)

	reading		conversation	
	levels	rises	levels	rises
control females	38.1	29.9	12.4	61.2
control males	42.3	32.0	21.8	60.2
deafened females	46.4	30.3	12.7	62.5
deafened males	64.3	19.6	11.3	72.1

Not only do the deafened have too many or too few of particular shapes, but they use them inappropriately. Level sequences in control reading, for example, tend to co-occur mostly with short tone groups, but there are much longer level sequences in deafened reading. The long level leading sequences probably contribute to the impression of monotony so frequently reported as a marker of deafened speech. Rising sequences in the conversation generally appear to be intended to signal affect in control speech, but in deafened speech are used to convey neutral content.

6.4.3. The shape of final sequences

The shapes of final sequences were classified into one of three types – level final sequences, falling final sequences and rising final sequences. Each type was expressed as a percentage for each subject's total final sequences. These data were tabulated according to sex, hearing and style. A four-way analysis of variance was carried out on the levels and falls. Sex and hearing were the between-subject variables and style (reading versus conversation) and final sequence type (level versus fall) were the within-subject variables.

Abnormalities in this area were minimal. Only one effect even approached significance, the interaction between hearing and style (F 1, 36 = 3.6, p = 0.066). The combined mean score for levels and falls in deafened conversation was too high. This means that in conversation deafened speakers do not use a high enough proportion of rising final sequences. Table 6.13 suggests the trend. It should be emphasised, though, that final sequences are subject to another, grosser abnormality: there are simply too few of them.

Table 6.13   Falling sequences – mean percentage scores for level and falling final sequences

	reading	conversation
controls	45.9	44.3
deafened	44.0	48.0

6.4.4. Conclusion

This section has shown that there are statistical abnormalities in the numerical distribution of pitch shapes related to prominences and leading sequences, and that there is a trend towards abnormality in the case of final sequences. The abnormalities entail inappropriate linguistic distribution of particular pitch shapes.

These abnormalities are tied up to the variables of style-shifting and sex. Deafened males in particular appear to be abnormal at the level of pitch shape to a greater degree than deafened females. All subjects have problems with style-shifting, but the deafened males have greater problems in this respect. Style-shifting problems are complex. The deafened underdo some aspects of normal style-shifting and overdo others. Controls tend to use more falling prominences, fewer level prominences, and fewer rising leading sequences when they read than they do in conversation: all of these trends are significantly weaker among deafened speakers. On the other hand controls tend to use level leading sequences proportionately more often in reading than in conversation: this trend is significantly weaker among the deafened.

It is worth noting that the data considered so far cohere reasonably well with the data from acoustic analysis of the F0 contour (see chapter 5). In reading, the acoustic analysis showed that deafened speakers lack compound features (where F0 continues unbroken through more than one inflection): they are replaced by simpler features, stretches which end with a fall or remain level throughout their length. Here deafened subjects' reading shows too many level leading sequences and prominences, and the trend among final sequences is for too many falls. Both point to a pattern where the bulk of the utterance shows little inflection, tending to end in a fall. In narrative, the acoustic analysis showed that deafened speakers used too many fall and rise-fall features. Though falling end features were grouped together in the acoustic analysis, it is worth noting that rise-fall features were more clearly too common than simple falls: in fact an analysis of variance on rise-fall features alone gave a main effect of hearing on the verge of significance. In this study deafened speakers' conversation showed too many falling prominent syllables, with the leading sequences disproportionately likely to be rising rather than level. Both suggest that here utterances show inflection, but gravitate too much towards a basic pattern of rise followed by fall.

These correspondences are rough, but substantial nonetheless. Three main points should be made about them.

First, they strongly suggest that the effects reflect points of some generality about different styles. At the most basic level, one might suspect that some effects were highly specific to the exact exercises or passages used. The correspondence answers that concern, and goes considerably further. The reading passages here were quite different in style from the passage considered in the acoustic study, and the spontaneous samples were conversation rather than a prespecified monologue (see section 3.5.). The fact that substantial parallels were found is therefore far from trivial.

Second, the correspondence tends to validate the acoustic technique as a simple and objective way of obtaining a broad picture of trends in intonation. One might have suspected that the simple method of breaking F0 into stretches would result in data with little or no relationship to phonetic descriptions of intonation: but again, the correspondence here suggests otherwise.

Third, it has to be added that the phonetic approach to intonation used here provides an additional level of description which simple acoustic analysis could not match. Specifically it identifies regularities involving relationships to the prominent syllable which are masked in the simpler technique. For instance, the fact that deafened speakers are disproportionately likely to end on the prominent syllable could not possibly have been established with acoustic techniques of the order that we used in chapter 5.

6.5. Pitch characteristics of components

This section describes acoustic data on pitch movement and pitch obtrusion associated with stressed syllables within selected tone groups. The section also describes subjective measures of pitch-related subtypes of prominent syllables for reading and conversation.

Initially our investigation focussed purely on the prominent syllable in a tone group. The main aim was to see whether the marking of the prominent syllable in deafened speech was abnormal. This aim often dictated the selection of the tone groups studied. However, it became apparent that differences in the prominent syllable in deafened speech were part of a wider pattern, and so analysis was extended to cover other stressed syllables in the tone groups selected.

6.5.1. Pitch movement in stressed syllables

A tone group was selected from one of the reading passages and measurements (in hertz) were made of the amount of pitch movement on all the stressed syllables in the tone group for each subject. The tone group was selected because the prominence was on the same syllable in both deafened and control speech and almost all realised it with a rising prominence. The tone group consisted of the words – *Billy*'s a*way down* to *Bang*or this *morn*ing. The stressed syllables are in italics. The syllable *Bang* is identified for everyone as the prominent syllable. Measurements were tabulated according to sex and hearing.

An analysis of variance was carried out on a subset of the stressed syllables. These were the last three stressed syllables, which was where exploration of the data suggested differences lay. A three-way analyis was carried out with sex and hearing as the between variables, each with two levels and word as the within-variable with three levels (i.e. *down*, *Bang* and *morn*). The analysis showed an interaction between hearing and pitch movement (F 1, 32 = 4.9, p = 0.034). Pitch movement for the deafened is too small. This is shown in table 6.14.

Table 6.14 Mean pitch movement in Hertz on all three stressed syllables

	mean movement
controls	39.73
deafened	25.12

The amount of pitch movement involved here is small for controls let alone deafened. This reflects the fact that in Belfast pitch movement does not seem to mark the prominent syllable in the way it does in RP (see section 6.2.2. above). Nevertheless there is a trend, independent of hearing, for the prominent syllable to have more pitch movement than its neighbouring stressed syllables. This is seen in the separate means for the three syllables involved (*down* = 21.4, *Bang* = 40.2, *morn* = 35.7). This trend failed to reach significance at p = 0.07. But the fact that it does not interact with hearing suggests that the deafened are at least normal in the way that they distribute pitch movement over the syllables even if they get the degree wrong.

6.5.2. Pitch obtrusion

Section 6.2.1. suggested the importance of pitch obtrusion in Belfast in marking the prominence in a tone group. For this reason deafened speech was analysed for pitch obtrusion to see if it was also a marker of prominence there. One tone group was selected for study because auditorily the prominence seemed to be singularly and typically marked for pitch obtrusion in control speech with the obtrusions taking the same direction. The tone group was – He asked his *father* to *switch* the *rad*io *on*, – taken from one of the reading passages. The last four stressed syllables (in italics) were selected for study. Of these the prominence always falls on *rad* in both control and deafened speech. Auditory analysis of this tone group (backed by acoustic exploration) suggested that each of the stressed syllables, apart from the last one, is marked in control speech by a jump down in pitch movement from the previous stressed syllable. The last one is marked by a jump up in pitch from the previous stressed syllable. This pattern of pitch obtrusion is typical of Belfast. The prominent syllable is typified by the fact that there is a series of downward jumps towards it and then a large jump up from it.

An analysis of variance on pitch obtrusion suggests that there is not enough pitch obtrusion in deafened speech. The degree of pitch obtrusion was measured in hertz. Each data point represented the hertz difference between the starting point of a stressed syllable and the starting point of the preceding stressed syllable. The direction of pitch obtrusion was not considered. The data were tabulated according to sex and hearing. A three-way analysis of variance was carried out. There were two between-subject variables – sex and hearing each with two levels – and one within-subject variable – syllable – with four levels (i.e. *fath, switch, rad, on*).

The analysis showed a main effect of hearing on pitch obtrusion (F 1, 32 = 5.1, p = 0.031). The deafened do not show enough pitch obtrusion. This is seen in table 6.15.

Table 6.15 Pitch obtrusion in deafened and control speech (mean pitch obtrusion in Hertz over four stressed syllables)

	obtrusion
controls	64.7
deafened	38.4

This effect shows only part of the abnormality of pitch obtrusion in deafened speakers. It shows that the deafened get the degree of obtrusion wrong, but sidesteps the question of whether they get the direction of obtrusion right. Some do not: they have pitch obtrusion upwards to the prominence rather than downwards. However that is probably best regarded as a different phenomenon from the widespread error of degree that the table shows.

Nevertheless some features of the use of pitch obtrusion are retained in deafened speech. They are indicated by the existence of effects which do not interact with hearing, i.e. similar patterns occur in the hearing and the deafened groups. A main effect of syllable (F 3, 96 = 7.4, p = 0.0002) indicated that all speakers showed less pitch obtrusion on the second syllable (*fath*) than on the others. There was also a simple effect of sex (F 1, 32 = 6.3, p = 0.018): females in general show more pitch obtrusion than males. In this way the deafened retain linguistic and social markers in their use of pitch obtrusion.

6.5.3. Pitch-related subtypes of prominent syllables

Section 6.4. categorised prominent syllables into four broad categories – rises, falls, levels and rise-falls. It is possible to distinguish within each of these categories on the basis of the pitch starting point of each prominence type and the ensuing degree of pitch movement. Figure 6.1 shows the subtypes for each prominence type.

All prominences in both reading and conversation were labelled for each subject according to their subtypes. Auditory analysis formed the basis of this labelling. Subtypes 1 and 2 have low starting points, subtype 3 has a mid starting point, subtype 4 has a high starting point and subtype 5 has an extra-high starting point. These levels are relative to one another and are assigned on the basis of a given speaker's overall pitch range.

Exploration of the data suggested that there might be differences between deafened and controls in two of the prominence types – the rises and the rise-falls. Two analyses of variance were carried out, one on each of these types.

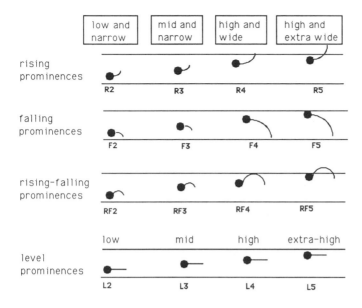

Figure 6.1 Prominence subtypes

These were done for reading style only, as this was where the major differences appeared to lie. Between-subject variables were sex and hearing.

There were no significant differences in the rise-falls, but the analysis of variance on the rises showed a significant interaction between hearing and subcategories of rises (F 1, 36 =14.0, p = 0.0006). The analysis was restricted to two subcategories, Rise 3 and Rise 4, as this was where the differences appeared to lie. The control pattern showed a greater proportion of rises in the Rise 4 category than in the Risc-3 category, but the deafened had roughly equal numbers in both subcategories. Table 6.16 shows the nature of the interaction.

Table 6.16 Differences in subtypes of rises (reading style)

	% rise 3	% rise 4
controls	13.7	25.1
deafened	15.1	16.8

It is possible to identify different linguistic functions associated with sub-types Rise 3 and Rise 4 in control speech. Rise 4 in control speech is associated with questions, with attitudinally marked statements, particularly surprise or excitement, and with expressing contrast when the prominence is moved leftwards in the tone group. In deafened speech, however, rises which start lower – particularly Rise 3 – are used in these contexts. The distribution of subtypes of rises is therefore not just statistically wrong, but linguistically inappropriate.

6.5.4. Conclusion

This section has shown abnormalities in pitch movement, pitch obtrusion and pitch height. The common theme in the data is one of constraint and limitation. The deafened limit the extent to which they move pitch on a syllable, limit the degree to which they jump pitch between syllables, and steer away from extremes of pitch height.

6.6. Synthesis

This chapter has shown that almost every aspect of intonation in deafened speech is abnormal. The abnormalities range from tone-group structure, to component shape, to pitch-related aspects of components. Nevertheless, the data also show that deafened intonation does remain normal at a very fundamental level. It retains a structure that can be analysed in the same ways as normal intonation. Thus, for example, there are tone groups, prominences and the same shape categories of prominences. The abnormalities seem to lie in the imposition of limitations on a fundamentally normal system. These limitations are of various kinds and suggest different levels of explanation ranging from adaptation of high-order rules to problems with low-level realisation. The section on tone-group structure shows that variation in structure is restricted and perhaps suggests the strongest case for high-order adaptation. The section on shape particularly shows that there are limitations to stylistic variation. The final section shows limitations in the degree of pitch change and most clearly suggests low-level problems of realisation.

Up to a point the study supports the widespread claim that deafened intonation is monotonous, but it indicates that monotony is at least partly at a rather abstract level. Reduced pitch change between stressed syllables may relate to the impression of monotonous speech. But there is another side to the impression of monotony. The data on tone-group structure suggest that the over-repetition of the same pattern which characterises deafened speech may also contribute to this impression. Monotony, therefore, may be a mix of abnormalities in pitch and pattern.

The results suggest two clear levels on which deafened intonation may contribute to impaired communication. First, it fails to carry out some linguistic functions that are executed by normal intonation. The data have provided clear examples of these. Secondly it fails to signal style-shift adequately. It is perhaps not surprising that listeners have so frequently identified deafened intonation as abnormal. This chapter has begun to indicate where the abnormality lies.

Chapter 7
Errors of articulation

7.1. Introduction

This chapter considers articulatory disorders in deafened speech. Articulatory disorders have been a particularly controversial issue in the literature on deafened speech (see Goehl – Kaufman 1984; Kaufman – Goehl 1985, Cowie – Douglas-Cowie – Stewart 1986; Zimmermann – Collins 1985). As chapter 2 has indicated, articulation is one of the aspects of speech which a priori one would least expect to be affected by lack of auditory feedback. The expectation is linked to theoretical questions about the role of auditory feedback in speech production and about the organisation of linguistic knowledge. This chapter provides a much fuller body of empirical evidence on the issue than has been available hitherto.

The fundamental aim of the chapter is to provide an overall picture of deafened articulation. The existing literature provides many disparate bits of information, but little sense of the whole picture. For example, some studies focus on errors in only one or two subjects, but give no sense of whether the errors described extend beyond these subjects to the deafened world at large. Some focus on only a few error types, but give no comprehensive view of deafened articulation. Some list substantial numbers of error types, but give little impression of the quantity in which these errors occur. Very few attempt to provide an exhaustive list of error types, and those that do are flawed in other respects. For example, our earlier work (Cowie – Douglas-Cowie 1983: 197–216) comes near to such a list, but it is based on a smallish sample, and it lacks proper quantification of error occurrences and information on the distribution of errors across subjects. Some studies indicate the phonetic environment for some errors but not for others.

In order to provide an overall picture of deafened articulation, the study addresses a number of specific aims. The first is to provide a comprehensive account of the error types in deafened speech and their phonetic distribution. The second is to describe the frequency of occurrence of errors in subjects' speech. The third is to describe the distribution of errors across subjects.

The approach used in the study reflects these aims. Five aspects of the approach deserve mention.

(1). A substantial sample of deafened subjects (28) is used (see section 3.3.1. for details). Almost all had losses over 80 dB in the better ear. This sample size allows one to be fairly certain that the full range of common errors has been identified. It also allows examination of the relationship between the distribution of errors and inter-subject variables.

(2). A substantial control sample (31) is used (see section 3.4. for details). A control sample is fundamental to identifying articulatory errors in deafened speech. Although there are many features of deafened articulation which are auditorily salient as errors, there are others where the picture is perhaps less clear and where control data is essential to clarify the distinction between normal and abnormal articulation. This study refers to control data where the dividing line between normal and abnormal is unclear. Existing descriptions of articulation errors are particularly weak on the use of control data to make such distinctions (though see Lane – Webster 1991).

(3). Analysis is carried out on a substantial body of speech material. This consists of the reading passage entitled "It was unfortunate..." and the description of a day in one's life (see section 3.5.2. for details). This material provides a sufficient speech sample per person (around 200 words on average) to allow a picture to emerge of the range of errors, their distribution across phonetic environment and their frequency of occurrence. The material from the two passages is presented collectively in this study, but the use of two types of speech material has allowed some attention to be paid to the variable of style, where it seems relevant (see section 7.4.3.).

(4). The material is considered quantitatively so that the frequency of various effects can be described and compared.

(5). The basic data come from auditorily-based phonetic analysis. This is supported by informal observation of spectrographs. Such an approach is suited to providing an overall picture, which is what this study aims to do. Clearly there is room for more formal detailed acoustic measurement of some of the features identified, and it is hoped that this study will stimulate further phonetic study of this type.

The findings are reported in three main sections, one on consonant articulation (7.2.), one on vowel articulation (7.3.), and one on more global articulatory errors (7.4.). The latter concerns errors that spread over more than one consonant or vowel. Such errors receive rather little attention in the literature, but they occur over a wide range of subjects, and occur in linguistic contexts that have import for the role of auditory feedback.

7.2. Consonant articulation

7.2.1. Categories of error

There are four main categories of error. These are omissions and extreme consonant weakening, distortions, substitutions and intrusions. The boundaries between these categories of error are not always discrete. For example, some distortions such as that for [s] may be accompanied by a general weakening of the consonant. This poses the problem of whether to classify it as a case of weakening and hence affiliated to omission or whether to classify it as a distortion. Nevertheless the four basic categories do seem to capture the major directions of errors and to be easily applicable in most cases. In cases of doubt we have decided which category the error most strongly tends towards. This criterion can be applied reasonably consistently.

The distribution of errors among these categories is summarised in table 7.1.

Table 7.1 Categories of consonant error

error category	total number of occurrences	total number of subjects making error
distortions	171	23
substitutions	133	21
omissions and extreme weakenings	116	19
intrusions	4	3

A number of points can be made about the distribution. Errors of intrusion are extremely rare. This makes a clear distinction between the postlingual deaf and the prelingual deaf where intrusion is common (see e.g. Smith 1975). The distribution across the other error types is reasonably even in terms of the number of people showing the error type and in terms of the overall numbers of distortions, substitutions and omissions and extreme weakenings. There are fewer omissions and substitutions overall, because there are slightly fewer subjects who show these error categories, but the average number per person who makes any errors of the type is roughly the same as that for distortions.

7.2.2. The relationship between categories of error and place and manner of articulation

Table 7.2 provides information that allows us to look at the relationships between categories of error and the place and manner of articulation.

Errors involving elements in the affricates [tʃ] and [dʒ] are counted under either the stop or fricative manners of articulation as appropriate. Errors classed as alveolar include the grooved alveolars [ʃ] and [ʒ]. There is some case for classifying these consonants separately as palato-alveolars, but they are grouped here with the alveolars for simplicity, and their individual contribution to alveolar error types is discussed below.

Table 7.2 Categories of error by place and manner

	stops	fricatives	nasals	approximants	laterals
omission and extreme weakenings	29 alveolar 4 velar	1 labiodental 32 alveolar	7 alveolar	33 alveolar	9 alveolar
distortion	4 bilabial			1 bilabial	
		3 labiodental			
	9 alveolar 3 velar	146 alveolar	1 alveolar 1 velar		
substitutions	3 bilabial		1 bilabial		
		1 labiodental 20 dental			
	94 alveolar 8 velar		1 alveolar	5 alveolar	3 alveolar
intrusions	3 alveolar				

This table shows that consonantal problems affect virtually the whole range of consonant categories in English. But it also suggests that some are more affected than others. Alveolar consonants are salient. However these raw numbers are influenced by the relative prevalence of various consonant phonemes in the language. Two other types of information are therefore also taken into consideration. These are (a) the raw numbers as approximate percentages of the total number of target consonants in a particular manner and place and (b) the numbers of subjects showing each of the errors. On the basis of all this information, the following four major groups of errors can be identified. No other error type comes near to constituting a significant group.

(1). Alveolar fricatives. This is the most affected group with a total of 178 error occurrences. Alveolar fricatives are mainly distorted (146 occurrences) although omission also forms a substantial error (32 occurrences). The vast majority of subjects (22) show at least some errors involving alveolar fricatives. The number of error occurrences represents a substantial proportion (approximately 20%) of the total target number of alveolar fricatives in the speech of these 22 subjects. The palato-alveolar grooved fricatives are involved in distortion and represent around one third of the cases of distortion, but are not involved in omission (for further details see table 7.6).

(2). Alveolar stops. This is the next most widely affected group with a total of 135 error occurrences. Alveolar stops are mainly substituted, although omission occurs in a sizeable proportion. A total of 19 subjects out of the total 27 show some error involving substitution or omission of alveolar stops. There are a few distortions of alveolar stops. The number of occurrences of errors involving alveolar stops represents approximately 10% of the total target number of alveolar stops in the speech of these 19 subjects.

(3). Alveolar approximants. These are affected to a lesser degree but nevertheless stand out as a noticeable error group. There is a total of only 38 actual occurrences, but around half of the deafened subjects (11) show errors involving alveolar fricatives, and the total number of occurrences represents a noticeable proportion of the total target number (around 10%) for these 11 subjects. Alveolar approximants are mostly omitted.

(4). Dental fricatives. These also constitute a noticeable problem.They are mostly involved in substitution errors. Again there is a small total of actual occurrences (21), but a substantial number of subjects (9) show errors in this region and in terms of the percentage of the total number of target dental fricatives for these 9 subjects, the raw numbers of occurrences represent around 4%.

7.2.3. Consonant problems – a detailed description

This section describes the nature of consonant errors in detail. It identifies particular consonants within the general groupings so far established, describes the nature of the abnormality and provides information on the phonetic environment of errors.The orthographic forms of the consonants referred to are underlined in the illustrative examples.

The section deals with errors in two broad groupings – the four major groups of errors summarised in the previous section and the remaining more minor errors.

Throughout this section consonants are considered in voiced/voiceless pairs rather than individually. Thus [s] and [z], for example, are considered a unit rather than two consonants which have to be treated separately. The reason for this is that it is not always easy to say which of two such consonants is the intended phoneme, because of a blurring of voiced/voiceless distinctions in some subjects' speech and because of a normal overlap in the realisations of the two phonemes. For these reasons they are grouped together here. Where there is good evidence to suggest that they are differentially affected by an error type, this is made clear.

7.2.3.1. Major errors

(1). Alveolar fricatives. Two errors affect these very frequently – distortion and omission.

(a) Distortion

Two alveolar groups are involved in distortion. These are the alveolar fricatives [s] and [z] and the alveo-palatal grooved fricatives [ʃ] and [ʒ].

[s] and [z] These consonants are distorted in a wide range of phonetic environments:
- word initially in prevocalic position (e.g. *six, zoo*);
- word finally in post vocalic position (e.g. *house, lose*);
- word medially between vowels (e.g. *noisy, bossy*);
- in consonant clusters occurring initially, medially and finally (e.g. *street, youngster, games*).

These consonants appear most frequently in the data in word-final position, and it is thus easy to get the impression that distortion is most common in word-final position. In proportionate terms, however, distortion of [s] and [z] is just as common in the other positions. There does seem to be a relationship, however, between distortion and proximity of these consonants to each other in a word or word-string. Thus, for example, words such as *analysis, younsters, necessary, six*, create problems, as do strings such as *half past six*.

Distortion of [s] and [z] takes a number of forms. Auditorily it is possible to distinguish several types of distortion. The first is a general weakening of [s]. This sometimes occurs on its own, but the general weakening more frequently takes place in the context of a post-alveolar backing of [s]. Another type is exaggerated sibilance. Auditorily one of its attributes appears to be added length.

[ʃ] and [ʒ] These consonants are most commonly distorted when they occur as part of the [tʃ] – [dʒ] affricate clusters in a range of phonetic environments e.g. as in *Jim, unfortunate, church*. Distortion also occurs in [ʃ] in initial, medial and final position as in *she, coronation* and *lunch*, and in [ʒ] in medial position e.g. *leisure*, though distortion is more common in the affricate clusters.

The main auditory impression of [ʃ] and [ʒ] distortion is that the consonants move in the direction of [s] and [z]. The movement forwards for these consonants coupled with the movement backwards for [s] and [z] suggests the possibility of convergence of these consonants in deafened speech, though Lane – Webster (1991: 863–864) show in an acoustic study of these consonants in deafened speech that speakers continue to differentiate the two consonants but merely less so.

(b) Omission

Omission affects three alveolar consonants, the group [s] and [z] and the consonant [ʒ]. It is most apparent in [s] and [z], and occurs sporadically in [ʒ].

[s] and [z] Omission of [s] and [z] occurs in a limited range of phonetic environments. Omission occurs almost exclusively in word-final position, although one instance was found of word medial omission in the word *noisy*. Within the word-final category there are two further restrictions, either of which may be in operation when word-final [s] or [z] omission takes place. These are:

– when the word is final in a sentence or precedes a pause (usually coinciding with the end of a grammatical clause), and when the general tempo is slowed and there is audible creak;
– when the word is relatively unstressed compared to the surrounding words e.g. *was born*.

Omission of [s] or [z] is not always absolute. One quarter of the [s] and [z] group counted as omission is made up of cases of extreme weakening.

[ʒ] omission This takes place in two contexts:
– in the cluster [dʒ] in initial position as in *Jim*;
– in medial position between vowels as in *usually*.

(2). Alveolar stops. These show two main error types – substitution and omission.

(a) Substitution

There are three types of substitution: [t] → [ʔ], [t] → [θ] and [d] → [z].

[t] → [?] By far the commonest of all substitutions is the use of a glottal stop in place of [t]. This occurs in the following environments:
- word-final position particularly after a vowel e.g. *bi*t, *ge*t. Replacement of [t] by a glottal stop in this context commonly occurs when the word is clause or sentence final or precedes a pause. Approximately two thirds of the total cases occur in these positions, although examples occurring in other sentence positions can be found.
- word-medial position either intervocalically as in *bitter*, or in consonant clusters e.g. *unfortunate*.

Glottal articulation has not been instrumentally examined in this study, but auditorily there do seem to be different degrees of glottalisation. While the majority of cases are clear glottal stops, there is a small group where glottalisation is accompanied by some form of [t] or [d] articulation.

[t] → [θ] This substitution occurs only once in the word *better*.

[d] → [z] This occurs twice, both occurrences in word final position in the phrases *groun*d *very fine*, and *ha*d *no time*. The latter might conceivably be a misreading of *has* for *had*.

(b) Omission
The alveolar stops [t] and [d] are omitted. Such omission takes place in a limited range of phonetic contexts:
- in word final position, e.g. *biscui*t, *eigh*t, *pas*t. (most common when the word is followed by a pause as in sentence final or clause final position);
- in consonant clusters containing other consonants with similar place of articulation but different manner:the clusters can be either medial or final in a word, but not initial. e.g. *youngs*ters, *regimen*ts, *don't*;
- in the unstressed word *t*o as in the phrase *don't* *like to leave the dog*;
- in [tʃ] and [dʒ] in initial, medial and final position e.g. *change*, *J*im, *un-for*tunate, *char*ge.

The nature of [t] and [d] omission is not always clear cut. As in the case of [s] and [z] omission above, [t] and [d] are sometimes extremely weakened rather than actually omitted, though these cases have been counted as omissions. Although they show up as faint spectographic traces, the ear is strained to identify them. Such weakened instances of [t] and [d] make up one quarter of the total number of [t] and [d] omissions.

(3). Alveolar approximants – omission. The omission of [r] is the only error in this group. Omission of orthographic r in postvocalic position is well known to be a feature of many normal accents of English. Normal Belfast English, however, as part of Hiberno-English, is well known to be a rhotacised accent, that is, orthographic r is present postvocalically. Omission of [r] in the following phonetic environments can therefore confidently be said to be an abnormality rather than a feature of normal Belfast English.

Omission of [r] occurs in the following phonetic environments within the word. Sentence position appears to be irrelevant.

- word-finally either directly after a vowel e.g. *for*, or word finally in a consonant cluster e.g. *work*;
- word-initially as part of a consonant cluster e.g. *through*, *Friday*, *break-fast*, *drink* but not word initially on its own;
- word-medially either intervocalically e.g. *period*, or word-medially in consonant cluster e.g. *quarter*.

Omission of [r] is mainly auditorily clear, but there are a few cases where some gesture towards [r] seems to be maintained.

(4). Dental fricatives – substitution. Substitution involves the use of [d] for the dental fricative [ð] and [t] for [θ]. These substitutions have a fairly limited distribution in terms of phonetic environment. With one exception, all occurrences are word-initial as in e.g. *then*, *them*, *through*, *thinking*, *that*, *thing*. The exception involves word-final substitution of [t] for [θ] in the phrase *with my*.

7.2.3.2. Other minor consonant errors in detail

Other more minor consonant errors are described in three groups, (1) the minor alveolar group, (2) the labial group, (3) the velar group.

(1). The minor alveolar group – omission, substitution, distortion and intrusion. This group consists of alveolar errors that do not occur in sufficient numbers to be classed with the major alveolar errors above. They include errors of omission, substitution, distortion and intrusion.

(a) Omission
Omission of [l] and [n] occurs.
[l] omission This occurs in a wide range of phonetic environments:
- word-finally after a vowel e.g. *school*;
- word-finally in a consonant cluster e.g. *myself*;
- word-initially in a consonant cluster e.g. *play*;
- word-medially in a consonant cluster e.g. *children*.

[n] omission. This is restricted to word-final positions. This may sometimes be in a cluster e.g. *la<u>n</u>d*. Sometimes it may occur at syllable boundaries e.g. *co<u>n</u>sultants*.

(b) Distortion

There are three broad types of distortion of alveolar stops. All involve the target sound [t]. They are:

[t] overaspirated. This occurs in the following phonetic environments:
– word-initial prevocalic position in e.g. *<u>t</u>oo*;
– word-final position when preceding a marked pause e.g. *well it must have been a couple of years I was like tha<u>t</u>*.

Overaspiration of [t] does not just involve too strong a burst of energy, but is generally accompanied by protracted aspiration.

[t] underaspirated. This is uncommon. It occurs in word-initial position where the norm in the local accent is accompanying aspiration e.g. *<u>t</u>able, <u>t</u>own*.

[t] distortions related to more general problems. There are two distortions of [t] which seem to be products of more global articulatory abnormalities. The first is retroflexion of [t]. This is uncommon and occurs in the wider context of general retroflexion of the speech, in particular of [r]. The second is the use of an ejective [t‘] or something very close to it. This is again very uncommon. It occurs in word-final sentence-final position and seems to be part of an accompanying larger problem with breath control.

(c) Intrusion

There is intrusion of the alveolar stops [t] and [d]. This occurs only at word boundaries e.g. *tonsils <u>d</u> out, stay <u>d</u> home*.

(d) Substitution

Substitutions affect [r], [l] and [n].

[r] is substituted by [w] in a range of environments e.g. *<u>r</u>eady, p<u>r</u>oblem, ag<u>r</u>ee*.

[l] is substituted by a glottal stop in word-final position as in e.g. *wi<u>ll</u>*.

[n] is replaced by [d] as in *fi<u>n</u>ish*.

(2). The labial group. Three types of error are found in this group – substitutions, omissions and distortions.

(a) Substitutions

These are of four types:

[p] → [?]. The substitution of a glottal stop for [p] occurs in word-final position only e.g. *u_p_*.

[w] → [m]. This substitution occurs only once in the phrase *and _w_ill not*. This suggests an error caused by over assimilation of the [w] in *_w_ill* to the nasal manner of the preceding [n] in *a_n_d* and is in keeping with larger scale assimilatory errors discussed in section 7.4. which extend beyond individual phonemes.

[m] → [b]. This occurs medially between vowels e.g. *co_mm_on*, and word-initially e.g *_m_aybe*, *_m_ake*.

[f] → [w]. There is only one example of this in *breakfast*.

(b) Omissions

Omission of [f] occurs. This occurs word finally in the phrase *hal_f_ past* where two labial consonants are together.

(c) Distortions

Most errors in this category affect the consonant [p] and are of the following three types:

[p] overaspirated. This occurs in word-final position, and tends, like over aspiration of [t] to involve too much energy protracted too long.

[p] underaspirated. This occurs in word final position.

[p] sounds like an ejective. As in [t] (above), this occurs in word final position and seems to be part of a larger problem with breath control.

Other distortions in the labial group may appear.

[w] distortion: [w] loses its liprounding and becomes too vowel-like.

[f] and [v] distortion: these fricatives move towards bilabial stops.

(3). The velar group – omission, substitution and distortion. Errors in this group consist mainly of omissions of [k] and some substitutions for [k] and [g], though there are a few distortions.

(a) Omissions

[k] is omitted in word-final position in e.g. *o' cloc_k_*, *wor_k_*, *ma_k_e*.

(b) Substitutions

[k] is replaced by [?] in word-final position e.g. *boo_k_*.

[k] and [g} are replaced by [x] in word-initial and word-final position e.g. *_c_ommon*, *tal_k_*, *bac_k_*.

(c) Distortions

Distortions of [k], [g] and [ŋ] occur.

[k] and [g] are given an affricate like articulation – [kx]

[ŋ] may have a hint of a velar stop at the end – [ŋg]. This is not part of the control dialect.

7.2.4. Synthesis of consonant errors

On one level, the data here agree reasonably well with the fullest previous description of consonant errors (Cowie – Douglas-Cowie 1983: 201–209). Both sources show a "backward shift" where the labiodental fricatives are replaced by alveolar stops, and alveolar stops (with some palatal stops) are replaced by glottal stops. Both studies show a complex of effects around the other fricatives and affricates, with the affricates replaced by grooved fricatives and reduced distinction between the grooved alveo-palatal fricatives and the alveolar fricatives. Distortion in that area is recognised more fully here, but it is noted in the 1983 report. Both studies show omission affecting the alveolar consonants, particularly the stops, fricatives and semivowels. Both studies agree that consonants with a forward place of articulation are relatively little affected. These correspondences suggest that the trends in question are reasonably firm. Although there is overlap between the speakers in the two studies, it is not sufficient to explain the extent of the correspondence. Only eleven of the twenty-eight speakers in this study participated in the earlier one, and in no case were the actual speech samples the same.

The new dimension which this study adds involves phonetic context. The point which comes through most clearly is how many of deafened people's articulatory difficulties involve managing word boundaries. This corresponds at least in broad terms to the observation from the previous chapter that the rise and fall of intensity shows major abnormalities. Theoretically it makes eminent sense to suppose that realisation at word boundaries is particularly variable and that auditory feedback is particularly relevant to setting balances correctly. For at least two relevant errors, evidence from the controls reinforces the point. In an informal follow-up observing spectographs of control speech, it was found that the controls had weakened final [s], [z], [t], [d] in sentence- or clause-final position or before a pause, though the weakening did not result in the extreme weakening or omission characteristic of the deafened.

7.2.5. The distribution and extent of the consonant problem

7.2.5.1. Numbers of subjects showing errors

This section shows the numbers of subjects showing each individual error across subjects, and examines the distribution in terms of intersubject variables.

Table 7.3 summarises distribution. It makes a number of points. There are a few (six in all) errors which show a substantial distribution across subjects. This distribution has a range from around two thirds of the subjects in the case of [s] and [z] distortion to just under a third of the subjects in the case of [t] and [d omission. The rest of the errors show minimal distribution.

Table 7.3 Numbers of subjects showing each error

number of subjects	error
18	[s] and [z] distortion
14	[ʃ] and [ʒ] distortion
12	[t] to [ʔ]
11	[s] and [z] omission; [r] omission
9	[θ] and [ð] to [t] and [d]
8	[t] and [d] omission
4	[n] and [l] omission
3	[p] to [ʔ]; [t] and [d] intrusion; [p] and [t] overaspiration; [r] to [w]; [k] omission
2	[d] to [z]; [ʒ] omission; [p] and [t] underaspiration; [t] and [p] to an ejective; [t] retroflexion
1	[t] to [θ]; [l] to [ʔ]; [n] to [d]; [w] to [m]; [m] to [b]; [f] to [w]; [v] to [b]; [f] omission; [k] and [g] to [x]; labiodental fricative and bilabial approximant distortion

Further analysis suggests that some of the errors show distinctive distribution patterns across subjects, depending on the age at onset of a subject. Two points can be made. The first is that some articulatory errors appear to be the hallmark of a particular small subgroup of the deafened sample. Three errors are involved. These are (i) [r] omission (ii) [l] omission and (iii) [t] and [d] intrusions. These are related to age at onset of deafness and occur predominantly in the speech of those deafened in childhood. Table 7.4 shows the pattern.

Table 7.4   Total numbers of subjects by age at onset showing errors of [r] and [l] omission and [t] and [d] intrusion

error	age at onset				
	5 or under	9 years	11 years	14 years	adult
[r] omission	6	2	1	1	1
[l] omission	3				
[t] and [d] intrusion	3				

The second point is more tenuous. It is that errors involving the distortion of alveolar fricatives can occur across the whole range of subjects. In fact everyone shows some alveolar distortion, even if slight, either of [s] and [z] or of [ʃ] and [ʒ], with the exception of some subjects deafened in early childhood. It seems that alveolar distortion is a hallmark of post childhood onset of deafness but not necessarily of childhood onset of deafness.

7.2.5.2. Numbers of error types for individual deafened subjects

There are 31 specific consonant error types listed in table 7.3. This section describes how many of these error types any one individual may show. Table 7.5 summarises the data. The table shows that all 28 deafened subjects do show some consonant error types, but suggests that the problem is more limited for some than others. The table indicates that the limitation is related to age at onset of deafness. There is a clear trend for larger numbers of error types to occur in those deafened in the period up to the mid teens.

Subjects show a common core of error types. This core is consistent with those errors which show the largest distribution across subjects as set out in table 7.3. The core consists of at least two of the following error types and, for subjects showing larger numbers of error types, may consist of all of the following types:

[s] and [z] distortion; [ʃ] and [ʒ] distortion; [t] to [ʔ]; [s] and [z] omission; [r] omission; [θ] and [ð] to [t] and [d]; [t] and [d] omission.

Table 7.5 Numbers of error types shown by individual subjects

age at onset	number of subjects	number of error types
up to mid teens	1	12
	4	10
	2	8
	1	7
	3	6
	1	5
late teens and after	3	5
	4	4
	4	3
	5	2

In the speech of those who the show fewest error types, distortion of the alveolar fricatives is the most likely error type to occur.

7.2.5.3. Numbers of occurrences of error types

This section describes the numbers of occurrences of each major error type. The data are presented in table 7.6. The description is limited to the major core-error types. The table gives a number of different types of information. First it gives the raw numbers for each error type aggregated across all subjects. Raw numbers, however, are not a very accurate guide to describing the size of the problem, as they will vary depending upon the frequency of the target phoneme. In order to provide a more accurate guide, the average number of occurrences of each target phoneme per subject is calculated and given in the second column of the table, and the range of error occurrences across subjects for each phoneme is given in column 3. This information allows one to calculate the highest and lowest proportions of the target phoneme produced erroneously. A further breakdown of the data is given in the last three columns and gives a more accurate picture of the distribution of subjects across the range of error occurrences. These columns show how many subjects had error occurrences which fell within the top third, the middle third and the bottom third of the range for each error type. Some of the numbers involved did not divide evenly into thirds, but in practice this did not constitute a problem.

Table 7.6 Numbers of error occurrences

	total number of errors across all subjects	average number of targets per subject	range of errors across all subjects	number of subjects who made error type in:			
				whole sample	top third range	middle third range	bottom third range
Alveolar fricatives							
[s] and [z] distortion	102	25	2–25	18	1	4	13
[ʃ] and [ʒ] distortion	44	12	1–7	14	5	1	8
[s] and [z] omission	32	25	1–6	11	3	4	4
Alveolar stops							
[t] to [?]	94	50	1–21	12	1	6	5
[t] and [d] omission	29	50	1–6	8	1	5	2
Alveolar approximants							
[r] omission	33	30	1–7	11	1	4	6
Dental fricatives							
[θ] and [ð] to [t] and [d]	20	60	1–6	9	1	2	6

A number of points can be made from the table. First, it is clear that if one looks at the top value in the range of error occurrences for each error type and considers this in conjunction with the target number per subject, some subjects clearly show substantial proportions of errors per target phoneme. For example, in the case of alveolar fricatives, the proportion can be as high as 100% for [s] and [z] distortion, approximately 50% for [ʃ] and [ʒ] distortion and approximately 25 % for [s] and [z] omission. In the case of alveolar stops the top values represent around 40% for glottalisation of [t] though only 14% for [t] and [d] omission. The top value for alveolar approximants represents around 25%. The highest value for dental fricative substitution represents around 10%. The proportions for [s] and [z] and [t] and [d] omissions might well be higher if one restricted the counts for target phonemes to final word contexts which is where these errors are most likely to take place. The last three columns in the table, however, indicate that there are very few subjects who come near to the top values in the range, and that there are many more who fall in the middle or bottom third of the range. Nevertheless, in the case of some errors, falling within the middle third of the range still means that a sizeable number of occurrences of the target phoneme are produced erroneously. For example, in the case of [s] and [z] distortion, falling within the middle third means that, on average, around half of the [s] and [z] phonemes are distorted, and in the case of the glottalisation of [t], falling within the middle third means that on average somewhere around 20% of [t] phonemes are glottalised. These figures are certainly not negligible; nor are the numbers of subjects who fall within the middle third categories.

Age at onset is related to the number of error occurrences that subjects have, but its relationship is not black and white. Subjects who become deaf before adulthood tend not to have minimal occurrences of an error type in the sense that they tend not to fall in the bottom third; but those who become deaf later may well have as many occurrences.

7.3. Vowel errors

7.3.1. The nature of the problem

There are four categories of vowel errors – substitutions, distortions, intrusions and vowel lengthening. It is particularly difficult in the case of vowels to separate out substitutions from distortions as distortions tend to be distortions in the direction of a substitution. In presentation the two categories are thus usually conflated and explanatory notes given where necessary.

7.3.1.1. Vowel substitutions and distortions

Individual vowel substitutions cum distortions are described below in groups which reflect the major patterns in the data. These groups are:
  (1). the front-upwards pattern;
  (2). the front-downwards pattern;
  (3). the front-central pattern;
  (4). the back group;
  (5). the diphthongs.
Since the vowel errors are limited in occurrence, all words in which they occur are listed. Since the vowel system of Belfast English is considerably different from that of Received Pronunciation, the normal form of the vowel cited is to be read as that which would occur in standard Belfast English. There are some cases where an error could conceivably be interpreted as a

Belfast dialect variant, but in the overall context of the speech of the subjects concerned, this seems unlikely.

(1). The front-upwards pattern. This pattern is characterised by the raising of front vowels. Auditorily these come across as straight substitutions. Five front vowels are involved.

[a] → [ε] This occurs in *that* and *past*.

[ε] → [i] The only example of this occurs in the word *depending*.

[ε] → [e] This occurs in *better, bed*.

[e] → [i] This occurs once in the word *taken*.

[ɪ] → [i] This occurs in *embarrassing, television*.

(2). The front downwards pattern. This pattern involves a lowering of front vowels. Again these come across auditorily as straight substitutions. There are four types of movement downwards. These are:

[i] → [e] This occurs in *three, teach, we, agree, tea*.

[e] → [ε] This occurs in *paper, laid*.

[e] → [a] This occurs once in the word *games*.

[ε] → [a] This occurs in the words *when, ten*.

(3). The front-central pattern. This pattern involves the centralisation of front vowels and increased centralisation of [ɪ]. This pattern does not always result in auditorily clear-cut substitutions of one vowel for another, but is more a matter of varying degrees of shift towards a particular substitution. The movements listed below are therefore indicative of a strong movement in direction of a substitution rather than an auditorily clear substitution.

[i] → [ɪ] This occurs in the words *three* and *repeat*.

[e] → [ə] This occurs in the words *eight* and *make*. It occurs in the context of over-fast speech.

[ɪ] → [ə] This occurs in the word *party* at the end of a sentence.

(4). The back group. The distinguishing feature of this group is that it involves back vowels and that the substitution movements involved are contained within the back vowel area. There are three movements involved. The first two involve the raising of back vowels. The third involves lowering of a back vowel. All these movements are strong movements in the direction of the vowel listed below rather than auditorily distinct substitutions.

[o] → [u] This occurs in *smoke, go, four*.

[ɔ] → [o] This occurs in *talk, quarter*.

[o] → [o] This occurs in *cope*.

(5). The diphthong group. This group is focussed on the diphthong [aÈ]. There are two distinctive movements associated with this diphthong.

One is the movement from the dipthtong to a simple vowel. This involves two types of substitution:

[aɪ] → [e] This occurs several times in the word *I*.

[aɪ] → [a] This occurs in the words *nine*, *times*, *I*. In the case of *I* it may be relevant that the [a] occurs in the context of a following [a] in the phrase *I agree*.

The second movement associated with [aɪ] is the converse, that is, a movement from a simple vowel to the diphthong. There are two particular substitutions:

[ɪ] → [aɪ] This occurs in the word *finally* [faɪnlaɪ]. It is of note that the inappropriate [aɪ] comes directly after an appropriate [aɪ].

[e] → [aɪ] This occurs in the word *play*.

7.3.1.2. Vowel intrusions

There are intrusions of three vowels – [a], [ə] and [e].

These all appear at word boundaries. Examples are:

it [e] *was*
we have [e] *two*
a coffee [a] *break*
and [e] *hoovered*
had [a] *Aunt Thelma*
have [ə] *to get up*

7.3.1.3. Vowel lengthening

Vowel lengthening occurs in four contexts:
  – in the first element of a diphthong;
  – in vowels which are naturally long in control speech; the length, however, is exaggerated beyond normal limits (this has been confirmed by spectrographic analysis);
  – in words which occur in sentence final position where there is a natural slowing down and extenuation of the vowel; spectographic analysis shows that this is exaggerated beyond control limits;
  – in vowels that would normally be short in Belfast English; this, however, is not as common as the three contexts above.

7.3.2. The extent of the problem

The striking thing about vowel errors is that their distribution across subjects is extremely limited. Table 7.7 summarises the relevant information. It first shows the number of subjects who have vowel errors including both vowel lengthening and other types of vowel errors. It can be seen that most of the errors occur in the speech of those who were deafened well before adulthood. The table then shows the numbers of additional subjects showing vowel lengthening only. It can be seen that vowel lengthening is the exceptional vowel error that extends beyond early onset. The actual numbers of error occurrences (excluding lengthening) are also very small. The total average number for the most affected group is only 6.

Table 7.7   Distribution of vowel errors by age at onset

age at onset	number of subjects showing vowel lengthening and other types of vowel errors	number of additional subjects showing vowel lengthening only	total number of errors excluding vowel lengthening
5 and under	5	–	30
late childhood	2	–	7
teens	3	2	4
adulthood	2	3	4

7.3.3. The nature of vowel errors – synthesis

The point that stands out about vowel errors is their limited distribution. Only lengthening is at all common outside the group with early onset. Length is a parameter which it is easy to imagine being controlled by feedback, though the fact that vowels are lengthened rather than shortened indicates that less obvious factors are at work.

The prevalence of vowel lengthening errors bears an interesting relation to the prevalence of boundary errors in consonants. Both point to timing and temporal organisation as a central problem, and it makes sense to suppose that that is at least as important in deafened speech as any tendency to forget or alter target articulator configurations.

Our earlier study also found vowel errors much less marked than consonant errors (Cowie – Douglas-Cowie 1983: 211–216), and so the finding seems to be robust. The question is why this should be so. One might well expect the opposite, since vowel duration tends to be longer, giving more opportunity for on-line control, and the opportunity for tactile feedback is less. One possibility is that vowel production is simply less sensitive to small errors in articulator positioning than consonant production. However that seems less plausible when one considers that some of the common consonant errors, particularly the "backward shift", involve very substantial articulator misplacements. Another factor may be that vowels occur less often at word boundaries, where difficulties tend to concentrate. However basically the fact is that the phenomenon is reasonably clear, and stands in need of a satisfying explanation.

7.4. Global articulatory errors

The previous sections have examined articulatory errors confined to individual consonants and vowels. This section is concerned with errors that spread over more than one consonant or vowel. Such errors are usually not classified although they do receive passing mention in the literature (Cowie – Douglas-Cowie 1983: 201–202).

7.4.1. Nature of global articulation errors

There are a number of categories of errors that can be identified. These are (1) large scale elision, (2) total distortion and (3) assimilation errors.

(1). Large scale elision. This refers to the elision of more than one phoneme. There are a number of subcategories:

(a) Elision of whole words
Whole words get elided. This happens when the words are in unstressed positions, e.g.
to *have had* Aunt Thelma → [tʊ had ant θɛlmə]
might come back *in an* hour → [matt kʌm bak a ə r]

(b) Final syllable elision
This is the elision of the final syllable in a word which has more than one syllable. It can occur when the word is in any syntactic position in a subject's speech, but is most prevalent at a sentence or clause end. The syllable is frequently replaced by audible creak. Examples are:

unfortunate → [ʌnfortʃən]
tested → [tɛs]
before → [bə f]
something → [sʌmp]
often → [of]
purposes → [pə rpə z]

(c) Reduction of bisyllabic structures
This group is characterised by the the reduction of two adjacent unstressed syllables in a polysyllablic word to one syllable. Examples are:
television → [tɛviʃə n]
video → [vɪde]

(2). Total distortion. This refers to words or sequences of words which bear very little resemblance to what they appear to be aiming at, judging from the context. Sometimes it is simply not possible to decipher what their target form is. Examples are:
make → [hed]
maybe → [bɛ?ə]

(3). Assimilation errors. Errors in this group may also involve elision and distortion but are characterised by the fact that they involve relationships between adjacent words. There are two subcategories.

(a) Syllable reduction at word boundaries
This refers to the merging of two words leading to syllable reduction. Examples are:
I agree → [ə gri]
a quarter to → [ə kwadʉ] and [ə kwardə]
couldn't hear → [kʉdnir]

(b) Vowel assimilation across words
This refers to adjacent words appearing to match each other in vowel phonemes (a sort of vowel harmony) when this would not be the normal case. Examples are:
had no → [hodno]
log book → [lʉgbʉg]

7.4.2. Extent of problem

Global articulatory errors occur in half the subjects in the sample. The distribution across subjects does not relate to any obvious variable. The actual numbers of occurrences within a subject's speech, however, are very small. The maximum number of occurrences for any one subject is 4.

7.4.3. Synthesis of global articulation errors

Theoretically these errors form an interesting group. Apart from the cases of total distortion, which are extremely rare, the errors seem to be interpretable in terms of normal trends of reduction and assimilation taken to extremes. Thus the elision or reduction of unstressed syllables and words and the merging of adjacent words can be seen as extreme representations of the normal phonological processes of reduction and assimilation in similar contexts.

It is important to consider whether some of the examples are possible in normal speech. Our control data does show cases of considerable reduction and assimilation, particularly in the day-in-the-life passage. There do not seem to be examples as extreme as the deafened examples listed, but it is difficult to be objective about drawing a line between what is acceptable assimilation and reduction and what goes beyond the range of acceptability. In the majority of cases, however, the deafened examples can be classed with some confidence as abnormalities. This is supported by the fact that the deafened examples spread into the reading passage, a style which in normal speech is not likely to be characterised by assimilation and reduction, and which in our control data is characterised by a trend in the opposite direction towards a citation-form style.

The main theoretical impact of these examples is to underline the role of word boundaries. Examples where the juncture and assimilation are so clearly problems reinforce the inference that difficulty with these issues underlies many of the consonant errors.

7.5. Conclusion

This chapter has provided an overall picture of deafened articulatory errors. Where it overlaps the fullest previous source, there is a good deal of agreement. However it provides greater detail in several respects, the most important of which is the role of context. The theoretical significance of these observations has been considered during the chapter.

The issue which has not been considered is the practical significance of errors. There is no doubt that numbers of errors are relatively small. Kaufman – Goehl (1985: 222) used our earlier error counts to argue that articulation errors are practically negligible in deafened people's speech. The numbers here are comparable, though some qualifications are in order. Most deafened people have something wrong with their articulation, especially their articulation of alveolar fricatives: the numbers represent substantial proportions of the target consonants for some subjects: and at least in some subjects, the total number of error types is substantial.

At root, though, counts are simply not the right basis on which to decide whether errors of articulation lead to real problems for the deafened. A key underlying point is that outright errors may effectively be the tip of an iceberg, cases in which a pervasive imperfection is expressed sharply enough to register as an inappropriate segment. This is particularly plausible if difficulties of timing and integration have a central role. The point is taken up in the next chapter using data from the acoustic study to establish whether local articulatory errors do relate to more pervasive trends. The chapter also takes up the question which is the real arbiter of whether articulatory errors matter practically: do they affect listeners?

Chapter 8
Social and emotional reactions to deafened people's speech

8.1. Introduction

This chapter returns to the theme of functional abnormality in deafened people's speech. Chapter 4 considered the simple and self-evidently important issue of intelligibility. Studying intelligibility is certainly a necessary element of any attempt to establish whether deafened people's speech is a practical problem. However it is not sufficient.

One might use the data to argue that very few deafened people have problems with their speech, since it can almost always be understood (at least with a little effort). However such an argument would reflect an indefensibly narrow approach to speech. If people's speech leads them to be avoided, or underrated, or mocked, then it is a problem even if it can be understood. The point is not as firmly entrenched in the clinical literature as one might expect, but it is by no means unprecedented: it has been made, for instance in connection with various speech problems, including lateral lisps, stammering, and abnormal voice qualities (Silverman 1976: 550; Blood – Mahan – Hyman 1979; Hurst – Cooper 1983). However it is implicit in the substantial and growing body of sociolinguistic and social psychological research which emphasises the negative effects that unacceptable speech varieties or behaviour can have throughout life – for instance in education (e.g. Edwards 1979), in court (e.g. Lind – O'Barr 1979), in employment (Kalin – Rayko 1980) and in personal interactions (Lambert 1979). Systematic extension of this approach to clinical speech is a natural and overdue development.

This chapter uses a limited but useful methodology to consider the social effects that deafened people's speech may have. Subjects listen to recordings, and afterwards fill out questionnaires concerned with their reaction to the speaker (see chapter 3, section 3.6.1.). There is a great deal of artificiality about this, but it provides fair amounts of reasonably tractable data. The next chapter complements it by using more complex and realistic types of situation, and by asking whether the trends that come through in this study are likely to transfer to real encounters.

An important use of data on reactions is in evaluating the abnormalities of form which earlier chapters have described. At root, what makes an abnormality of form important is that it disadvantages the speaker. If it does not, then there is no point investing large efforts in its treatment. The second main part of the chapter takes up this issue. Regressions are used to explore relationships between formal abnormalities and functional problems. Larger quantities of data would be needed to establish this kind of conclusion with any confidence, but the relationships that emerge are interesting, and until larger studies are available they may be a better guide to practice than pure intuition.

8.2. The study of the listeners' impression: method

The subjects involved were those who took part in the shadowing experiment used to provide a measure of intelligibility. Details are given in chapter 3. The speakers were 47 postlingually deafened people and 19 control speakers (see section 3.3.1. for details of deafened subjects and section 3.4. for details of control subjects). The listeners were 660 normal hearing listeners, ten per speaker. Each one shadowed one speaker reading five passages and giving three narratives in his or her own words (see section 3.5.1. for details of the speech sample). After that, a questionnaire was presented and the subject used it to record his or her impressions of and reactions to the speaker.

The questionnaire was developed using previous sources concerned with reactions to deaf and deafened people's speech (Davison 1979; Nicholl 1981; Cowie – Douglas-Cowie 1983: 192–196), stereotypes of deaf and deafened people (e.g. Bunting 1981), and general sociolinguistic work on reactions to speech (e.g. Giles – Powesland 1975; Scherer – Giles 1979). It contained 67 items (see section 3.6.1. for details of the items). They can be summarised under three main headings.

(i). Listeners' emotional reactions to deafened speakers. Questionnaire items in this category probed, for example, reactions of embarrassment, pity, frustration, sympathy, confusion.

(ii). Listeners' assessments of deafened speakers. Items in this category asked about speakers' competence, their personality and social relationships, their educational and occupational status, and their psychological and physical states (e.g. depressed, anxious, mentally deficient, stroke victim, spastic).

(iii). Listeners' assessments of their speech and language. Seven questionnaire items dealt with aspects of speech. They asked whether the speech seemed generally normal, and whether it suffered from any of the following defects: difficult to understand; bad (slurred) articulation; strange quality of sound; monotony; bad control of pitch; bad control of volume. These items were intended to capture the major problems which the literature suggests might occur in deafened speech, but to express them in a way that would make sense to listeners with no knowledge of phonetics.

Another five items related to speakers' ability to express themselves. They dealt with vocabulary, grammar, description, organisation of ideas, and imaginativeness. Differences on these dimensions would be expected to affect the speakers' ratings, and so it is important to take them into consideration: but it would be surprising if these abilities were systematically affected by post-lingual deafness.

There were five possible reponses to each item. Subjects chose the one they felt was most appropriate. We scored them by counting 5 for the most favourable of the responses, 4 for the next most favourable, and so on down to 1 for the least favourable. All of the analyses used scores averaged across listeners (i.e. each speaker was assigned one score per questionnaire item).

8.3 The study of the listeners' impression: results

For purposes of analysis speakers were divided again into hard of hearing and profoundly deafened, using the same 80 dB cut off as in the shadowing experiment.

The obvious question is whether the hearing impaired fare worse than normal speakers in these various respects. The general answer is that they do. The profoundly deafened have much more extensive problems than the hard of hearing, but both are different from controls. This is indicated by two-way analyses of variance which take account of all the questionnaire items. These show that overall the profoundly deafened group fared worse on the listeners' assessments than the hard of hearing ($F_{1,45} = 6.5$, $p = 0.014$) and that the hard of hearing fared worse than the controls ($F_{1,39} = 9.6$, $p = 0.004$). But each comparison between groups is associated with a significant interaction ($p < 0.0001$) between hearing and item, indicating that the effect of hearing impairment differs from item to item. The main task of analysis is to unpick these differences and provide a more specific picture of the adverse judgements that deafened people face because of their speech.

8.3.1. Speech items in the listeners' impression questionnaire

A natural first step is to consider the questions about speech as such. There were seven questions about speech. We carried out three t tests for each of these questions – one comparing the controls and the profoundly deafened group, one comparing the controls and the hard of hearing group, and one comparing the profoundly deafened group and the hard of hearing. Table 8.1 summarises the results. It should be noted that, although the table shows a large number of t tests, the situation is not one where logic of post-hoc tests applies. There is no risk of reading unwarranted conclusions into a single test that is significant by a statistically inevitable accident, and it would be worse, not better, to "allow" for the large number of comparisons by using Neumann Keuls or Scheffé type tests.

Table 8.1   Assessments of speech

The outcomes of t tests (one tailed) are represented as follows: *** means p<0.001; ** means 0.01>p >0.001; * means 0.05> p > 0.01.

item	mean scores (3 = neutral, 1 = definitely has defect)			t tests		
	C (controls)	H (hard of hearing)	P (profound)	P vs C	H vs C	P vs H
normal speech	2.9	2.4	1.9	***	**	**
hard to understand	2.9	2.1	1.6	***	***	**
slurred articulation	3.3	2.4	1.9	***	***	*
strange sound quality	3.1	2.5	2.2	***	***	*
monotonous	2.6	2.5	2.1	**	–	*
bad control of pitch	3.1	2.8	2.5	**	–	*
bad control of volume	3.1	2.9	3.0	–	–	–

There are two main points to be made about these findings.

The first is that our naive listeners were aware of abnormalities in the way our deafened subjects spoke. That is a useful supplement to the data from the shadowing experiment: it rules out any suggestion that the shadowing technique is oversensitive in the sense that it reveals abnormalities which are actually imperceptible to the ordinary listener. Similarly, it supplements the data of the last three chapters by indicating that the problems which they reveal are apparent without special instrumentation or listening skills.

The second main point is that different problems were differentially salient. This is relevant to an important issue, which is identifying the aspects of deafened people's speech which are practically significant. Particularly in conjunction with other data, some conclusions can be drawn in this area. However there are also issues which raise difficulties.

The specific deficit which listeners mark most strongly is intelligibility. Again, this complements indications from the shadowing technique that intelligibility is a real issue for deafened people. It shows that the shadowing technique is not magnifying differences which are subjectively insignificant. If anything it lacks sensitivity: the rather marginal difference in measured intelligibility between controls and hard of hearing corresponds to a difference in subjective judgement which is very clear indeed.

Deafened speakers' control of volume showed least abnormality – in fact it was essentially indistinguishable from that of the controls. This corroborates the point which was made in chapter 5 on acoustic analysis, that our recordings were not substantially affected by gross abnormalities of overall volume (see section 5.3.2.), and consequently our technique of normalising at data capture was reasonable. It is also broadly consistent with the perceptual study by Leder – Spitzer (1990: 171–172) where perceived abnormalities of intensity were smaller than abnormalities in any other respect that was considered. However it is contrary at least to a naive reading of the claim cited in chapter 2 that "The onset of deafness among adults does not usually interfere with the ability to speak except that some will tend to shout" (Espir – Rose 1976: 40). It is of course true that control of volume can be a problem, particularly when an adjustment is needed to a new or unusual level of background noise. The point which this evidence seems to put beyond reasonable doubt is that intensity can also cease to be a salient problem once the speaker has adjusted to a particular context.

On the other dimensions, our data agree with those of Leder – Spitzer (1990) that there are perceptually apparent abnormalities. However the two studies suggest opposite orders of severity. Intonation and pitch were clearly the most affected aspects of speech in Leder – Spitzer's ratings. In ours, the corresponding items were control of pitch and monotony: and they were less affected than anything but volume. Conversely Leder – Spitzer's judges rated articulatory abnormality a less salient problem than anything but intensity. In ours, the corresponding item was slurred articulation, and it was rated the most salient of the specific problems.

The most satisfactory response to this difference is to assume that the two studies are giving different and essentially complementary kinds of information. On articulation, our study shows that there is an abnormality which is perceptually salient and which naive listeners consistently label slurred articulation. Leder – Spitzer's study adds that clear-cut segmental errors (of the kind that their listeners had been engaged in transcribing before they made their ratings) are not the kernel of the problem: unfortunately it does not illuminate what the kernel is. Leder's study shows that there is abnormality in deafened people's intonation: ours indicates that it does not primarily consist of monotony, contrary to the widely cited assumption noted in chapter 2 (see sections 2.2.1. and 2.2.2.). Their study shows that pitch abnormalities are apparent to the trained ear: ours, that they are not salient to naive listeners.

This interpretation of the data is reasonable, but it is not certain. The problem of reconciling the studies highlights the limitations of direct ratings as indices of the significance of speech problems. It is the effect of speech on the man in the street which matters, since very little of the average deafened person's life is spent interacting with speech clinicians. However the man in the street has a limited ability to describe what affects him about speech. In sum, if one has ratings whose meaning is clear their social relevance is doubtful, and vice versa. This highlights the case for taking a more roundabout route to assessing the significance of speech problems, and that theme is taken up later in the chapter.

8.3.2. Factor analysis

Looking beyond the speech items to the questionnaire as a whole, the first priority is data reduction. Intuitively it seems most unlikely that the responses given by each subject to the 67 questionnaire items reflect as many independent types of reaction, each quite separate from the other reactions that the questionnaire probed and from any other reaction that it might have probed, but happened not to. It seems much more likely that the subjects' sixty-odd overt responses flowed from a smaller number of underlying types of reaction, each of which had some bearing on several of the overt responses which were studied, and would have one on various other responses that were not investigated.

Factor analysis offers a way of inferring underlying types of reaction which would explain the questionnaire data. The technique involves finding a relatively small number of dimensions which explain most of the differences between individuals (in this case, differences between the various speakers who were rated in the questionnaires). These dimensions are called factors. They are chosen so that each factor is reasonably closely related to a few of the original items, and factors are given an intuitive interpretation by looking at the items which are closely related to them. In the course of the analysis each speaker is assigned a score on each factor. The correlation between the speakers' scores on a given factor and their scores on a questionnaire item is called the loading of the item on the factor, and loading is the measure of how closely related an item and a factor are.

In this study, each factor should ideally correspond to one of the basic ways in which listeners react to speakers. High loadings can have two kinds of interpretation, depending on the items involved. If two items involve a judgement about the speaker, and both have a high loading on the same factor, this suggests that both ratings are strongly influenced by a single underlying type of reaction (which corresponds to the factor). But if an item concerned with speech loads highly on the same factor, the natural inference is that that feature of speech contributes to producing the reaction.

Factor analysis was carried out using Varimax extraction followed by an Orthotran oblique transformation. Ten questionnaire items were excluded in order to ensure sampling adequacy. The analysis yielded eleven factors, but four of these accounted (directly) for less than four per cent of the variance, and are best ignored.

The seven remaining factors are summarised in table 8.2. The items associated with a factor are those whose loading on it is greater than 0.45. This cut-off associates most items with one and only one factor. The factor summaries are based on these items and occasionally others with slightly lower loadings which appear to clarify matters.

The simplest use of this breakdown is as a guide to grouping items for analyses of variance. Three two-way analyses of variance were carried out on each set of items associated with a major factor. The controls were compared to each hearing-impaired group, and the two hearing-impaired groups to each other. Results showed that the profoundly deafened were rated significantly worse than the controls on every set of items, and significantly worse than the hard of hearing on every set of items but the one concerned with competence. The hard of hearing differed significantly from the controls on only two sets of items, those concerned with competence and those concerned with disability. Hearing by item interactions were examined in order to check whether the items associated with each factor behaved relatively consistently (in the sense that differences between groups of speakers were relatively constant across items). This is essentially a test of whether the groupings suggested by factor analysis represent a sensible way of partitioning the data. With one minor exception, the items in each grouping behaved reasonably cohesively.

Table 8.2   Factors extracted from analysis of the questionnaire

summary description of factor	characteristics attributed to high scorers:	
	speech & language	social & personal
competence	good vocabulary, grammar, description, & organisation of ideas	organised, intelligent, likely to reach high levels in education (4 items) and employment (4 items).
warmth	not monotonous	friendly, cheerful, cooperative, able to handle close friendships, not depressed.
social poise	–	self confident, amusing; not timid, withdrawn, or anxious.
stability	–	reliable, sensible, able to handle close friendships and working relationships.
disability	poor articulation, strange quality, hard to understand, not normal.	would evoke sympathy; might be deaf, mentally deficient, spastic, autistic, or a stroke victim.
subnormality	poor control of volume and pitch	might not have achieved normal primary education
social threat	–	listener anticipates that meeting speaker might cause embarrassment or shock , would be apprehensive about it.

The main effects establish a basic picture. For profoundly deafened people at least, speech constitutes a problem far beyond its actual intelligibility. It tends to create impressions of incompetence; lack of warmth and poise; instability; psychological disorder; illiteracy; and disability which may have a substantial cognitive component. For people who are already handicapped in their interaction, that is a thoroughly undesirable burden. For the less than profoundly deafened the picture is less extreme, but their speech still creates an adverse impression of their competence and suggests forms of disability which they do not actually have.

Regressions were used to check whether this changes when we take account of variables other than hearing status which are known to bear on speech. The analyses reported here use five such variables: socio-economic status; sex; age at time of testing; average pure-tone threshold in the better ear; and age at onset of deafness for the profoundly deafened (both other groups had scores of zero on this variable). These were chosen after exploratory work with a wider range of variables: none of the others contributed significantly to predicting any of the dependent variables which were considered. Two sets of regressions were carried out. In the first set, the dependent variables were the factor scores which (theoretically) give pure estimates of the underlying reactions associated with each factor. The second set used what will be called factor item scores. For any given factor, a speaker's factor item score was the average of his or her scores on the various items associated with that factor in table 8.2. Table 8.3 summarises the results.

Table 8.3 Regression analyses on factor scores and factor item scores. Each entry shows the probability that a variable's contribution to predicting a factor score is due to chance. A blank indicates that the probability is greater than 0.1.

	pure factor scores					factor item scores				
	status	age	sex	loss	onset	status	age	sex	loss	onset
competence	.0007	.003				.0004	.002		.002	
warmth			.09					.009	.06	
social poise									.01	
stability			.09					.003	.04	
disability				.0001	.01			.08	.0001	.02
subnormality									.01	
social threat						.04			.004	

The two sides of the table give essentially similar conclusions about variables other than hearing loss. Youth and high status favour impressions of competence; females are perceived as warmer and more stable, but are perhaps likelier to be judged disabled; and early age at onset is associated with a stronger impression of disability. However the effect of hearing loss fares very differently on the two sides of the table. The right-hand side reinforces the conclusion drawn from the analyses of variance: it suggests that level of loss affects virtually all the kinds of reaction we have identified even when the other variables are taken into account. The left suggests that only one kind of reaction, the impression of disability, is genuinely related to loss.

The logic of the contrast reflects the nature of factor analysis. Factors are constructed to be minimally intercorrelated. Hence if level of loss is strongly enough related to one set of factor scores, it cannot be related to other sets of factor scores. By contrast factor-item scores are (from a factor analytic standpoint) compound: they may be dominated by one factor, but others make a contribution too. From this standpoint what the right of the table shows is that the impression of disability tinges even judgements which are primarily linked to other issues, and the effect is strong enough to create differences between the groups. The main alternative is to conclude that the logical model underlying factor analysis is not precisely appropriate in this context – which is not to deny that it may be an extremely useful approximation.

It is theoretically interesting whether a single basic reaction does underlie all of the hearing-related differences in the data, and the question will be revisited later. However in practical terms the right-hand side of the table is the important one. Even allowing for other potentially relevant variables, the effects of hearing loss on speech mean that a variety of judgements are likely to be more adverse than normal.

Evidence on listeners' reactions makes it possible to revisit questions about speech by a different, and fundamentally sounder route. At root, questions about the significance of speech defects hinge on the way they affect listeners. Hence the best way to establish that a speech abnormality is practically significant is to establish that it leads to adverse reactions to, and evaluations of, the speaker. We now consider what appears to produce various types of adverse reaction.

One source of evidence is the factor analysis itself. It links some impressions of the speaker to items which involve speech and language. Table 8.2 highlights the point by separating out these items. The straightforward assumption is that the speech and language items which are associated with a factor produce the impressions and reactions which are listed alongside them.

This kind of link is worth considering, but it can be deceptive. Judgements about speech could be a result of judgements about the person just as easily as the other way round. A supplementary study carried out by Beagon (1989) showed that something of the sort does happen in the case of judgements about language. Straightforward interpretation of the factor analysis suggests that judgements of competence are based on differences in linguistic skill: and this is possible in principle, because listeners heard narratives in the speakers' own words as well as reading passages which were the same for everybody. Beagon examined the possibility. She wrote down the narrative passages for each speaker, and asked people to make judgements based on these written narratives (using a modified version of the original questionnaire). In that context, deafened speakers were rated just as well as controls on grammar, organisation of ideas, and so on. So it is not the case that deafened speakers score low on competence because their linguistic skills are poor: what happens is that their linguistic skills are rated low because listeners have a low impression of their competence. The low impression of competence must presumably come from aspects of speech, but the factor analysis does not suggest what they might be.

That kind of problem seems less likely to be severe in the cases where speech variables as such are associated with a factor. It makes sense to suppose that monotonous intonation suggests a lack of warmth; that poor control of volume and pitch suggests a major learning disability; and that abnormal voice quality and articulation lie behind the impression of disability. However the problem of interpretation exists in principle, and so the associations have to be treated sceptically unless they are reinforced by evidence from an alternative approach. Such an approach is taken up in the next section.

8.4. Form/function relations

This section examines relationships between speech and listeners' responses directly. We have taken measures of speech attributes, mainly from the acoustic study (see chapter 5) but also from the study of articulatory errors (chapter 7), and examined links between them and functional measures of speech – mainly measures based on questionnaire data, but also shadowing scores. Ideally measures based on the intonation study (chapter 6) would also have been used, but, because of the limited overlap between subjects, that would have restricted the sample which could be used unacceptably. The sample was already uncomfortably small because it was only possible to use people who had taken part in both the shadowing study and the acoustic analysis. There were twenty-four people in that category, 21 deafened and 3 controls. The great majority of the deafened were profoundly deafened: details of the deafened subjects in the sample are in chapter 3 (see table 3.1). The three controls are identified in table 3.3 by the fact that they are the only three to have taken part in both the acoustic and the intonation study (marked as participating in both studies A and I).

The basic statistical technique is stepwise regression. Each analysis takes an initial set of independent variables concerned with the form of speech, and progressively adds in those which improve its ability to predict a dependent variable. The dependent variables used were the factor scores, the scores on questions concerned with speech and language, and two measures of intelligibility – average intelligibility on the reading passages and average intelligibility in the cartoon narratives. Stepwise regression makes it viable to consider more potential independent variables than multiple regression could, but it is still necessary to restrict the number. From the acoustic work, we considered the fourteen main measures where the deafened and hearing speakers were significantly different (they are identified in the discussion below). When a number of measures were closely related, we selected the one which seemed to show the common pattern most clearly. The measures were derived from the reading passage. From the articulation study we derived two measures: the number of errors in producing the fricatives and affricates, which are the commonest single source of difficulty; and the number of different types of consonant error that each subject made.

Linking subjects' descriptions of speech to objective measures is not an essential, but it throws useful light on the interpretation of both the objective data and the subjects' descriptions. Table 8.4 summarises the significant predictors. The immediately striking finding is that all but two of their descriptions were linked to a single variable, the number of types of consonant errors that each subject made. Presumably this variable has such widespread relevance because articulation-related errors are salient enough to colour other judgements about speech. Two attributes are linked to lack of compound features in the F0 contour (i.e. passages where F0 continues unbroken through more than one inflection). The feature may be connected with articulation because it indicates that voicing was abnormally fragmented, and its link with monotony suggests that repetitive use of short units of speech is at least an element of this notorious but ill-specified problem. Most of the other connections are self-explanatory except for the association between monotony and absence of fricative errors, which is presumably a reminder that statistics must occasionally throw up meaningless accidents.

Table 8.4 Predictors of subjects' ratings of speech attributes

quality judged	attributes associated with negative judgement
normality	consonant errors
intelligibility	consonant errors
articulation	consonant errors, low spectral differentiation in the fricative band (level-relative), few compound features in the F0 contour
quality	consonant errors, protracted rises in the amplitude contour
control of pitch	consonant errors, level-relative change (peak-to peak) in the F0 band
monotony	few compound features in the F0 contour, absence of fricative errors
control of volume	excessive rises in the amplitude contour, high median F0 (relative to mean for same-sex controls)

While the focus is on speech, it is worth touching on relations between acoustic measures and the measures based on phonetically defined errors. Somewhat unexpectedly, spectral differentiation in the "fricative band" showed no reliable relationship with fricative errors. However there was a relationship between number of types of consonant errors and the measures which show abnormality in the upper spectrum – spectral differentiation in the fricative band and the F2 band; average energy in F2 band and the level-relative measure of change in it (maximum/average); and the midpoint of the average spectrum. A regression using these five variables falls just short of predicting the number of types of consonant errors significantly (F 5,18 = 2.58, p = 0.063). This relationship is illuminating on both sides. On one side it suggests that the anomalies connected with F2 have a connection with articulation rather than being a phenomenon of voice quality alone. On the other side it suggests that outright consonant errors are, so to speak, the tip of an iceberg – cases where imbalances which pervade the acoustic analysis become extreme enough to affect phonetic classification.

Descriptions of language are interesting because they appear to be affected by abnormalities of speech despite the considerable direct evidence that subjects had on speakers' linguistic abilities – evidence which, as Beagon (1989) confirmed, indicates that the deafened speakers and the controls are linguistically comparable. It is clear, and not surprising, that most of the relevant attributes involve intonation and articulation.

Most of the attributes which promote negative judgements are characteristics of deafened speech, as were all but the anomaly involving fricatives in table 8.4. However table 8.5 shows two attributes which break this pattern, and which are not so easy to write off. The deafened have a high number of "fall end" intonation features (i.e. fragments of F0 which form a fall or rise-fall pattern). That is the trend which is associated with positive judgements of vocabulary and organisation (perhaps because rises are a feature of working class speech in Belfast). The deafened also tend to have a wide F0 range, and that, understandably, is associated with imaginative language. These cases provide a reminder that departures from the norm need not be for the worse, and so it is worth checking whether abnormalities are detrimental before attempting to eliminate them.

Table 8.5   Predictors of subjects' judgements about speakers' language

quality judged	attributes associated with negative judgement
grammar	consonant errors
vocabulary	consonant errors, few compound features in the F0 contour, few 'fall end' features in the intonation contour
organisation	fricative errors, few compound features in the F0 contour, few 'fall end' features in the intonation contour, high median F0
description	few compound features in the F0 contour, protracted rises in the amplitude contour
imagination	narrow F0 range

Table 8.6 summarises regressions on the factor scores which were derived from the main body of the questionnaire. It is striking that the associations are generally reasonably meaningful. The impression of competence seems to be related to the underlying timing of speech. The sense of warmth is reduced by fragmentation of the intonation contour and simplification of spectral change. Another inverted relationship occurs here: articulation which lacks consonant errors seems to suggests a lack of warmth. "Poise" involves being self-confident, amusing, and not anxious or withdrawn. Its absence is signalled by a simplified pattern of change in amplitude (signalled by increased variance in its distribution) and narrowed F0. Lack of stability – being unreliable, not sensible, etc. – is associated with excessive change low in the spectrum, which is affected by fluctuation in both amplitude and pitch (the particular variable used was the level relative peak-to-peak measure). The impression of disability is associated with articulation errors, with both acoustic and phonetic analyses agreeing that the fricative region is particularly significant.

A final set of regressions was carried out on the intelligibility scores from the shadowing experiment, using the average intelligibility scores from the reading passages and the average from the narratives as dependent variables. Both were predicted by the same combination of variables. Shadowing errors increased with number of types of articulation error, and with average energy in the F2 band. High energy in that band is one of the most characteristic features of deafened speech. However shadowing errors were reduced when rises in the amplitude contour were large, and it is another striking characteristic of deafened speech that these rises tend to be high.

Table 8.6 Predictors of subjects' judgements about speakers' personalities

quality judged	attribute associated with negative judgement
competence	protracted rises in the amplitude contour
warmth	few compound features in the F0 contour, narrow spread of change across the spectrum (peak-to-peak measure), absence of consonant errors
poise	narrow F0 range, high variance of amplitude
stability	high change in the F0 band
disability	consonant errors, fricative errors, low spectral differentiation in the fricative band (level-relative)
subnormality	–
social threat	–

Two immediate points emerge from these regressions. The first is that almost all of the variables which mark clear abnormalities in the form of speech appear to be functionally relevant. Of the sixteen independent variables which were chosen, only three never appeared as a predictor: the midpoint of the average spectrum, and two level-relative measures associated with the F2 band – peak-to-peak change in the band and spectral differentiation in it. Even these are not so much irrelevant as superseded by a variable which gives a better measure of essentially the same thing – that is number of types of consonant error. This is confirmed by the fact that if we exclude the auditorily determined variables, the level-relative measures concerned with F2 take over one of their key roles, as predictors of the disability factor.

Data like these go a considerable way towards answering arguments of the kind used by Kaufman – Goehl (1985: 222), who conceded that articulation errors might occur but used frequency counts to argue that they could not be practically important. Whatever one's intuitive inclinations, it is basically an empirical matter whether a speech abnormality has appreciable consequences. The evidence presented here indicates that most of the major abnormalities in deafened people's speech do have appreciable consequences.

The second immediate point is that a complex mix of positive and negative effects may accompany deafened speakers' departures from normality. It has been noted that some trends in intonation are associated with positive judgements about language. It is also noticeable that large average rises in the amplitude contour are associated with enhanced intelligibility. One has to wonder whether these effects mark adjustments designed to optimise speech. If so, they have mixed success. Large average rises in the amplitude contour may promote intelligibility, but they are also associated with judgements of poor pitch control; and if (as seems likely enough) they are linked to rises of abnormally long duration, then they are indirectly associated with impressions of low competence. Similarly while wide pitch range may have benefits, excessive fluctuation in the F0 band is associated with impressions of instability. These balances underline a logical point which we have stressed elsewhere (Cowie – Douglas-Cowie 1983: 223–225): if control is fundamentally limited, adjusting to avoid one problem is quite likely to aggravate another.

An essentially academic, but interesting point concerns the suggestion from Table 8.3 that problems due to hearing loss may only affect a single underlying reaction, the impression of disability. That view is weakened by the evidence on form-function relations. The reason is that there appear to be distinct attributes of speech associated with distinct types of reaction, even if pure factor scores are used as a measure of those reactions. A number of interesting questions arise from this point, but since they cannot be answered from the available data they are probably best left unstated.

8.5. Conclusion

Two different kinds of qualification have to be attached to this chapter.

The first applies to all of it. The method of eliciting reactions is unquestionably artificial. It is reasonable to ask whether the reactions would carry over into a more realistic situation – so long as it is understood that the question is not a rhetorical one. The evidence suggests that they will carry over. As Giles – Sassoon (1983: 311) put it, "the effect of accent is exceedingly robust and knowing a Cockney speaker is middle class does not deliver him from the stereotyped discourtesy of low status ratings." There is a pointer in this chapter to parallel effects with deafened speech. Listeners had a good deal of evidence on the speakers' linguistic competence, and it indicated that deafened speakers and controls were comparable in that respect. Nevertheless the deafened were rated low on all aspects of linguistic ability, indicating that in this context too, global impressions based on speech can over-ride more directly relevant evidence.

This is not an issue that should be left in doubt, and so it is taken up specifically in the next chapter. But if that loophole can be closed, then the chapter makes a strong case for accepting that deafened people are disadvantaged by their speech, in a variety of ways.

The second kind of qualification applies to the form-function study. Regressions are unstable unless the numbers of subjects is an order of magnitude larger than the number of variables involved. As a result the form-function study is, simply, too small to be at all conclusive. The issue which it addresses is an important one, and it is important to insist that evidence, not intuition, is the proper bar at which to present questions about the significance of particular speech abnormalities. The relationships which it derives provide good starting hypotheses for further research, and until that research is done they are the best available guide to the facts that we have. However there is no doubt that further research with much larger samples is needed to derive conclusions which can be safely relied on. It is currently under way.

Chapter 9
Speech impairments due to hearing loss: their effect on person perception in information-rich contexts

9.1. Introduction

It is well known that the way people speak can affect the way others react to them and assess them (e.g. Knapp 1978: 330–353; Giles 1979; Scherer 1986). Chapter 8 provides a preliminary indication that this may give rise to problems for deafened speakers. However showing that such problems occur in real life raises difficult design problems. This paper reports attempts to confront those problems in the context of speech affected by deafness.

It is a standard design principle that to study the effect of one variable, others should be held constant. In the context of speech defects, that is most easily approximated by having speakers read a set passage and presenting listeners with a recording of the passage. Such techniques have demonstrated that listeners evaluate normal hearing controls more positively than prelingually deaf children (Blood – Blood – Danhauer 1974; Davison 1979), or adults with acquired deafness (see previous chapter).

But although these results suggest that the speech defects associated with hearing loss are a social handicap, they do not prove it. The reason reflects an important logical point. If one wants to understand the effect of a particular variable, then holding others constant is a necessary principle of design, but not a sufficient one.

The problem hinges on the way cues combine. It is natural to assume that combination is at least roughly additive: if a person's speech creates a negative impression when people have no other information to go on, then it will always make people's assessment of him or her slightly more negative than it otherwise would be. But a moment's reflection shows that other possibilities exist. Many of the responses people make to a disembodied voice either are, or depend on, attempts to explain its perceived peculiarity. These explanations may be completely superseded when additional information becomes available. For instance, people listening to deafened speakers on tape tend to agree that they may be spastic. But this explanation is ruled out when they meet face to face. Here information from voice and from other cues do not combine in a simple arithmetical way: instead they combine according to logic. The main problem with studies of disembodied voices is that we do not know how much of the interaction between voice and other cues follows a logical pattern rather than an additive one.

Experiments are needed to resolve this issue, but it is not easy to design appropriate experiments. The main difficulty is that we cannot easily dissociate the speech defects associated with deafness from other characteristics which are relevant to impression formation. The ideal experiment would compare two situations involving the same deafened person, in one of which he spoke normally; and in the other, with the defects which are characteristic of hearing impaired people. This is impossible because hearing impaired people cannot adopt unimpaired speech at will. A hearing actor could attempt to mimic deafened speech, but it is doubtful whether this could be done with acceptable accuracy. Nor is speech the only stumbling block. There are other behaviours which tend to be associated with hearing loss and which seem likely to affect the way listeners will explain an observed speech abnormality. The most obvious is difficulty registering speech. Hearing loss can be simulated (van der Lieth 1972; Erber 1987), but it is doubtful how close the simulation is. We also know that permanent hearing loss tends to change communicative behaviour in various ways – some adaptive, involving "hearing tactics" (see e.g. McCall 1984; Rice 1988), some apparently not (see chapter 10). Research also shows that deafness tends to create psychological disturbances (see chapter 1), and these are likely to have perceptible consequences. In sum, many factors are likely to affect the way listeners explain a hearing-impaired person's speech abnormalities: and we cannot expect to create situations which are realistic in all of these respects, but in which the speaker's voice is normal.

It is nevertheless possible to gain clues about the interactions between voice and other cues from studies which introduce those cues in a partial, but controlled way. The studies which are reported here (Experiments 1 and 2) introduce key cues in two different ways.

In the first, listeners are "interviewed" either by a deafened speaker or by a matched hearing speaker. The interviewer's questions appear to follow on from the subject's comments, but in fact they do not: they simply follow a preset script. The experiment makes it possible to examine listeners' reaction to a deafened and a hearing speaker in a case where the listeners have a virtually normal range of visual information about speakers, and the content of speech is held constant. However this content is artificial, and the results of defective hearing hardly come into play. The experiment also allows another comparison to be drawn. The same deafened speaker who acts as interviewer in the experiment reported here, also participated in the shadowing experiment, where listeners heard only his voice. It is therefore possible to make a comparison between reactions to his disembodied voice and reactions to him in a face to face encounter – albeit a contrived one.

In the second experiment, listeners watch video tapes of either deaf or hearing adolescents talking. The content of what they say may be conveyed in three ways: by speech alone; by subtitles alone; or by speech and subtitles. Here again listeners have visual cues, albeit more limited than before; but now the speech has genuinely informative content. Each speaker gives a monologue describing in her own words how she spent her holiday. The monologues are highly revealing, both in their phrasing and in their substance. Subtitling is an imperfect, but useful substitute for conveying this content in a neutral voice. Once again, potential effects of defective hearing are controlled by avoiding them.

Both studies used a questionnaire to measure listeners' reactions to the speakers. In each case it was closely related to the questionnaire that was used in the shadowing experiment (see chapter 3, section 3.6.1) with modifications to suit the manifestly different context.

9.2. Experiment 1 – The interview experiment

9.2.1. Method

Subjects. Two senior social workers served as interviewers. Both had experience and training in interviewing. One had normal hearing, the other a profound loss originating in adolescence. They will be referred to as D (for deafened) and H (for hearing) respectively. Details of Mr. D can be found in Chapter 3. He is subject no. 17 in table 3.1 in chapter 3. Interviewees were twenty two first year students at Queen's University. Half were interviewed by Mr. H, and half by Mr. D. They knew nothing about the aim of the study: anyone who appeared to have any inkling of it was rejected.

Apparatus. Interviews were held in a TV studio and interviewees were videotaped during the interaction. After it they filled out a questionnaire based closely on the listeners'-impression questionnaire used in the shadowing experiment (see chapter 3, section 3.6.1. for details of the questionnaire). Full details are given in McDaid (1987: 46–48). It consisted of 14 blocks of questions. There were five or six thematically related items in each block. The first three blocks dealt with the interview as such, and were different from the shadowing questionnaire. The remaining 11 were concerned with impressions of and reactions to the interviewer, and were the same as the items in the listeners' impression questionnaire.

Procedure. Interviewees were asked to participate in an interview. They were met and led into the studio by an experimenter. At this stage they were told that the experimenters were interested in how people react to different types of interview, and so the interview would be filmed and the interviewees would be asked about their impressions afterwards.

The interviewers followed a set script which was designed to give the impression that questions followed on from the interviewee's answers, though in fact they were predetermined. A written version of the script was among papers on the table between the participants which the interviewer consulted at intervals. Only minimal departures from the script were made.

After the interview the experimenter re-entered and led the interviewee to a separate room where he or she filled in the questionnaire. After this, it was explained that the aim of the experiment had been to compare reactions to deafened and hearing interviewers.

9.2.2. Results

Responses were coded numerically, using 1 for the most negative response to the interviewer and 5 for the most positive. They were subjected to analyses of variance, each dealing with a single block of thematically related items.

Two sets of comparisons were made. First, reactions to the deafened interviewer were compared with reactions to the same speaker's voice after the shadowing experiment. Second, reactions to the hearing and deafened interviewers were compared.

Table 9.1 summarises results from the first comparison (I stands for "the interviewer").

One overall trend is clear: Mr. D's presence consistently produced a better impression than his disembodied voice.

The significant effects involving item mean that there is structure in the data at a finer level than the overall blocks. The interactions are particularly important because they indicate that the change from disembodied voice to live encounter does not simply improve ratings: rather it changes the profile of ratings. The fact that such changes occur makes it necessary to ask whether there is any real relationship between ratings in the live and taped situations, a question which will be addressed below using correlational techniques. The interaction involving voice, though, can be considered immediately. Figure 9.1 summarises the data from the relevant block (block 12).

Table 9.1 Comparisons between ratings of Mr. D on tape and in an interview. Non-significant effects are shown by a "–" sign, significant effects (p < 0.05) either by a "+" sign or by specifying the direction of the effect.

block	main effects		interaction
	live vs. taped	item	
4. expected reactions in a future meeting with I	live > tape	+	–
5. I's sociability	live > tape	+	–
6. I's competence and energy	live > tape	–	–
7. I's educational level	live > tape	+	+
8. I's employment level	live > tape	+	–
9. I's social competence	–	–	+
10. expected feelings in a future meeting with I	live > tape	–	+
11. I's language skills	live > tape	–	+
12. I's speech	live > tape	+	+
13. affective disorders	live > tape	–	–
14. cognitive disorders	live > tape	+	–

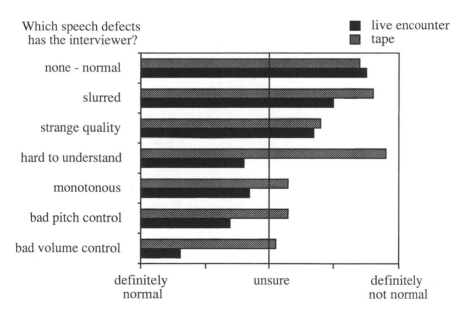

Figure 9.1 Ratings of Mr. D's speech *per se*.

Of the four most negative ratings in the taped experiment, three changed very little. Mr. D's presence may have made a favourable overall impression, but it did not prevent listeners from finding his voice strange in quality, slurred, and generally not normal. On the other hand, the sense that it was hard to understand, which was strong in the taped condition, did recede. The remaining features were not badly rated in the taped condition, and their ratings became quite positive in the live encounter. These are often presented as the main abnormalities in deafened speech. The previous chapter argued from the evidence of taped studies that this is inappropriate. The point can now be reinforced by evidence from face to face interaction, where naive listeners appear to be even less aware of monotony, bad pitch control, and bad volume control.

The comparison between speakers is summarised in table 9.2. The immediately striking point is that Mr. D was rated higher than Mr. H in the first three blocks. The natural inference is that he was being rated a better interviewer. Observing the sessions suggests that this was a reasonable judgement. Mr. H in fact commented on his own nervousness. However this was not translated into an overall advantage in the remaining blocks which deal with the person rather than the interview as such. Mr. D fared better overall in seven of these eleven remaining blocks, but neither in the individual blocks nor overall was there a significant speaker advantage.

Two blocks in particular are worth closer attention.

Block 12, which deals with speech, is clearly one. The interaction reflects the fact that Mr. D was rated significantly more negatively than Mr. H on sound quality, slurring, and overall normality. He was also rated significantly harder to understand. This underlines the fact that his speech was perceived as abnormal even in this context. It is also interesting that he was rated more positively than Mr. H as regards monotony and the control of pitch and volume. The effects were not significant, but their direction emphasises the point that these are not abnormalities which strike naive listeners in deafened people's speech.

The second block which deserves closer attention is the block dealing with cognitive problems. It is important here that Mr. D was not recognised as deaf. Only three of the eleven listeners were unsure or considered that he might be deaf, exactly the same as the number who gave those responses to Mr. H. It is also revealing that eight of the eleven were unsure or considered that Mr. D might have had a stroke, whereas only two came into that category with Mr. H. If the data are recoded in the terms which have just been used, distinguishing between those who are unsure or think a handicap likely and those

Table 9.2   Comparisons between the deafened and the hearing speaker in the interview. Non-significant effects are shown by a "–" sign, significant effects (p < 0.05) either by a "+" sign or by specifying the direction of the effect.

block	main effects		interaction
	deaf vs hearing	item	
1. aptness of questions	D > H	–	–
2. quality of replies	D > H	–	–
3. feelings after interview	D > H	–	–
4. expected reactions in a future meeting with I	–	+	+
5. I's sociability	–	+	–
6. I's competence and energy	–	+	+
7. I's educational level	–	+	–
8. I's employment level	–	+	+
9. I's social competence	–	+	+
10. expected feelings in a future meeting with I	–	+	–
11. I's language skills	–	+	–
12. I's speech	–	+	+
13. affective disorders	–	+	+
14. cognitive disorders	–	+	–

who think it unlikely, then the difference over the stroke item is highly significant. Whatever the statistical niceties of this situation, it seems a fair judgement that interviewees felt something could well be wrong with Mr. D, with a stroke the most obvious possibility and deafness a remote one.

Most of the other interactions involved exceptions to a general pattern of higher ratings for Mr. D. They suggest an undramatic but recurring sense of instability. Mr. D was rated higher overall in block 13, but less likely to have no particular problem. Mr. H was (quite accurately) rated significantly more anxious in the same block. Mr. D was rated less sensible and organised (block 6) and less likely to manage long-term relationships well (block 9). Subjects were more positive about meeting him in most respects, but would be more likely to keep a meeting with him brief (block 4). It is interesting to speculate on what gives rise to this unease, but there is clearly no firm evidence.

Another way of looking at the structure which these interactions reveal bears on a question which was raised in connection with the speech items: how strong is the relationship between the ratings which Mr. D receives in the two types of presentation, live and on tape? This is important because if the relationship were weak, then it would seem unlikely that Mr. D's voice, in and of itself, contributed very much to the way he was assessed in a live encounter.

The question cannot be answered definitively, but some light can be cast on it by considering the data from both comparisons – taped versus live and hearing versus deafened. Two correlations provide the key evidence. Each measures how much consistency the profile of ratings retains through a major change – in one case the change from tape to live encounter, in the other the change from one speaker to the other.

Consider first the correlation between the ratings of subjects who heard Mr. D on tape and the ratings of those he interviewed. This will be called the cross-medium correlation. It is modest ($r = 0.4$) but highly significant ($p < 0.005$). It is apparent graphically that some points are outliers, and four of these are suspect because of floor effects or ambiguity. Removing these increases the correlation to $r = 0.52$.

The second correlation to be considered is between the two speakers' ratings in the interview (again excluding the suspect items). This will be called the cross-speaker correlation. It is very similar in magnitude to the previous one, with $r = 0.51$.

Each of these correlations will reflect two obvious sources of consistency. Both will reflect trends linked to the way items would be answered whoever was being rated (for instance, almost any speaker would be rated more likely to have achieved primary than university level education). But each can also be taken to involve another factor. It may be assumed that the cross-speaker correlation is raised by the fact that both of the speakers used the same words in the interview. But that source of consistency does not contribute to the cross-medium correlation, since the live and taped conditions involved quite different words. The second contributor to consistency across those conditions was the fact that the same speaker, Mr. D, was involved.

The similarity between the correlations therefore suggests an interesting summary: using the same voice (as in the cross-media case) appears to have influenced reactions about as much as using the same words (as the speakers in the cross-speaker correlation did).

9.2.3. Discussion

This experiment makes two main kinds of point.

The first is that deafened people's speech production can be a more salient marker of their handicap than their speech perception. Listeners quite clearly did notice abnormalities in Mr. D's speech, but they did not notice clues which suggested that he might be deaf. The speech abnormality was not only detectable, but presumably regarded as a possible sign of underlying problems.

The second kind of point concerns the social effect of the perceived speech abnormality. Here it is important to stress that the experiment marks a "best case" estimate of interaction for deafened people. The experiment successfully avoided exposing Mr. D's poor speech reception. It allowed him to exercise a skill which he possessed to a high degree, and it compared him with someone who (on the day at least) was a less skilled interviewer. It is also true that Mr. D was highly motivated to create a good impression, whereas Mr. H had no great stake in the exercise. The result of providing these advantages was an assessment of Mr. D personally which was on a par with Mr. H's. There are also hints that interviewees found Mr. D disturbing in some ways.

It would be wrong to suggest that this is a very negative picture, but it is not wholly positive either. Essentially it suggests that deafened people need their best efforts to create an average impression even before their hearing tells against them. Failing any other obvious source of negative impressions, speech seems the likeliest reason why Mr. D did not achieve an outright advantage, and the fact that there is a substantial cross-medium correlation is a positive indication that reactions were influenced by his speech.

9.3. Experiment 2 – Subtitling experiment

In experiment 1, speech content provided no valid cues to the interviewer's personality. Experiment 2 was designed to provide content which did offer cues. Visual information was also provided, though on a video tape rather than in person. This allowed us to study whether cues from speech would affect impression formation in the presence of these apparently more valid and informative indicators.

It has to be emphasised that this study is only partly comparable with others we have reported. The speakers were different from those whom we have considered elsewhere. We were not given access to full audiological information, but their hearing losses appear to have been moderate to severe, and they originated early enough to affect speech acquisition (see chapter 3, section 3.3.3.). The questionnaire was also only partly comparable with the ones considered previously – in fact it was the prototype for the one used in the shadowing study (see chapter 3, section 3.6.1.). Nevertheless the results are worth including because they make points which are highly relevant to the general issue of speech in acquired deafness.

9.3.1. Method

Apparatus. Video recordings were made of four schoolgirls, each narrating a monologue about her holidays. They were all 13–14 years old. Two had normal hearing and two were partially hearing (see section 3.3.3. for details of deafened subjects). They had prepared the stories beforehand, but for the recording they told them unscripted. After recording, three versions of each tape were made:

(i) Text only (TO). Here the text was presented in subtitles beneath the speaker, but the sound track was silent.

(ii) Sound only (SO). Here there were no subtitles, but the sound track was presented.

(iii) Sound and text (ST). Here both subtitles and sound were presented.

A questionnaire was used to assess reactions to the speakers. It was similar to the one used after the shadowing experiment but slightly shorter. It consisted of nine blocks, each containing an average of six items on a related theme. Subjects responded by circling one of five responses.

Design. There were two between-subjects variables. The speakers were divided arbitrarily into two pairs, with one partially hearing and one normal hearing speaker in each. Each pair was rated by three equal groups of subjects, one for each form of presentation (TO, SO, and TS). Each subject filled out two questionnaires, one for a partially hearing and one for a hearing speaker. It is known that presentation order can make a substantial difference to ratings in this kind of experiment (Davison 1979: 96–97), so it was kept constant: the normal hearing speaker was always presented and rated first.

Subjects. Subjects were 102 students who carried out the experiment during first year psychology laboratory classes.

Procedure. Subjects were tested in groups. Each group was told that the experiment was about people's ability to evaluate speakers from what they say, and two questionaires were given to each subject. The first recording was then presented on a large video screen, and when it was finished subjects completed the first questionnaire. The procedure was then repeated for the second recording.

9.3.2. Results

As before, responses were scored on a 1–5 scale, with 1 representing the most negative response and 5 the most positive.

To obtain an overall picture, analysis of variance was applied to a summary consisting of 27 scores per speaker. Each score was the average of responses to a particular block of questions for a particular speaker in a particular mode of presentation. (In fact each corresponds to one of the points in figure 9.2 below.) There was a significant interaction between hearing and mode of presentation (F 2,4 = 12.9, p = 0.018). Analysis of simple effects shows that this occurred because mode of presentation has no effect on ratings for the controls (F 2, 4 = 0.91, p = 0.47) and a strong effect on the deaf speakers (F 2, 4 = 29.1, p = 0.004). The effect took the form of markedly higher ratings in the TO condition, where their speech was not heard, than in either of the others. This confirms the general point that their speech did have a significant negative effect on their reception despite the favourably received content of what they said.

For closer inspection nine analyses of variance were carried out, each dealing with one block of items. At this level three types of effect emerged consistently. There was a significant effect of item in all nine analyses and a significant interaction between hearing and item in seven. Neither is particularly informative. Most of the hearing-by-item interactions were due to high points in a general pattern of moderate advantage for the normal hearing speakers.

The striking finding rests on interactions between hearing, presentation, and pair, which were significant in seven analyses (counting a marginal one where F 2, 96 = 2.82, p = 0.064). Figure 9. 2 shows the relevant means. Each line represents responses to a single speaker. The partially-hearing speakers are marked with dashed lines and squares, the controls with solid lines and diamonds. The leftmost point shows ratings in the text only condition, the central one is the sound only condition, and the rightmost point is the text and sound condition. The non-significant interactions are in panels (g) and (h), and the marginal one is in (e).

The pattern associated with these interactions can be summarised on two levels. The broader summary is to say that the two deaf girls differ from each other and from the hearing girls in the way mode of presentation affects them. This can be formalised in terms of correlations. Subtraction yields scores which indicate how answers to a particular question are changed by replacing sound with subtitles (SO – TO) or by adding subtitles (SO – TS). This gives an array of 18 scores per speaker. Table 9.3 shows the correlations among these arrays. It shows that there is a good deal of consistency in the way mode

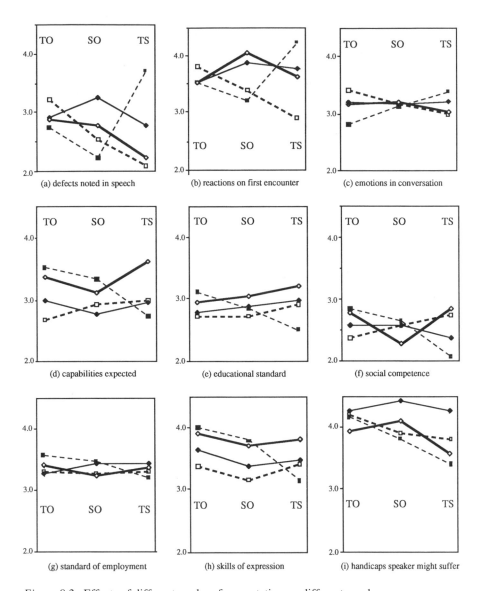

Figure 9.2 Effects of different modes of presentation on different speakers

of presentation affects responses to the controls. However there is very little relationship between the modes of presentation which be efit deaf speaker 1 and those which benefit the controls, and deaf speaker 2 tends o suffer in presentations which benefit the controls and vice versa.

Table 9.3   Correlations among scores which indicate how subtitling affected responses
to different speakers.

	control 2	deaf 1	deaf 2
control 1	.55	.04	−.52
control 2		.24	−.55
deaf 1			-.43

Closer inspection suggests that the curious mirror image relationships indicated in table 9.3 are linked to highly non-additive relationships between the
content of speech and its form. Consider panel (a). In the text-only condition,
shown by the left-hand column of points, one of the partially hearing was
rated the best of the speakers – indicating that the content of her monologue
created a very favourable impression. Her rating was considerably worse in
the speech-only condition, and worst of all the speakers in the case where
speech was added to the text. That kind of pattern is repeated in every panel
but the last. The monologue given by one partially hearing girl seems to have
created favourable emotional responses, and she was rated best in the text only
condition in three questions (panels a–c). The other partially-hearing girl's
monologue apparently created impressions of competence, and in the text-
only condition she was rated best in five questions (panels d–h). But in both
cases, the addition of voice converted this advantage into a deficit: the speaker
with the highest rating in the text only condition had the lowest in the text-
plus-subtitles condition. The pattern is still present in two of the blocks where
the interaction is not significant. The lack of a significant effect in panel (h),
where the pattern appears qualitatively strong, reflects the fact that ratings of
subjects' grammar are almost unaffected by adding voice: that is sufficient to
prevent the trend which occurs with the other 'language' items reaching significance.

It therefore appears that when content which evokes positive responses is
combined with abnormal speech, the result is far from additive. Instead the
speech abnormality may negate the effect of content, so that what would have
produced a strongly favourable response evokes a strongly negative one. Possible explanations are considered in the discussion. A weaker, but interesting
converse is worth mentioning. The shift from text-only to speech-only presentation improved a deaf speaker's ratings in just four instances (panels c–f).
In each case the deaf speaker in question received the lowest rating of the four

speakers in the text-only condition – as if poor voice increased acceptance of content which would otherwise be somewhat offputting.

There were numerous other significant effects, but the great majority were interactions involving "item" which were neither easy to interpret nor particularly revealing theoretically. Details are available in Brankin (1985: 17–28). However ratings of speech as such deserve special mention, particularly the ratings of speech given in the speech-only condition. Four items closely paralleled items used in the previous study. These speakers were rated higher than Mr. D in the questions on intelligibility and slurring; slightly lower in the question on control of volume; and in ratings of monotony, one was considerably higher than Mr. D and the other considerably lower. Not too much should be made of the comparison between these ratings, given that they were obtained under quite different circumstances. However it seems fair to offer them as evidence that the order of abnormality involved here is not radically unlike the order found in speakers who have more profound losses than these speakers, but acquire them later.

9.3.3. Discussion

On a coarse level, this study shows that partially-hearing speakers were rated worse when an informative monologue was presented in their own speech rather than visually – in contrast to normal-hearing speakers. The finer detail carries a hint of the mechanism involved.

The clearest possibility is that listeners may be disturbed by perceived mismatches between speech and message. This would mean that instead of offsetting the effects of an abnormal voice, words which would be well received in themselves may have created a worse impression than words which fitted the voice in which they were spoken. Conversely abnormal speech may offer an explanation of content which would not in itself be well received, and incline people to accept it more readily.

This is a post-hoc interpretation of distinctly curious situations (particularly those where text and speech were presented together). It needs both to be tested directly, and to be explored in less artificial ways – if that is possible. But it provides a relatively natural explanation of complex data, and makes a degree of intuitive sense.

9.4. General discussion

Experiment One suggests a conclusion which has some positive aspects. It suggests that a deafened person can nullify the effects of poor speech by the various non verbal cues that he can present in a real interaction. However Mr. D's greater interviewing skills produced only parity of general ratings with Mr. H, and there appears to have been a thread of unease running through reactions to him. It also seems clear that abnormal speech can signal to listeners that a person suffers some kind of handicap when his or her problem with hearing is not apparent.

Experiment Two suggests a markedly more negative picture. Voice was capable of negating good impressions which were made by the content of speech alone. The data suggest that listeners may have been disturbed by mismatches between voice and message. If so, the implication is that the problem cannot be overcome by improving the content of speech: in fact, that may aggravate the problem rather than alleviating it.

The natural inference is that if hearing-impaired people cannot improve their speech, their key to acceptability lies in good self-presentation by nonverbal and related means. This is disturbing, because research described in the next chapter suggests that deafened people's non-verbal self presentation itself tends to be abnormal.

Overall, the results of these studies give no grounds for discounting the problems suggested by research with taped voices. It appears that voice continues to affect reactions in the presence of other information. But it seems very probable that the combination of voice and other cues is, as initially suggested, not additive. It remains to be seen what arises from the combination of abnormal voice and the behaviours noted in the previous paragraph. But it seems very possible that it contributes significantly to deafened people's problems.

Chapter 10
Acquired deafness and interaction

10.1. Introduction

Chapter 1 emphasised the point that acquired deafness has a broad impact. The underlying malfunction of hearing has a multitude of non-obvious consequences. They are non-obvious in the sense that it is easy not to anticipate them, though most of them are understandable once they are recognised. Impaired speech is one consequence which has been considered. This chapter broadens the perspective to consider some of the consequences which arise as people try to function with severely limited speech communication. These consequences reflect two main themes which are familiar, but all too easy to overlook. First, communication is not an emotionally neutral act of data transmission. It has profound links to the way people see themselves, both as individuals and in relation to others. Second, communication involves at least two parties, and usually a sequence of contributions which interlock in a complex way.

The chapter draws mainly on material from informal sources. These include observations of the tape-recorded conversations with deafened subjects that accompanied the psychosocial questionnaire study, and our own observations over a decade of communication with deafened people. The chapter also draws on a pilot study on the interactive communicative skills of three deafened subjects with hearing people.

The chapter falls into three main parts. The first considers the modes of speech reception that deafened people use and the problems associated with them. The second studies how impaired reception tends to affect the active inputs that deafened people make to interactions, in terms for instance of turn-taking and non verbal behaviour. The third section broadens the perspective again to consider the wider impact of the communicative problems that have been outlined.

10.2. Modes of speech reception

Deafened people can use a wide range of techniques to comprehend what others say to them. These include lipreading, sign language, fingerspelling, pen and paper and use of a third party. This section reviews them briefly, noting the characteristic problems associated with them. Hearing aids are also mentioned briefly for completeness. The comments come from the tape recorded conversations.

10.2.1. Sign language and fingerspelling

In some respects learning a manual language looks like the ideal response to acquired deafness. However the majority of the psychosocial questionnaire subjects (80%) report that they do not use sign language or fingerspelling, and many of them show considerable antipathy to the idea. One subject, for example, states: "I don't agree with sign language ... I prefer lipreading ..."

The reason is partly practical. Some subjects point out that signing would be no use to them in the normal hearing world because no one would understand them:

> I don't know anyone who has sign language. It wouldn't be any benefit to me ... it's limited, because lipreading you need all the time. You can't go on a bus with sign language because you go to pay your fare, the driver will not say it's so many fingers. He'll say to you its 40 or 45. You have to get that, you have to be able to read that man's lips.

The other practical reason given is that signing or fingerspelling are difficult to learn. One lady says: "It's impossible for me ... I couldn't concentrate on her lips and concentrate on her fingers".

However there also seems to be an antipathy which is tied up with the desire to remain part of the normal hearing world and not to become associated with the prelingual deaf community. The deafened frequently comment that signing is part of the prelingual deaf world, that they have nothing in common with the prelingual world, that unlike the prelingual deaf, they grew up in a normal hearing world and want to remain part of it. Some make it clear that signing is too closely related to the prelingual deaf for comfort and are fearful about the consequences. One subject says: "I think I would lose my voice if I was with deaf people. That's why I won't learn sign language".

A related point is that signing is a visible sign of being deaf and not everyone likes admitting to it. This is suggested by the following statement, made by someone who does sign:

> Most people who become deaf prefer lipreading and carrying on as normal except that they have a hearing loss ... I think they are making it hard for themselves ... I think we should encourage them to face up to the fact that they are deaf. If lipreading isn't the ideal answer, then I recommend sign. Not everyone is enthusiastic about it because its official ... you can see it.

An interesting counter-example comes from one man deafened in adulthood who describes the use of fingerspelling to communicate with his child: "My little girl of eight and I learnt it in half an hour ... very very shaky, but we communicate with each other when other people get stuck". It is intriguing that this exception to the rule involves communication with children, not adults. There is perhaps a suggestion here that signing is acceptable for children, but not for the real world of adults. Our experience also suggests that few adult family members are as receptive to learning manual methods of communication.

The general point here is that manual communication is surrounded by a multitude of difficulties. The deepest problem is probably the sense that signing is a marker of an alien world and not part of the hearing world in which the deafened feel they belong. This reflects a curiously black and white view, as if there are two options – either do or do not use manual language. It is striking that so few of those deafened in adulthood contemplate a half-way steps. Perhaps this reflects an underlying fear that any step towards signing increases the risk of being syphoned off from the normal hearing world.

10.2.2. Lipreading

Lipreading is a vital line of communication for most of our informants. Many are intensely aware how much it means to them. As one lady puts it: "If I hadn't been able to lipread, no one would have been able to communicate with me". Another subject states that lipreading "helped me over the depression, being able to communicate with people." However, lipreading is an extremely limited mode of communication. Chapters 11 and 12 consider some of the theoretical background. This section aims to convey a more intuitive sense of the problems that our informants raise in connection with lipreading.

Lipreading is a major topic in the conversation tapes. People point to several areas of difficulty. Some are too well known to need discussion. Informants stress their dependence on various environmental and social conditions. The lighting in the room must be good, the interactants need to be relatively close to each other, the person whose lips are being read should have no obstacles in or around the mouth such as cigarettes or food or a beard, it is difficult to cope with more than a a one to one interaction between deafened person and hearing person. Informants also stress that lipreading is a strain. As one subject says: "It's a great strain on the eyes because you have to watch people's mouths ... it makes you feel tensed up when you're concentrating on someone you're finding difficult to follow ... its a round of concentration all the way". This issue of strain is related to topics which are taken up in chapters 11 and 12.

Three topics which are less widely discussed are also raised:

(1). Learning to lipread. Thirty-two deafened subjects reported attending lipreading classes, but only nine mentioned receiving benefit from the class. This is consistent with the general finding that training has a very limited effect on lipreading (see chapter 11). However it has less obvious side effects. Several of those who received little or no benefit from the classes considered it a failing on their part, and that reinforced their general depressed state.

The classes are also discussed as a social experience rather than a means of instruction. Some comments are highly positive. One subject says the classes provided: "The opportunity not just to communicate via the medium of lipreading but also to meet people who had exactly the same problem ... It became a major social event apart from an educational one which was fantastic". However the social experience can also be negative. One subject who was deafened in his thirties says: "I went ... all these elderly people came in and I said to myself, this is the wrong place and they sat down and I said is this the lipreading class and she said yes we're all hard of hearing ... its too old for me ... and I didn't go back". This reinforces a point made in the context of signing: the communicative adjustments that deafened people face are intimately bound up with matters of social identity.

(2). The manner of speech. Speech is a multichannel medium. It not only carries a surface message, but also conveys a variety of other information – e.g. the attitude of the speaker, the speaker's social standing, whether what is being said is a mere aside or a matter of importance. While some of this information can be conveyed by appearances and expressions and gestures, much is conveyed through subtleties of voice. Deafened people's comments suggest that in lipreading, such information is largely lost. This is perhaps most obvious in the way they talk about trying to read the expressions on people's faces to get the meaning. In the absence of tone of voice they appear to rely heavily on expression but often find it missing. One subject says: "They [i.e. the hearing] are trying to communicate it back and their faces are dead. They have the same expression all the time and there's no fluency in their actions".

(3). The impact of lipreading on hearing people. There are frequent comments in the conversation tapes that the hearing do not make it easy enough for the deafened to lipread them. One man observes that people are "inhibited" or "they think you're rude when you're really trying to lipread them." Others report that the lipreader often needs words repeated, but that the hearing resent this. As one subject says: "You get tired of asking people to repeat themselves … they get annoyed when you keep asking them". Another says: "When my husband had been talking to me, I would have had to ask him what he said, he lost his temper and he would say, 'Never bother'".

These comments focus on the way lipreading limits deafened people. However they imply another side of the coin: lipreading limits the normal-hearing interactant. A few comments in the tape recorded conversations acknowledge this explicitly. One person notes: "I would imagine that it takes a bit of effort on their part to repeat things to someone who can't hear too well, to go out of their way to face that person …" Another comments: "You can't expect people to tell you everything that's going on for people have to concentrate themselves".

Our own observations over a decade of contact suggest the nature of the limitations. There are a number of ways in which normal communication for the hearing interactant is badly disrupted. It is a physical strain always having to face the right way and speak slowly with clear lip movements. Speaking for a lipreader tends to limit what you actually say or to impose limitations on the particular way you construct what you want to say. For example, if a lipreader is having difficulty, one way to help is to cut out the normal social niceties of speech, the usual tags, hedges, and qualifications and simply get to the point. This is a considerable curtailment of the normal informal spontaneity of communication in everyday situations. It is often tempting to carry the process further and leave out genuinely significant information, rather as one might respond to the perpetual questions of a child.

Certain contexts make it particularly clear how lipreading constrains all concerned. Consider, for example, the practicalities of daily communication in a family which includes a deafened person who is wholly dependent on lipreading. All concerned are strained by the constant effort that lipreading involves both for the deafened and the hearing. The hearing person has to have abnormal patience. The deafened person either has to make constant requests for help or be left out. This is perhaps particularly difficult for people whose self esteem is threatened in other ways, for instance, people who are unable to fulfill socially expected roles because of their deafness. One deafened person indicates the problems that lipreading causes when interacting with his children:

> Sometimes I don't even understand what they are arguing about, because they are speaking too fast for me to lipread, so it is left to [his wife] to sort it out or perhaps it is something to do with school and when they tell me about it, I perhaps miss part of it and ask them to repeat it and they will say "Oh forget it Daddy, I'll tell Mummy".

Lipreading means that the parties concerned cannot focus on other things at the same time. The constant demand for the lipreader to watch the speaker's lips and for the speaker to face the lipreader means that a husband and wife, for example, cannot watch a TV programme and have a casual interchange of their opinion of it at the same time.

It is easy to regard many of these as small problems, and in a sense they are. However when they are constant, they add up to a very considerable load, and a considerable incentive to take the easy option of avoiding interaction.

10.2.3. Use of a third party

Another technique used by deafened people is to communicate via a third party. 38% of the questionnaire respondents report sometimes or frequently experiencing situations where people spoke to them through a third party. For the most part the third party tends to be a family member.

Communication via a third party seems to be particularly widespread in two situations. One is using the phone. The other is on official appointments, e.g. of a personal nature such as visiting one's doctor, or of a business nature, e.g. seeing the bank manager. The way that third party communication works is usually that the third party repeats slowly what the outsider says to the deafened person and the deafened person then replies directly to the outsider. This means of communication is important for many deafened people, but it has severe drawbacks for them and it creates problems for both the other principal interactant and the third party.

As far as all parties are concerned, this is a very laborious way to communicate.

But the major problem centers around the demarcation of the roles of the deafened person and the hearing person and how the outsider interprets these roles. The deafened person tends to regard the third party as a mere interpreter, but the outsider frequently treats the third party as the actual interlocutor and ignores the deafened person. This problem is voiced strongly by one deafened subject in relation to hospital receptionists: "The one who makes my appointments doesn't even speak to me ... she speaks to my daughter as if I wasn't there".

The situation is equally difficult for the third party who may be torn between the role of interpreter and the outsider's pressure to conform to a normal form of communication between the two hearing parties, and may be drawn into answering for the deafened person. Deafened people's frequent comments that the outsider will not address them personally suggests that the outsider finds the situation difficult. The situation on the phone can verge on the bizarre for the hearing outsider. Many deafened people insist on speaking for themselves on the phone but use a third party to interpret what the outsider is saying. This creates the situation that the hearing third party answers the phone and conveys the outsider's message to the deafened person. The deafened person then speaks directly on the phone to the outsider, then hands the phone to the third party who takes the outsider's reply and conveys it to the deafened person who then responds directly to the outsider and so on.

Apart from the fact that the whole procedure is extremely cumbersome, there are a number of particular problems with this situation for the outsider. These all relate to the fact that it is impossible to signal anything directly to a profoundly deafened person on the phone. For example, if the deafened person's speech is difficult to make out, there is no immediate way of conveying this, and it is embarrassing to have to tell the third party that you could not understand what was said. Normal conversations on phones usually consist of frequently interspersed signs of assent in the form of *yes, yes, uhuh, mmm* etc. When you know that the other person cannot hear your mumbles of assent, it feels extremely odd saying them to a vacuum. Staying silent is equally peculiar. Finally when you respond via the third party, it is extremely difficult to know how to respond. Do you tell him or her (i.e. the deafened person) such and such, or do you speak to the third party as if he/ she was the deafened person? These problems with third party phone conversations are exacerbated by the fact that the third party is not infrequently the deafened person's child. We have on occasion relayed messages to a deafened person via a four-year-old third party. Talking to an adult via a child is a peculiar situation.

The use of a third party is clearly important for the deafened person's communication with the outside world, but in view of the practicalities of how it works, it would be surprising if it did not have negative effects on all parties concerned.

10.2.4. Pen and paper

42% of the psychosocial-questionnaire respondents report using this mode of communication with some degree of frequency. For two people, both profoundly deafened, this is the primary mode of communication. Children's wipe-off boards are popular.

As an occasionally used mode, it can be a useful supplement to lipreading. Sometimes there may be one particular word that a deafened person has difficulty making out, and pen and paper can make the difference between comprehension and total misunderstanding or incomprehension. But beyond the occasional word, pen and paper is an extremely socially demanding and limited mode of communication. To ask hearing people to write down everything that they want to say is a large imposition on their time, energy and good nature. Even if they comply, they are not likely to keep up the interaction for very long because of the sheer slowness of it and the physical fatigue. Subtleties, innuendoes and complexities are likely to be left out in the effort to write down the bare facts. Nevertheless this very inefficient and restricted mode is the life line to communication for two of the subjects.

10.2.5. Technical means of boosting communication

It is notorious that hearing aids have drawbacks as well as advantages (e.g. Kaplan 1985; Littlejohns – John 1987: 33), but for completeness we reflect the kind of comment that our informants made on the topic.

Many comments emphasise the communicative benefit of hearing aids, for instance: "You'd be lost without them, they're a great benefit", or "It [i.e. hearing aid] has given me a new life". Several make the point that hearing aids improve self-confidence in a general way. One man comments that having a hearing aid gives him "a certain amount of assurance, a bit more confidence." Another woman says that "From [the time] I got this I won't avoid anybody". These comments are from people with moderate losses, but some with more severe losses comment on the psychological benefit of a hearing aid in making them feel less dissociated from the real world. One such man says: "I had it [i.e. hearing aid] up to full volume and I wore it and I put the T.V. up loud … there was no way I could lipread, but it made me feel better".

There are, however, many negative comments about hearing aids. Several people regard hearing aids as the outward sign of a socially stigmatised group. One subject puts it very bluntly: "I feel self conscious about it [i.e. hearing aid] ... I keep thinking people are looking and saying , Look at that fellow there, that fellow's one of them [i.e. the deaf]". Another comments: "I don't have many hang ups about things, but where hearing aids are concerned ... maybe its stupid pride or something ... I just don't want to be seen with a hearing aid". A second set of comments deals with the way hearing aids distort sound and the problem of getting adjusted to what they provide. One subject says: "I wasn't able to use the hearing aid properly for four or five years ... I was depending on the hearing aid at first replacing my hearing instead of magnifying sounds".

Others talk of the "artificial" sound. Linked to the idea of distortion is the problem that hearing aids are poor in noisy settings because they magnify the background noise.

Finally, a somewhat ironic type of comment is that "when people see you have a hearing aid, they expect you to hear everything."

10.2.6. Summary

Deafened people have open to them a range of modes of communication. As a result they are rarely faced with absolute inability to receive important information. The problem is rather that normal patterns of communication are disrupted, and that disruption places them in socially anomalous positions whichever way they turn – and not only them, but also those who interact with them.

10.3. Deafened people's communicative behaviour

The previous section focused on deafened people's problems of reception. However it is important to realise that in interactions, impaired reception often leads to abnormal forms of interaction. Disordered speech is part of this pattern of abnormal contributions to communication, but only part. This section considers some other aspects of the pattern. It focuses on profoundly-deafened subjects who rely solely on lipreading for interaction with the the hearing world. Two bodies of material are used. First, there is a formal pilot study of the communication of three deafened subjects. Second, there are informal observations based on tape-recorded conversations between deafened people and an interviewer, and on general personal observations.

10.3.1. The pilot study

A pilot study was carried out using three deafened subjects. Each was video taped in two dyadic interactions. The three selected were all totally deafened and relied on lipreading for communication. They are subject nos 4, 5 and 11 in table 3.1. The subjects were chosen because they were good lipreaders and relatively self confident, and so the data deal with the best scenario for lip-readers.

Each lipreader took part in two interactions. The first was with a person with whom he/she was very familiar. The second interaction was with an unknown person for a similar period of time. Each interaction lasted about half an hour, and involved two subtasks. In the first, the subjects had to enact three short scenarios; in the second they were to converse about anything they wanted.

The interchange between hearing and deafened was scored according to a checklist of features which probed both verbal and non-verbal behaviour. These features were generated by informal observation of deafened inter-actions. Verbal behaviour included whether interactants responded relevantly to each other's comments, how frequently they interrupted, whether they over-lapped the other speaker's comments, whether they ignored comments. Non-verbal behaviour included eye contact, head movement, smiling, fidgeting. A full list of the verbal and non-verbal behaviours which were noted with any frequency is given in table 10.1. Scoring consisted of a count of the frequency of each feature in a subject's behaviour, and it was carried out for both parties in each interaction, deafened and hearing.

Frequency counts for verbal features are summarised in figure 10.1. The order on the horizontal axes of the graphs corresponds to the order in table 10.1. The figure shows scores for both interactants in two contexts i.e. to a known individual and to an unknown individual. It is immediately apparent that the deafened subjects behave distinctively. Verbal features 9–17 are al-most completely absent in the hearing interactants but clearly present in the deafened interactants in both contexts. These cover a range of responses – ig-noring a comment, interrupting, making a non-committal answer, asking for clarification, overlapping the other speaker's comment, pursuing their own line of discussion without reference to the context, terminating the exchange. The deafened also appear to behave distinctively with respect to verbal fea-

Table 10.1 Verbal and non-verbal features (numbered in order of appearance in Figures
10.1 and 10.2)

verbal features	non-verbal features
1 gives direct answer	1 makes eye contact
2 gives answer and develops it	2 smiles
3 asks question relevant to topic	3 makes head movement
4 repeats something said by other	4 gestures
5 changes subject	5 makes body movement
6 returns to a previous comment	6 fidgets
7 comments on related topic	7 frowns
8 makes aside	8 looks puzzled
9 returns to a previous topic	9 looks tired
10 ignores a comment	10 looks anxious
12 interrupts	11 looks aggressive
13 makes a non-committal comment	12 touches other
14 asks for clarification	
15 overlaps other speaker's comment	
16 develops own line of discussion	
17 terminates exchange	

tures 1 and 2 – giving direct answers and relevant answers. With unfamiliar interactants, they provide too few direct or relevant answers. With familiar interactants they give an unusually high number of direct or relevant answers. This probably reflects communicative adjustments by the normal-hearing interactants: their communicative behaviour positively demands answers from the deafened interactants, presumably as a means of checking that the deafened have actually understood what was said. For example they ask direct questions which should be met with an answer if they have been understood.

Distinctive profiles on verbal features are perhaps not very surprising. Limited comprehension might be expected to lead to the behaviour apparent in verbal features 9 to 14. However it has to be recognised that this kind of behaviour tends to convey an impression of disruptiveness and/or uncertainty, and it is not always easy for a hearing interactant to accept. An item which is not shown on the graphs deserves mention in this context. It is admitting that one has not understood something. This occurs only three times in the whole length of the interactions, each time by a different deafened person to an unfamiliar interactant. This reinforces the point made in the previous chapter that interactants are likely to encounter nonspecific signs that something is wrong far more often than signs which indicate directly that the problem is impaired hearing.

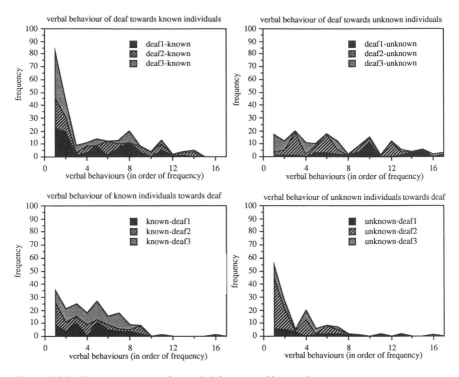

Figure 10.1 Frequency counts for verbal features of interactions

Frequency counts for non verbal features are given in figure 10.2. The order on the horizontal axes of the graphs correspond to those on table 10.1.

Non-verbally the deafened make a range of responses to both known and unknown interactants which were rare among the normal-hearing interactants – particularly fidgeting, frowning and looking puzzled (features 1–4). With the unknown interactants they exhibited low levels of what were elsewhere the commonest behaviours – eye contact, smiling, head movement and gestures. Again, this distortion of normal "body language" would be expected to present difficulties for a hearing interactant, at least if he or she did not have a very firm sense of the reasons for it.

The study bears a clear relation to the indications in chapter 9 that good non-verbal self presentation offers a way of overcoming the adverse impression that deafened people's speech tends to create. The data here suggest that deafened people's general self presentation is more likely to compound the adverse effects of poor speech production than to over-ride them. To put it an-

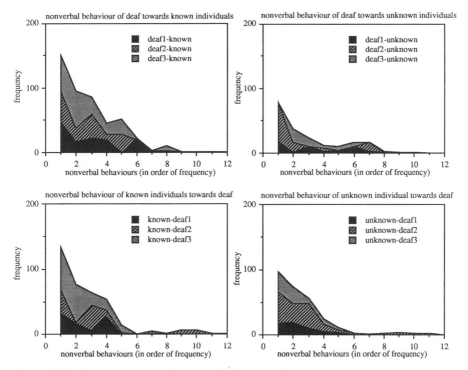

Figure 10.2 Frequency counts for nonverbal features of interactions

other way, deafened people's speech is part of a pattern of abnormality in the active conduct of interactions.

10.3.2. Observations from other sources

The pilot study highlights a number of characteristic abnormalities in deafened people's interaction, but others which we have observed are worth describing. Two are considered in this section. The first relates to turntaking in conversation and pursues the theme of domination by the deafened; the second to the social behaviour of deafened subjects.

(1). Turntaking. It is very noticeable from the tape-recorded conversations that some deafened subjects fail to signal that other participants can take the floor. Normal turntaking signals such as slowing down or pausing are often considerably weaker than in normal speech. Even the syntax sometimes seems to be designed to prevent others taking the floor. For example, one subject does pause but frequently precedes the pause with *and* which signals that there is more to come and halts interruption. Others fill pauses with abnormally extended mumbles of *ahhhhhhhh* or *mmmmmmm* which prevent interruption. Another way that some deafened prevent others from taking turns is to read what they want to say rather than speak it. This is an extreme method, but is used by two subjects. On two occasions, when the interviewer told a subject that she would be returning next week, the subject had prepared a long written statement of what she/he wanted to say and proceeded to read it out. This gave very little chance for interruption. A less extreme version of the same strategy is to deliver a monologue with at least parts which are clearly pre-rehearsed. We have heard a number of informants deliver what are very nearly the same descriptions on several occasions. Although we have no direct evidence, it is difficult to resist the impression that the passages have been rehearsed at length in private, and are used as a whole whenever the occasion arises.

There is some suggestion that the prevention of turntaking by deafened people is a deliberate stategy used to dominate the conversation. One subject who gives very few turntaking cues says : "I have to dominate the meeting. I make myself the artificial centre of attention so that people will just speak to me ..."

It is not surprising that the deafened want to dominate interactions. It is an effective way of keeping control of the situation and hence minimising the extent to which unknown elements can creep in and destabilize the situation, making large demands on the deafened person's comprehension. The effects on hearing interactants, however, are unlikely to be welcome.

(2). Socially inappropriate behaviour. Our experience of deafened people includes several cases of behaviour which is socially inappropriate. Particularly striking are examples of taking the initiative in other people's houses in things that would normally be left to the owner of the house. For example, early on in our experience with the deafened, we observed that a deafened visitor turned off our electric heater without asking permission. Another departed from the main group of people and went to watch television in the kitchen without signalling that she intended to do so, or confirming that this would be alright. Another was found looking for sugar in our cupboards without having asked if he could. Such initiative perhaps stems from the fact that it is simply easier to do things for oneself than to have to go through a painful and difficult communication about trivialities. But it results in behaviour that some might construe as rude and most would certainly find odd.

10.3.3. Summary

This section provides evidence that deafness tends to affect the way a person behaves in interactions. The effects range from the very immediate, such as abnormal patterns of eye contact which are enforced by lipreading, to longer term and indirect effects, such as a tendency to bypass social niceties that would entail verbal communication. That is not surprising when one thinks about it, but like so many points about acquired deafness, it is easy not to think far enough to realise that it is likely.

We do not have formal evidence that interactants notice these features, and more to the point that they are influenced by them. Informal experience strongly suggests that they are likely to be aware of some kind of abnormality, and to find it disconcerting, without necessarily being able to pinpoint the source of their unease. It would be worth having firmer evidence on the point, but that raises difficulties of the kind that were discussed in the previous chapter.

10.4. An overview of deafened communication

The previous sections have looked at specific aspects of deafened people's communication. This section takes a broader view and considers their consequences.

A considerable body of literature shows that acquired deafness causes substantial problems, ranging from problems in the family and problems at work to emotional problems (see chapter 1). There are fewer attempts, however, to explain why it should do so. This section suggests that recognising the profound and multiple ways in which acquired deafness affects communication is a key part of the explanation.

An important first step is to acknowledge that it is not immediately obvious why deafness should be such a major problem. Deafened people can speak and read. Between residual hearing and lipreading, most of them can make out most spoken sentences given time. In short, given the will to use them, the resources to communicate are there. It is not self evident why such a permeable barrier should cause problems. The point is not academic. Among those involved, it surfaces in perennial complaints such as "he can hear well enough if he tries" from the hearing party, and "he won't take the trouble to speak clearly" from the deafened. From there, they are left to construct their own explanations of the problems, and these are often censorious and destructive. Among outsiders, it may well contribute to the public indifference which deafened people of all groups report (Cowie – Douglas-Cowie – Stewart 1987: 146–148) and to professional reluctance to devote extensive resources to acquired deafness.

There are singularly few attempts to confront this theoretical issue, and those that there are tend not to confront the practical problem which has just been noted. Knapp (1948: 208–209) argued that serious emotional problems need not follow from deafness unless the deafened person's underlying personality structure was unhealthy. It is scandalous that such a statement should still be repeated with apparent approval when we know that clinical depression afflicts a majority of people with a sufficient level of loss (Thomas – Gilhome Herbst 1980: 79; see chapter 1). Oyer – Oyer (1985: 148–151) propose adopting a crisis-oriented approach, but little detail is offered. Some sociologically oriented writers argue that handicap is imposed by the normal community (e.g. Finney 1977), often invoking Goffman's discussion of stigma (Goffman 1968). The danger of this approach is that it lays responsibility for the deafened person's problems on normal-hearing parties who themselves may be suffering severely. On the other hand, Kyle – Jones – Wood (1985) proposed a model of adjustment which consists essentially of feedback allowing the deafened person to find an appropriate (reduced) level of interaction. This approach carries the opposite danger of suggesting that smooth adjustment should occur unless the deafened person wilfully refuses to accept his or her limitations. Approaches which stress conflicts over roles and status (e.g. Beattie 1981: 278–285; Schlesinger 1985) tend to suggest that all parties are behaving in an essentially irrational and rather unsavoury way.

This section reflects a different approach, which is to begin by thinking through the effects of the central communicative handicap that affects deafened people and those close to them. It seems reasonable to suggest that this line of approach should be exhausted before implying that the problems brought about by deafness are signs of ill will or poor coping or inadequacy on the part of hearing or deafened parties. Five themes may be brought out.

(1). Effort. An effort of will can make an enormous difference to communication between a deafened and a hearing person, but it tends to be extremely difficult for either party to sustain the effort required. Section 10.2 has already indicated some specific details of effort. This section draws out some generalisations. On the deafened person's side, comprehension, even with residual hearing and a hearing aid, is a detection task involving a rapid sequence of degraded signals in a very noisy background. Sustaining such a performance for long is notoriously exhausting. There is a particularly interesting parallel between deafened people's experience and the experimental finding that the effort of maintained performance in a detection task under noise tends to lower resistance to frustration (Wholwill et al. 1976). Deafened people who rely on lipreading may also face problems later in the comprehension process because lipreading appears to interfere with short term storage and their ability to go beyond the speaker's actual words and grasp the intended meaning of an utterance (see chapters 11 and 12).

The hearing party's problem is less obvious, but experience leaves us in no doubt that talking to deafened people can be exhausting. The same point is made by Beattie (1981: 307–308). Three general reasons can be suggested. First, there is the problem of straining to understand what is being said. Chapter 4 has shown problems with the intelligibility of deafened speech. Secondly, it is necessary to keep monitoring, and often over-riding deeply ingrained action patterns. This is rather like a negative transfer situation in skilled performance. It is particularly interesting that it involves a change of timing, a kind of adjustment which is notoriously likely to provoke negative transfer (Newell 1981: 224–225; Summers 1975). Thirdly, dealing with misunderstandings involves considerable intellectual effort. It falls on the hearing party to spot them, which is not always easy. It may be still harder to infer what the deafened party thinks was said and to decide how the conversation should continue. From both hearing and deafened points of view the sheer effort of communication creates a strained environment which is unconducive to easy relationships among the interactants.

(2). Metalinguistics. There is much more to communication than exchanging propositions. Intonation (Frick 1985) and voice quality (Scherer 1986) may convey the speaker's attitude or indicate how a proposition is to be taken. Section 10.2.2 suggested that lipreading loses out on this level of communication. This is probably why the deafened often report difficulty with jokes. The manner of making a comment may often be at the core of a message. For example, if one makes the passing comment "it's a nice day", the interchange has already failed if one has to repeat it several times. A related point is that you cannot convey affection by whispering sweet nothings if they have to be repeated loudly and precisely. The words may come across eventually, but the gesture is dead.

The metalinguistic problem is two-sided. We have shown that deafened people's speech tends to be abnormal in stress and intonation, which are key elements in conveying a sense of the person speaking and his or her feelings (chapter 6): and more directly we have shown that it tends to evoke various adverse reactions and evaluations (chapters 8 and 9). The suggestion that deafened people have particular problems with socially significant variation in style (chapter 5) is highly significant in this context. This chapter has added evidence that there tend to be difficulties in other aspects of communication which have a powerful influence on the judgements we form of a speaker, that is the non-verbal signs which are transmitted and the co-operative mechanics of turntaking.

Considering the two sides together suggests how difficult deafness can make it to establish a real rapport between speakers. Morgan-Jones (1987) makes the point that genuine closeness, particularly in a marriage, is often expected to mean effortless understanding. That kind of understanding is mediated by fluent, accurate communication at a metalinguistic level. That becomes very difficult when one party is deaf.

(3). The cost of failed exchanges. Even if a high proportion of exchanges succeed, those that fail exact a heavy cost. In the psychosocial impact study, these costs figured prominently among the things that people felt had a very bad effect on their lives (see chapter 13). Direct costs are feeling embarrassed or stupid when you misunderstand something. Indirect costs stem from the difficulty of knowing whether you have misunderstood something or not. This is associated with fear of having missed vital information or warning sounds, and fear that what you say in a conversation will be inappropriate. All of these items fall in a small group of questionnaire items which a fifth or more of the questionnaire sample felt had a very bad effect on their lives. Failed exchanges may also have costs for hearing parties. Beattie (1981: 304) gives a telling quote: "The children come in from school and chatter. They tell me things and a week later I realise I didn't hear a word. Sometimes it's things they need for school".

(4). Negotiating obligations. Communicative difficulties raise what is essentially a thorny moral problem. When parties have very unequal abilities, it is difficult to agree what each owes the other. A common example, discussed in section 10.2.3, involves answering the telephone. At what point has a hearing party the right to refuse to act as intermediary on the telephone for a deafened person? There is no simple answer, and there is no generally accepted convention to fall back on. Moreover deafness makes the business of negotiating agreements extremely difficult.

(5). Evaluating strategies. The literature often describes inappropriate reactions to deafness, such as denial of the handicap, overprotectiveness on the part of family and friends, or isolation of the deafened person. What is rarely acknowledged is that these all represent reactions which at least in the short term can appear constructive. It is not trivial distinguishing between adaptive responses and those which lead to disaster. This reflects a widespread problem. Adjusting to disability is, as Creegan (1966: 112) puts it, a "continuous process of fairly arbitrary trial and error; of blind alleys and exasperating frustrations." However deafness makes the process particularly hard to regulate because it isolates the parties involved, so that it becomes extremely difficult to formulate judgements about the present state of affairs and to develop strategies for the future.

These themes are not in themselves a sufficient explanation of the problems that acquired deafness causes. They need to be integrated with the strengths of the other accounts mentioned above. There is also an element related to the general effects of sensory deprivation (see, e.g., Zubek 1969) which needs to be considered. But it is surely reasonable to insist that this kind of analysis is a necessary component of any serious attempt to understand the problems of acquired deafness. It is difficult to see how one can identify appropriate types or amounts of support, and still more difficult to see how one can judge whether people are coping well or badly, if one has not thought through what the problems are.

10.5. Conclusion

This chapter essentially sketches a broader context in which our research on speech production belongs. Functionally, abnormal speech production is part of a problem of abnormal communication which follows from acquired deafness. Abnormal speech production is a significant issue insofar as it compounds that wider problem. The previous chapter acknowledged that the interaction might conceivably be positive, with abnormal speech production being cancelled by positive self-presentation. We have tried to indicate that this is not something one should expect to happen automatically and as a rule.

The chapter is in effect a link between the focus on abnormal speech production which we have maintained so far, and the issues which are considered in the final three chapters. It has indicated that other aspects of acquired deafness impinge on communication in complex ways, and that is taken up in two chapters which consider lipreading from that perspective. The chapter has also presupposed that qualitative social and emotional aspects of interaction are important for deafened people, not just its ability to convey practically important information. That theme is taken up in the final chapter.

Chapter 11
Do they mean us? Preliminaries to a theory of lipreading that is recognisable to deafened lipreaders

This chapter is a step towards linking two bodies of information which sound as if they should be closely related, but which turn out to have surprisingly little in common. One is the academic literature on lipreading. The other is the experience of a deafened person who relies on lipreading for most of his daily information, as a co-author of this chapter does. For convenience he is referred to as FR when we draw on his experience.

The chapter reflects FR's conclusions from a year as research associate at Queen's University. As such it presents academic literature through the eyes of a layman with some claim to be considered an expert in the field. It makes no claim to be dispassionate, but it is worth recognising that lipreading is not a neutral subject for deafened people.

The term "deafened" needs to be emphasised. There is a strong tradition of practically-oriented research on lipreading among the prelingually deaf, focused on the ability of lipreading to support language acquisition (see, e.g. Mogford 1987). But that problem is not relevant to deafened people, and the problems which do concern them have tended to receive less academic attention, despite the fact that the deafened far outnumber the prelingually deaf (Davis 1983; Thornton 1986).

The chapter does not set out to criticise academic research on lipreading. It has been dealing with real and important issues, and it has made clear progress. The point is simply that there are many other issues, at least as real and important from a lipreader's point of view, and as legitimate from a psychologist's, which have not been taken up. There is also a rich source of evidence waiting to be tapped: the experiences, and particularly the errors, of practising lipreaders. It is now well established that records of errors can be an important source: for example they have been used to study speech (McKay 1970; Cutler 1981); reading (Goodman 1976; Cowie 1985); typing (MacNeilage – de Clerk 1964); and action plans (Norman 1981). It would be eminently reasonable to extend the approach to lipreading. We have used a few informally collected examples to make the point: they prompted the larger collection which is discussed in the next chapter.

In at least some cases, another point also needs to be made. The research literature often uses terms which are legitimate if they are understood in an abstract or specialised way, but misleading if they are taken to relate to everyday experience in any direct way. This is non-trivial because most of the people who need to lipread are literate adults. They are able to benefit from information that is couched in terms they can relate to their own experience, but they can also be confused by material that they misunderstand. The problem can be compounded when information is transmitted via intermediaries who are neither practising lipreaders nor research psychologists – such as doctors or teachers of lipreading. So it is important that someone should clarify the relationship between researchers' concepts and the experience of lipreading described in ordinary language.

At least twelve topics seem crucial for a satisfying treatment of lipreading. It is convenient to order them roughly from those which contemporary theory covers best to those which it covers least (see 11.1 to 11.12 below).

11.1. The sound-like quality of lipreading

It is deeply entrenched in popular thought that each of the five senses produces a distinct kind of experience. Touch tells us what objects feel like, vision tells us what they look like, hearing tells us what they sound like. But this idea is a barrier to understanding lipreading. In point of fact lipreading speech gives the same kind of experience as hearing speech – at least for a lot of the time.

For a profoundly deaf lipreader, this is a matter of experience. It is brought home when someone very familiar speaks, and the voice comes across as if it were heard – yet in fact they spoke soundlessly. Recent research has reinforced this point very clearly, through two main effects which occur when normal hearing subjects lipread.

First, it has been shown that lipreading affects what normal subjects hear. When people are shown a speaker saying *ma*, but the sound track says *ta*, what they hear is *pa*. This is called the "McGurk effect" (McGurk – McDonald 1976; Summerfield 1983: 138–144). It shows that information from ear and eye merge thoroughly to give a single type of impression which we call "hearing" speech.

Second, it has been shown that lipread material behaves like auditory rather than visual inputs in short term memory. A lipread addition at the end of a heard list, a "suffix", impairs recall of the last item nearly as much as a heard suffix, and much more than a written suffix. Similarly a heard suffix impairs recency in a lipread list, where a written suffix does not (Gathercole 1987).

All this is practically important for a very simple reason. It means that people who are learning to lipread should not be looking for a new kind of experience. At its best, the experience of lipreading is close to the experience of hearing the speaker – in fact, it is rather as if you weren't lipreading.

11.2. Lipreading and residual hearing

The McGurk effect shows that sound and hearing can combine in surprising ways. This can work greatly to the advantage of the lipreader who has some residual hearing. Eye and ear often supply different parts of the information needed to recognise a sound, and they can complement each other to give quite an accurate impression even though neither the eye alone nor the ear alone would give a very helpful picture. This effect is familiar to lipreaders, but it can be extremely puzzling. Theorists have now explained the basic logic behind it (Summerfield 1983; Bailey 1983), though the fine detail is still in dispute (Summerfield 1987).

This point is still being digested by professionals concerned with hearing. FR has a loss of 120 dB, and so he is regarded as having "no useful hearing". With losses of that level, traditional clinicians tended to see little point in prescribing a hearing aid. But subjective experience has always suggested that the sound which remains audible makes a difference, a point made strongly by Ashley (1985: 61) on the basis of his own experience. It is reassuring that research is confirming this experience, and explaining its basis. Sound patterns which have very little significance in their own right can nevertheless complement information which is picked up by eye, and the brain is able to combine these distinct sources into a whole which is very much greater than the sum of its parts.

11.3. People have different basic aptitudes for lipreading

There is a public perception that training is the essence of good lipreading. (In the stories, all the best secret agents are "trained lipreaders".) This does not square with the experience of deafened lipreaders, and research is increasingly backing them up. In interviews reported by Cowie – Stewart (1985), there was, if anything, an inverse relationship between attendance at lipreading classes and proficiency at lipreading. Many find that they can lipread without consciously learning (e.g. Rice 1988: 23) and see little point in attending classes; others remain strikingly poor lipreaders after attending classes for years. It is unfortunate that both groups often seem to feel guilt over their approach – the former because they should have attended and learned to do it properly, the latter because they feel they must not have tried hard enough.

Research now seems to be showing that lipreading depends on a complex of skills which are very unevenly distributed through the population. Gailey (1987) has argued that there are large differences in the low level skills required to register significant patterns in fleeting mouth movements. Lyxell – Ronnberg (1987a; 1987b) have assembled evidence that various higher level "cognitive determinants" exist. These include working memory (Lyxell – Ronnberg 1987b) and at least two forms of "guessing ability" (Lyxell – Ronnberg 1987a).

11.4. Ambiguity

This is a major theme in the literature. Much has been written about the ambiguity of the lip shapes which correspond to individual sounds. This is typically expressed in lists of "visemes" – that is, the distinct visible patterns that are informative to a lipreader. There are different estimates (see e.g. Walden et al. 1977: 130; Gailey 1981: 117–134): but broadly speaking there seem to be about a third as many visemes as there are separate elements of sound in spoken language. In other words, individual visemes are ambiguous – they have about three possible meanings on average.

But the reality experienced by a lipreader does not correspond simply to that ambiguity. There is a rich and practically important set of phenomena to be described here: the immediately following sections (11.4.1–11.4.4) highlight some key points.

11.4.1. For a good lipreader, real ambiguity is much less than the literature suggests

It is possible to understand very complex utterances with little or no uncertainty. A recent case noted by FR provides a useful illustration. His daughter came in in the evening and told him: "Mrs X was not at school last week because she had palpitations of the heart". He understood the sentence, including the name, without repetition or conscious effort. This is far removed from the kind of performance suggested by saying that each viseme has on average about three possible readings.

There is an important theoretical point here. When information from lip movements is combined with other types of information that can reasonably be used – such as what is and what is not a word in the language, what is and is not a meaningful sentence, what is and is not a sensible thing to say in the context – there are very rarely approximately three sensible readings of each lip movement. No-one seems to have worked out how many there usually are, but experience suggests that it is very rare to get a misunderstanding that is completely plausible and quite wrong. In other words, a lipreader's problem is not generally that the information is not there – it is the practical difficulty of getting the information which is there in the time available.

It may be useful to cite an exception which proves the rule. Recently someone said to FR: "I've connections there", which he lipread as "I've got a throat there". These two offer very nearly the same sequence of visemes, and they are both grammatical. But intuition suggests that it is rare to find such a close approximation to real ambiguity. And the ambiguity is not complete because the second reading makes little sense, particularly in the context of the conversation in question – which is why it was picked up as a misreading immediately.

11.4.2. *There are several subjectively different ways of not "getting" what has been said*

This is important from the point of view of a lipreader, because these different kinds of problem lead to different kinds of response. It is also of considerable interest for psychologists concerned with the representations that cognitive processes form and store.

One clear possibility is that the lipreader will form a definite but incorrect impression. This is common, and it is illustrated in the example immediately above.

A possibility which is highlighted by theory is that the lipreader will be aware of ambiguity. This seems to happen in very restricted ways, mainly as a variant on the first possibility. A lipreader who has learned about the ambiguity of visemes may realise that what he or she "hears" is only one of the possibilities. For example, a lipreader may hear *Sean* and be aware that the speaker could just as well have said *John*; or may hear *Bobby* and know it could have been *Mummy*. But it seems doubtful whether this consciously constructed awareness of ambiguity can be developed very far. For instance, the "connections" example above could not have been handled by working out the alternative possibilities associated with the reading that was "heard". It is an important question whether this deliberate recognition of ambiguity is the main skill taught by traditional lipreading classes. If so, then the apparent limitations of this strategy would have obvious implications.

A certain amount of experience suggests that some sort of uninterpreted representation can be stored and accessed without the lipreader's awareness for some time. One pointer to this kind of representation is the experience of simply not getting what a speaker is saying – lip movements seem to be simply shape changes devoid of meaning or structure, as if interpretation were simply not reaching a level that conscious interpretation can access. A subtler pointer occurs when the lipreader is aware of an unresolved problem at a certain point in a sentence, but as more information comes in the missing word or phrase "clicks". For instance FR recently picked up the end of a sentence – *de-mister yet*. Shortly afterwards the rest "clicked": the whole was *Have you done anything about that de-mister yet?*

This kind of experience suggests that a weakly interpreted representation has been stored, ready to be accessed when context suggests (in some sense) a plausible interpretation that can be checked against this trace. But though this is theoretically interesting, it appears to be rather uncommon: we have noted only a few clear examples in a period of several weeks.

11.4.3. Many mistakes are not at the level of confusing visemes

A good number of mistakes are at the level of getting the right number of visemes, or the right relationships between them.

A very common mistake which illustrates this is missing a syllable. For instance, FR has recently misread "Paul Hammill" as "Paul Lamb"; "guitar" as "Darts"; and "Stevenson" as "Steven".

These examples raise two general problems which have received surprisingly little attention in the context of lipreading. One is the problem of establishing rhythm. It has been argued that contours of rhythm and intonation play a central part in understanding speech by ear (Darwin 1976: 192–194, 214–217; Noteboom – Brokx – de Rooij 1979). It is not at all clear what replaces them in lipreading. The second problem is segmentation. It is far from trivial to establish the boundaries of a word in lipreading, particularly given that a word is often flanked by soundless mouth movements concerned with preparing or terminating the utterance. And within a word, it is far from trivial to separate out the movements concerned with individual sounds, particularly in consonant clusters such as those in *straw* or *inked*. One study hints that the ability to establish the right number of components in such a cluster may be independent of the ability to recognise single consonants (Cowie et al. 1982: 68).

Even further from the problem of recognising letters, lipreading often seems to involve taking a short cut to the message – somehow bypassing all sorts of questions about individual words, let alone sounds. This can radically improve the efficiency of lipreading, but it can also lead to dramatic mistakes. The experience can be puzzling and difficult to describe, but it links up to a wealth of material in cognitive psychology. Empirically it is reminiscent of the claim that skilled readers read the message, not the individual words (Kolers 1970: 109–118) or that they are primarily concerned with constructing representations of the meanings which stimuli convey, and only incidentally with the physical characteristics of the stimulus (Cowie 1985: 101–105). Theoretically, it recalls accounts which consider comprehension as filling in slots in a schema or script (e.g. Schank – Abelson 1977). These connections may do a good deal to illuminate lipreading. They suggest, for instance, that ambiguity in practice may occur at two levels: at the level of invoking the right script, and at the level of registering cues to major variables in that script. They may also prove a useful way of developing issues which are raised below, particularly in points 11.5.–11.7.

11.4.4. *Some extremely surprising pieces of information do seem to be available to a lipreader*

A prime example involves intonation contours, which FR's hearing loss suggests he should be quite unable to detect. Yet he can mimic the intonation patterns which are characteristic of some mutual acquaintances with considerable accuracy. This may be because they tend to be parallelled in head movements – the head tending to be raised and the lips stretched in time with a sustained final rise in intonation.

11.5. "Top-down" influences

These are acknowledged in the literature (e.g. Cowie et al. 1982; Summerfield 1983: 151–153), though they receive considerably less attention than issues connected with bottom-up processing. This may reflect the influence of concern with prelingual deafness, where the ability of lipreading to function with a limited knowledge base is crucial. But for whatever reason, the experience of top-down processes is not well conveyed in the literature. Subjectively it can take several fairly distinct forms. These are worth separating out for at least two types of reason. Theoretically, they suggest that different types of memory stores and representations are being used. Practically, they are important for explaining how to go about speechreading: failing to distinguish them can easily give a completely misleading impression.

For example, Lyxell – Ronnberg (1987a) have published a paper called "Guessing and Speechreading." The suggestion is that once a lipreader knows the alternatives allowed by the visemes which he or she detects, the rest is guessing. This may be true in a very rarefied, special sense of the term "guessing", where it is used simply to mean taking a decision that may possibly not be right. But in the ordinary sense of the term guessing, it is not something a good lipreader does very often. The experiences associated with using top-down processing are usually quite different, and they take several forms.

The first, and the commonest, has been mentioned already. The lipreader watches a sentence being spoken, and knows what it means. Subjectively, there is no working out involved. In order to do that, the brain must be using knowledge about what is probable – in English, in the context of the conversation, and in the particular setting. But the lipreader is not aware of any such thing: he or she simply knows what was said.

This point can be difficult to absorb because it contradicts deeply entrenched assumptions about perception. Psychologists, and philosophers before them, have long tended to assume that cognition involves two distinct kinds of process – truly perceptual processes driven by the data reaching the senses, and "higher" processes driven by stored knowledge (Cowie 1987a: 52–55; 1987b: 100–106). This picture suggests that lipreading should split into a truly perceptual skill, whose output reflects the ambiguity of individual lip movements; and more cognitive skills, which use stored knowledge to disambiguate.

This description probably holds in a special, abstract sense (Gailey 1987), but a simple interpretation of it seriously misrepresents experience. It is just not true that a lipreader's immediate perceptual impressions are simply related to what can be extracted by bottom-up processing from lip movements: they also reflect an automatic and unconscious fusion of sensory inputs with "higher" knowledge – of possible words, of normal syntax, of what makes sense in the context. Theoretically, this is reminiscent of McClelland – Rummelhart's (1981) model of word recognition where downward and upward flowing information interact wholly automatically, under the control of a single type of process. It is natural to argue that a model of that kind seems much more relevant to lipreading than the conventional approach which separates perceptual and cognitive processes, and steps have been taken in that direction (Massaro 1987).

Unthinking use of top-down processing seems to be the norm, but there are other experiences that may be linked to using high level knowledge.

(1). Knowing that something can't be right. This was mentioned under 11.4.1. in the *connection / got a throat* example: the lipreader's knowledge of the context told him that what he had perceived could not be what was intended.

(2). Reasoning out what must have been meant. This tends to start with knowing that something can't be right, but it is sometimes possible to go beyond that and work out what must have been said. An amusing example arose when FR was being told about a friend's trip to London where he had, apparently, threatened to take his mother to a brothel. But knowledge about lipreading and family relationships allowed him to work out that the prank was aimed at the speaker's brother .

(3). Waiting till something "clicks". This has been mentioned before under 11.4.2. The double mention reflects the fact that the phenomenon depends on both the code generated by bottom-up processes, and the way that top-down processes can access that code.

(4). Consciously trying to predict what will come next. This is reminiscent of the old "analysis by synthesis" strategy, but it generally involves predicting topics rather than word sequences. For instance, at a dinner table, one can register that requests to pass something are likely to refer to the salt during the main course, but to the sugar during after dinner coffee. This kind of prediction is only possible in circumstances where there are strong contextual constraints. The psychologically interesting point is that conscious preparation seems to facilitate exploiting these constraints, indicating that there are limits to the potential of passive interactive activation type processing.

(5). Conversational strategies. Special forms of top-down processing can operate when the lipreader limits likely options by asking closed questions, and various related conversational conversational strategies.

11.6. Lipreading is an interaction between conscious and automatic processes

This is implicit in what has been said above, but it needs to be made explicit. Failure to do so leads to various confusions. There is an intriguing blind spot in academic discussions which propose multi-factor theories (Cowie et al. 1982; Lyxell – Ronnberg 1987a, 1987b; Gailey 1987). They infer distinctions among components by examining the way different sources of information are used, but ignore the manifest distinction between conscious and automatic processing (perhaps because of a Helmholtzian belief that automatic processing is simply conscious reasoning gone underground). It is revealing that the index of Dodd – Campbell's major collection (1987) contains no entries for "conscious", "awareness", "deliberate", "automatic", or any other term that obviously bears on the present distinction. The issue becomes more serious in non-academic texts on lipreading which focus on what the present analysis suggests are conscious accessories to the core, automatic skill of lipreading – particularly reasoning out what must have been meant, and predicting what is to come. These are useful refinements, but it would be unfortunate if readers tried to make them the foundation of their whole approach to lipreading.

11.7. Memory and processing capacity

There has been research on the role of memory in speechreading, but it very limited. Lyxell – Ronnberg (1987b) have shown that tests of working memory correlate with lipreading performance, and a number of researchers have studied the codes in which lipread material is stored (see Gathercole 1987). This leaves large, practically important issues untouched. Above all, FR's experience is that it is impossible to lipread and think at the same time. Theoretically, this makes sense in terms of the resources that must be mobilised in order to disambiguate incoming data. Practically, it means that lipreaders have a limited opportunity to carry out the inference and interpretation that are central to normal speech comprehension (see, e.g. Douglas-Cowie – Cowie 1984). This gives rise to particular problems with meanings which are stated indirectly, and, notoriously, with registering jokes. It also has implications for discourse, because in effect the lipreader is less able to prepare a reply or evaluate implicit pointers to the way the conversation is expected to develop.

11.8. Directing attention

Attention in general terms is crucial for a lipreader. It is fatal to let the mind wander because lipreading demands full capacity, and once the thread of a conversation has been lost, it may be very difficult to recover.

Visual attention in particular is critical. Lipreading depends heavily on active looking in the simple sense of directing gaze appropriately. It is normal for the eyes to wander when a listener is not giving the speaker his or her full attention, or is preparing a reply (Ellis – Beattie 1986: 35–38). This is fatal for a lipreader, who needs to maintain a wholly unnatural kind of sustained visual attention. This does not simply mean looking continuously at the speaker, though. Seeing the surroundings can provide essential contextual information, so the lipreader has to allocate his or her attention appropriately between person and surroundings. This is a demanding skill about which very little seems to be known.

11.9. The speaker's state is a key variable

The things that are most striking to a lipreader are the importance of being confident and the near impossibility of lipreading when one is tired. The psychological literature has very little to say about these.

On the other hand, the literature does contain hints that lipreading is very sensitive to the state of the speaker. Gailey (1981) examined the correlations between people's scores on nonsense syllables and their scores on meaningful materials. She found that these varied radically for reasons that were not at all obvious. In one experiment, they went from very high to very low depending on whether subjects saw the meaningful material or the nonsense syllables first. Another running sore is the fact that some studies find a high correlation between intelligence and lipreading, others find none. Psychologists have no good explanation. But the effects square with the experience of lipreaders – subjectively, lipreading is an extremely delicate balance, and it is not surprising if it is affected by changes that experimenters hardly notice.

11.10. Lipreading requires intense effort

It is very tiring and stressful. This is a common observation, but there seems to be no experimental verification of it; no attempt to incorporate it into cognitive theories (which components cause the trouble?); no attempt to understand its consequences for the structure of communication which involves lipreading; and little attempt to analyse its part in the upheavals which affect families with a deafened member (though see Chapter 10 and Cowie – Stewart 1987).

11.11. What makes lipreading easy/difficult?

Viewing conditions are discussed, but subjectively they seem much less important than lipreadability of the speaker. This involves not only the speaker's lip shapes, but issues such as whether the speaker puts the lipreader at ease (or seems at ease with the lipreader).

An intriguing point is that the literature discusses the visible signs of lipreading as if they were a constant. Perhaps it seems like that to a hearing person who makes the lip movements, and expects the lipreader to make sense of them. So we get lists of visemes specifying the sounds that can be distinguished on "the" lips. Whose lips? To describe what is available to a lip–reader, it is necessary to recognise that different speakers offer different things. Some are vastly easier to read than others, and a sort of rough average is a poor description of that reality. It would be a challenging task to map out the different forms that sounds can take on different speakers' lips, and to show how that can affect comprehension. Such a description would be extremely useful both for deafened people and for those who need to be lipread by a deafened person. Yet researchers have little to say about it.

A closely related point is that familiarity makes an enormous difference to lipreading. The research literature does not discuss the basis of this, but it both practically important and extremely interesting from a psychological point of view – a real, honest-to-goodness case of perceptual learning, waiting to be studied.

11.12. What is learned in lipreading?

Some parts of the literature suggest that learning can do very little to improve deafened people's lipreading. In particular, there are studies which indicate that experienced lipreaders score little or no better than novices on tests (e.g. Lyxell – Ronnberg 1987b: 52–53). We have replicated this: FR, who (experience suggests) rates very highly among deafened lipreaders, took a test which was also administered to second year psychology students with no experience of lipreading. Ten per cent of the class outscored the experienced lip–reader.

This kind of result needs to be taken seriously, but it also needs to be seen in context. The test involved lipreading individual words and sentences from a TV screen. This kind of procedure taps only a special, restricted subset of the experienced lipreader's skills. There may be a sense in which these are core skills, but we have tried to indicate that lipreading is an activity where the core needs to be set in an appropriate support structure. This is what we suspect is strengthened by experience, because we do not for a minute believe that the students who outperformed FR on the test would equal his ability to cope without hearing if they were suddenly forced to.

In the last analysis, this is the main motivation for studying the issues raised in this chapter. If people are to be helped to lipread, it is essential to identify the aspects of lipreading that can be learned. Research to date has not done this particularly effectively. We hope that the framework sketched here may point towards productive lines of study.

Chapter 12
Integrating central processes into accounts of lipreading

12.1. Introduction

The previous chapter drew on the experience of a deafened person who relies on lipreading, and argued that important aspects of that experience are under-represented in the literature. The point is not that existing research is unimportant or irrelevant, but that "there are many other issues, at least as important from a lipreader's point of view, and as legitimate from a psychologist's, which have not been taken up." (Chapter 11). Cognitive psychology seemed to provide a framework capable of accommodating a substantial part of the complexity that lipreaders experience.

This chapter develops that idea formally. Its focus is the role of central processes in lipreading. It is axiomatic that the visual signal used by a lipreader is less informative than the input provided by hearing. As a result, processes which deploy "higher" knowledge have to do more work in lipreading than they do in listening. But although the importance of higher order knowledge is generally accepted, its role has not been mapped out in any great detail. This chapter reports four studies which examine aspects of the way central processes operate in lipreading.

Two general points need to be made about our aims. First, we are concerned with lipreading by people who have full adult linguistic competence. It is a very different issue how lipreading functions as a medium for language acquisition, and we do not claim to address it. Second, we are concerned with lipreading supplemented by little or no auditory input. We are aware of contemporary interest in the integration of visual and auditory inputs (e.g. Summerfield 1983). However, there are substantial numbers of people whose auditory input is minimal (see Chapter 1). Our deafened lipreaders fall in that category. Understanding their position is not trivial. It is also theoretically important to determine what can be achieved without auditory input.

The chapter falls into two main parts. The second part is more fully developed. It describes research on the interaction between lipreading and other mental processes. Its theme is that lipreading is psychologically complex in a way that object recognition, for instance, is not. Object recognition is logically complex, but the processes involved are carried out smoothly and automatically so that they barely impinge on our conscious mental life, and they are no obstacle to carrying out other mental activities at the same time. Lipreading is different. It demands mental resources which are needed for other basic activities, such as thinking and remembering, and so as the previous chapter put it "it is impossible to lipread and think at the same time". We report three studies which confirm this point by showing the effect of lipreading on inference, memorisation, and performance on a secondary task.

The first part of the chapter is concerned with a question which is more basic, but more difficult: what part do central processes play in the core process of lipreading, interpreting facial movements as speech? The side-effects considered in the second part occur because of the way higher order knowledge is used in this core process. This is a complex area, and it is difficult to obtain evidence which illuminates it directly. But although it would be logically possible to study the side effects without considering the core process, it would be unsatisfying. Hence the next section describes a study which at least generates reasonable hypotheses about the way higher order knowledge enters into the immediate task of interpreting facial movements as speech.

12.2. Higher order involvement in interpretation *per se*

Classical academic approaches to lipreading centre on the problem of classifying elementary patterns of facial movement ("visemes") in terms of the speech sounds they could represent. The process is considered primarily as a "bottom-up" one in which the information used to classify a particular sound is at least mainly information that is currently arriving at the senses – not only vision but also residual hearing.

This approach is useful, but clearly it is highly incomplete. It would be appropriate if lipreaders were trying to reconstruct an arbitrary sequence of sounds, but that is not what they actually do outside laboratory settings. In general they have access to several other layers of information – notably information about the lexicon and the syntax of the language, about the semantics of meaningful utterances, and about the current topic of conversation. It is not clear how much of the evidence which derives from classical studies can be transferred directly to the situation of meaningful lipreading where these information sources are available.

One obvious question is how ambiguous the visual signal is when it is combined with these other sources. Working within the classical model tends to highlight the issue of ambiguity, because elementary facial patterns certainly tend to correspond to more than one elementary speech sound. However, if the visual signal only needs to discriminate among words in a particular language, and even then only among words which are plausible in context, then it may well carry information which is sufficient in principle to do that. The issue is important because ambiguity occupies a central place in the way lipreading is explained to people who need to use it. If ambiguity were actually a minor issue when central processes are fully engaged, then it would have implications for the way we explain lipreading.

A subtler set of issues involves the form in which information from the senses reaches processes which have access to higher-order knowledge – about words and perhaps contextual issues. The simplest extension of the classical picture is that lipreaders reconstruct an arbitrary sequence of sounds from the visual signal, without reference to higher-level knowledge, and that provides the input to more central processes which have access to other sources of information. However it would seem to be more efficient if units concerned with word recognition could access information that acknowledges ambiguities in the input, since then they would not have to undo the large number of wrong decisions which must arise if firm classifications are made on inadequate information.

If the perceptual system can do this, then it raises questions about the relevance of one of the classical techniques for studying lipreading. It is traditional to use deliberately meaningless "nonsense syllables" to obtain information about the basic process of categorising visemes which is unconfounded by the effects of meaning. The problem is that on the argument outlined above, this could be studying a secondary route (in which sight-to-sound translation precedes the use of meaning), and so it need not tell us about the sensitivities and limitations of the units which analyse visual patterns in the primary route (in which high level knowledge and visual information are used together to reconstruct meaningful utterances).

There is a branch of the literature which has studied questions like these for some years. It has used correlational techniques to estimate how much various components contribute to overall performance in lipreading (e.g. Cowie et al. 1982; Gailey 1987; Lyxell – Ronnberg 1987b). However this technique is less than fully satisfying: the description it gives of a component is essentially a number quantifying its contribution, and the numbers vary very substantially between and even within studies for reasons which are far from obvious (Gailey 1981). It may be necessary to develop better qualitative descriptions before we can quantify satisfactorily.

This study takes up an approach to developing qualitative descriptions which has been used extensively in modern psychology: the analysis of errors made in relatively natural settings (see e.g. Cutler 1981; Norman 1981; Cowie 1985). It uses a collection of errors made by practising lipreaders in the course of communicating. A study of natural errors raises various kinds of issue, and these are considered as they arise; but the central point is that the approach allows us to consider lipreading as a complex interplay in which multiple types of information need to be recovered and integrated in real time.

The error collection assembled here is naturalistic in a very broad sense. It involves people who normally rely on lipreading for speech reception, and they are using it to obtain information rather than to recreate sound sequences. The material they are lipreading is not constructed according to rules which would introduce obvious biases in the balance of variables such as phonetic composition, word length, sentence structure, and so on. These properties are useful. On the other hand, no effort has been made to ensure that material is representative in any stricter sense, and it is not obvious what would be gained if it were.

12.2.1. Method

Errors were provided by three deafened lipreaders, referred to here as A, B and D. They are respectively nos. 4, 5 and 17 in table 3.1. All have profound losses. They were chosen because experience indicated that they were excellent lipreaders. Three techniques were used to collect errors.

(1). D kept a "diary" record of mistakes made at home with his family. He kept a full record of errors in two specific conversations, and noted other errors as far as possible over a two-month period.

(2). All three lipreaders were recorded on video during a session of about 45 minutes when they were read passages (for experiment 2) and talked to the experimenters. They were encouraged to ask for clarification whenever they were uncertain. They volunteered what they thought they had heard in a large proportion of the requests for clarification. The errors recorded from these sessions were those which the lipreaders made explicit in these ways.

(3). D held three conversations which were recorded on audio tape. In these we adopted a slightly more formalised approach to recovering errors. If he had any doubt about a sentence, he repeated what he thought had been said. The other party could then confirm or correct as appropriate.

All errors were transcribed onto record cards. The classification systems which were used to analyse errors will be described below.

12.2.2. Results

Table 12.1 shows overall numbers of errors which were recorded in specific conversations.

Table 12.1 Frequency of lipreading errors. † indicates that figures are based on the lipreader's own record.

lipreader	A	D						B
		(a)	(b)	(c)†	(d)	(e)	(f)†	
duration of interaction	45min	45min	45min	20min	65min	45min	30min	45min
number of requests for clarification	36	32	24	25	14	7	4	2
number of errors in attempts to repeat	9	15	15	11	3	1	1	2

These figures are not precise. Most obviously they do not include instances where an error was made but it passed unnoticed, or where the lipreader decided clarification was unnecessary. On the other hand only one error which fell into this category later became apparent to the people who were interacting with the lipreaders, which suggests that these figures are not a serious underestimate of errors which affect the lipreader's grasp of the message – which is a more relevant measure than a count of words registered exactly. With this qualification, the figures make some broad points about lipreading in practice.

The right-hand side of the table indicates how low error rates can be. In one of these entries an exceptional lipreader, B, was interacting with people she had never met before, though they were making an effort to be understood. The two leftmost entries were obtained in the same setting, and it is revealing to compare B with D and A, who are excellent lipreaders themselves.

The fact that there are lipreaders as good as B raises two interesting points. First, it puts in perspective the claim that lipreaders confront a problem of ambiguity. If virtually perfect lipreading is possible, then the stimulus for lipreading is not ambiguous in any straightforward sense. This supports the view expressed in the previous chapter that "a lipreader's problem is not generally that the information is not there – it is the practical difficulty of getting the information which is there in the time available." Second, lipreaders like B are relevant to the issue of lipreading and learning. As the previous chapter noted, it is difficult to show that deafened lipreaders as a whole lipread better than people drawn from the general population and given a little very basic familiarisation. However it is our impression that the very best deafened lipreaders achieve a level that is quite different from the general population. B is a case in point. Other researchers seem to have similar experience of "star" lipreaders, but they have not been documented in depth.

It is also worth noting how error rate depends on context. D's entries illustrate some of the relevant factors. The very low error rate in (f) illustrates the importance of the speaker. The conversation was with his wife. Conversation (c) was also with a highly familiar speaker, his son, but it produced D's highest error rate. This illustrates the importance of subject matter: the conversation was about drumming, and most of the mistakes involved words which were familiar to D, but used in technical senses which were not familiar. The error rates for (b) and (e) make an interesting point. If we measure words understood per request for clarification, the recordings give comparable rates – 86 and 82 words per request respectively. The difference which appears in the table reflects the fact that in (e), interacting with an unfamiliar person, D took a far greater share of the speaking and had to do less lipreading. The other person spoke about 650 words in a 45-minute session which both parties knew was largely about his ability to lipread her speech. This strategy of dominating conversation was been mentioned in chapter 10: the evidence here provides a concrete example.

Turning from simple numbers of errors to their nature, we look first at the question of whether lipreaders must automatically translate the visual signal into representations which are sound-like (or linguistic), or whether they can use representations which reflect the ambiguity of the input considered apart from linguistic and contextual knowledge. The previous chapter noted a type of example which suggests that lipreaders can access such representations. These are cases where the meaning of a sentence is not picked up when it is said, or is picked up wrongly, but "clicks" later. That can only happen if the lipreader has stored, and can access, information about the pattern of movements which was observed.

D noted no new examples of this kind despite the fact that he was aware of their interest, and looked out for them. An appeal via the local newsletter for deafened people produced one more example. On that evidence it seems unlikely that lipreaders are often able to revisit the pattern that they see and interpret it correctly second time round. However two related phenomena were noted.

(1). In a large proportion of difficulties, the lipreaders reported no acoustic or verbal interpretation of what they saw. They simply "did not get" what was said. There appears to be a knock on effect. If part of a sentence is lost in this way, what follows is likely to be "lost" too. This observation provides one reason to question whether acoustic code is generated automatically and bottom-up from visible inputs. It suggests the possibility that mechanisms which generate acoustic code only operate if they can "lock on" to the input in a way that satisfies internal standards of plausibility.

(2). Both B and A tended to mimic or repeat the lip shapes of each word as it was spoken. When they had difficulty with a sentence they tended to repeat the process before asking for a repetition. This suggests a conjecture worth exploring: pre-acoustic information may be stored in a motor form, and the record may need to be replayed physically in order to be interpreted linguistically.

These observations are an aside to the main body of data, in which the lipreader identified a word (or phrase) which was different from what was actually said (the source). We will call these simple errors. They highlight three tasks which are important for correct lipreading. We will call them segmentation, the task of dividing a continuously changing visual pattern into segments which signify units of sound; simple recognition, the task of recognising which sound a segment signifies; and contextual inference, the task of using what is already known to limit the range of possibilities that are associated with a new word.

A broad classification of simple errors suggests that breakdowns in these three tasks are surprisingly similar in frequency. 31% of simple errors involved the wrong number of syllables, signifying a breakdown in segmentation. In 41% a substantial part of the word which was reported bore no straightforward relationship to the lip movements which had been made, indicating a breakdown in simple recognition. In 32%, the word which was reported would not fit naturally into the sentence in which it belonged, indicating a breakdown in contextual inference. The data allow us to look more closely at each of the categories.

It will be noticed that the task of segmentation was not mentioned in describing the classical view of lipreading. This is not unfair. Segmentation is certainly recognised as a problem in pragmatic descriptions of lipreading, but more formal analyses concentrate much less on it than on the ambiguity of elements. The data here suggest that that is an imbalance worth redressing. It will appear later that there is a link between emphasis on meaning and emphasis on segmentation.

Three main points can be made about the segmentation errors. First, they were evenly split between cases where a syllable was added (16% of simple errors) and and those where one was omitted (15%). Second, they were not evenly divided across positions in the word. Both omissions and intrusions occurred at the end of a word more often than they did either at the beginning or in the middle. In fact in 55% of the cases where a missing or extra syllable could be clearly located, it occurred at the end of a word. This marks final syllables as a particular problem.

The third main point concerns the finer resolution involved in discriminating between a single consonant and a consonant cluster. This emerged as a major difficulty. Fully 45% of errors involved either the replacement of a cluster by a single consonant, or the replacement of a single consonant by a cluster. The former was commoner: it occurred in 29% of errors, where the latter occurred in 21%. One might expect that lipreaders would tend to err in the direction of simplification, but although the difference is in that direction it is small. The main point is that the level of timing involved in distinguishing between single consonants and clusters is clearly a problem.

It is difficult to assess how radical segmentation errors can become, because the more extreme they are the harder it is to be sure that the elements which might correspond in source and response actually do. However it is worth illustrating the more radical kinds of breakdown which may be occurring. In two cases a consonant cluster appeared to be transformed into a syllable, *fla*mingo becoming *fili*pino and *br*eathtaking becoming *bir*thday (the components presumed to be involved are italicised). Somewhat similarly a single vowel appeared to be distributed over two syllables, *soo*n becoming *too* rev*iew*. Transposition between consonants may have occurred when shor*ts* was read as jo*ss* *st*ick and then joy *st*ick; alcoho*lic* was read as ice hoc*key*, suggesting transposition of a consonant and a vowel. Words may also have been transposed when *you do* was misread (on two separate occasions) as *did you*, and *I haven't* as *have I*.

It is also worth mentioning that sometimes the rhythmic pattern seems quite likely to be acting as an input to the recognition process in its own right. For instance, *is this a sensible task* was read as *are these detectable signs; approaches* was misread as *emotions; necrophiliac* was misread as *nymphomaniac; shook her head* was misread as *turned her eyes*. Except in the last case, most of the corresponding elements in source and response are visually similar; but that in itself does not explain the very close rhythmic match which is apparent. It would be interesting to have clearer evidence on the idea that rhythmic pattern can be recovered quite accurately and function as a relatively distinct input to the recognition process.

We now turn to the issues of simple recognition and contextual inference. Table 12.2 provides a useful summary of the relationship between them.

Table 12.2   Simple errors where the context is known well enough to judge how well the misreading fits the context

	almost all elements of source and error phonetically close	several elements of source and error not phonetically close
makes sense in context of sentence	17	29
does not make sense in context of sentence	14	9

The categories in the table, particularly the distinction between errors which are phonetically close and others, are informal and imprecise. The classifications were checked by an independent judge, but not too much can be rested on them. More formal measures are considered below. However the table as it stands makes three main points.

Firstly, the table suggests that the phonetic structure of an error tends to depend on its contextual properties. The implication is that the way simple recognition operates may depend on the role that contextual inference is playing. The more formal analysis below takes up that theme.

Secondly, the table illustrates the balance between simple recognition and contextual inference. Errors are rather more likely to be contextually apt but visually inaccurate than they are to be visually accurate but inappropriate in context. The sensible inference is that the two sides of the process are not grossly unequal in influence. There is a qualification, though. Most errors in the right-hand column still have some phonetic resemblance to the correct reading, whereas a considerable proportion of the errors on the bottom row make no sense at all in context. In effect, it seems that simple recognition has the power to generate readings which are totally inappropriate semantically: but contextual inference has very little power to generate readings which are totally inappropriate phonetically.

Thirdly, the table gives some indication of the extent to which lipreaders face genuine ambiguity. The errors in the top left hand cell are cases where the information available comes close to leaving a real ambiguity. They account for about a quarter of the errors which we can classify in these terms. Conversely three quarters of the errors made by even these good lipreaders occur not because the information is inadequate in principle, but because they are unable to integrate it in the time available.

More formal analysis was based on confusion matrices for the errors which are summarised in table 12.2. The matrices take account of all the elements in each word or phrase which was considered an inherent part of the error, including elements which were lipread correctly. The procedure of tabulating errors involves a good deal of subjective judgement, since it is often difficult to decide which elements in the erroneous response correspond to which elements in the source (the comments on segmentation errors illustrate the problem). However there is no reason to believe that the decisions introduce any bias systematic enough to influence the conclusions which are drawn from the matrices. Once basic matrices had been drawn up, viseme categories were superimposed by identifying groups of phonemes which were expected to be confusible on phonetic grounds and which appeared from the data to be mutually confusible in this study. This too involves a degree of intuitive judgement, but again there is no reason to believe it introduces a systematic bias.

The main concern of the analysis was to clarify interactions between simple recognition and contextual inference. That involves developing the vertical contrast in table 12.2. The question is whether there are differences between the phonetic characteristics of errors which make sense in context, where presumably information derived from the context has played a part in generating the error; and the phonetic characteristics of errors which do not make sense in context, where we have to asume that information derived from the context has played relatively little part. There is also a secondary concern, which involves the horizontal contrast in table 12. 2: is the difference between phonetically close and phonetically distant errors simply a matter of degree, or do some relationships break down more readily than others?

It is useful to begin with data for consonants. Five main viseme categories were used. They were:

SP   – simple palatals [k], [g]
SA   – simple alveolars [t], [d], [s], [z]
B   – bilabials [b], [p], [m]
GF   – grooved fricatives and affricates [ʃ], [tʃ], [dʒ]
LD   – labiodentals [f], [v]

Three phonemes were also considered as individual groupings because they occurred freqently and in this data, they showed no strong association with any other phoneme. They were: [r], [l], [n].

Responses were classified using five categories. They were:

C   – correct;

CV – correct viseme class, but not actually correct;
O   – omitted;
WV – wrong viseme class;
I   – intrusion (i.e. there is no obviously corresponding element in the spoken source).

When error counts are given as percentages, the baseline is the number of corresponding elements in the extracts which were written down when the errors were transcribed onto cards. Type I errors are excluded from the baseline because otherwise high error rates in category I would lead to low indices in the first four categories, which is quite inappropriate.

Comparing contextually apt and contextually inappropriate errors shows that some categories are remarkably stable. Correct responses run at 36% in both sets of errors. Errors in the wrong viseme class run at 25% for contextually apt errors and 24% for contextually inappropriate errors. Intrusions run at 17% in both sets. These similarities are a reassuring indication that the data are sound: differences which do appear are likely to be meaningful.

The remaining categories show a clear pattern of difference between contextually apt and contextually inappropriate errors. In contextually inappropriate ones, 28% of substitutions fall in the category CV – correct viseme class, but not actually correct. The proportion falls to 16% in the contextually apt errors. Conversely, only 12% of the substitutions which occur in contextually inappropriate errors are omissions (i.e. an element in the source is replaced by nothing in the response). The proportion rises to 23% among contextually apt errors.

These broad trends are of great interest theoretically, for two main reasons.

Firstly, the omissions are a species of segmentation error. Their distribution makes the point that segmentation appears as a minor problem among the errors where context seems to be playing a minor role, but a very substantial one when context plays a larger role. This is why giving meaning a central place in our description of lipreading is linked to giving segmentation a central place too.

Secondly, the shift in CV substitutions suggest that processes concerned with meaning have access to a fairly full description of the visual input, not just an attempted translation into a sound-like code. Not only that, they are at least sometimes more sensitive to the details in that description than processes which translate visual information into sound patterns without reference to meaning. If that were not so, the errors where meaning played a guiding role could not show this heightened discrimination between the actual phoneme which was generated and others which are visually very similar.

A fuller picture emerges from considering individual consonant categories separately, and at that level issues other than the shift between omissions and CV substitutions emerge. Table 12.3 summarises the data.

The first four columns deal with trends which seem to depend on whether errors are contextually apt. It can be seen that the trend for greater omission runs through most of consonant types. The exceptions in the case of the semi-vowels [r] and [l] prove the more general rule: it is intrusion, not omission, which is commoner there, but the rule that segmentation-related errors are commoner in contextually apt errors remains. The overall reduction in CV errors is largely due to a strong trend in the simple alveolars, where they run at 16% and 41% in contextually inappropriate and and contextually apt errors respectively. With other consonants which are articulated too far back to be obvious, a different issue emerges: whether contextually apt errors are more or less likely to contain elements from a completely inappropriate viseme class. Palatals show a definite drop in these errors with use of context. They make up 86% of responses to palatal elements when the response is inappropriate contextually, against 30% when the response is appropriate. The grooved fricatives and [n] show trends in the opposite direction, though the former are not common enough for the trend to be particularly solid.

The other type of observation which emerges involves the prevalence of certain types of element. [r] is common in sources which generate errors that are both contextually apt and phonetically close (where it forms 20% of elements): in the other logically related combinations (contextually apt but not phonetically close, etc) the levels are low and steady (at 8%, 5% and 10%). It looks as if the phoneme may serve as a peg on which it is easy to hang meaningful interpretations. Conversely the alveolars are commoner in sources which receive contextually inappropriate responses than they are in sources which receive contextually apt ones (they form 43% and 36% of consonants respectively), as if they tended to discourage fitting meaningful interpretations. Sources which contain bilabials are like sources which contain [r] in that they tend to receive a higher than average proportion of phonetically close reponses, whereas the opposite occurs with the consonants in mid-table which are articulated far enough back to be hard to see. Related trends involving labiodentals are shown, but the numbers are too small to carry much weight.

The visual summary of these points in table 12.3 indicates that there appears to be a good deal of order in these matters: they do not look like an arbitrary collection of statistical accidents. It seems well worth pursuing the hypothesis that different phonetic categories may take different roles in the process of linking visual input to meaning.

Table 12.3 Characteristics of phonetic categories ('+' indicates that the category behaves as the column heading describes; '−' that it does the opposite; and 'o' that there is no strong trend)

	use of context in interpretation				prevalence in source	
	promotes omission	promotes intrusion	reduces WV errors	reduces CV errors	promotes use of context	promotes overall accuracy
bilabials	+	o	o	o	o	+
labiodentals	+	o	o	o	+	−
simple alveolars	+	o	o	+	−	o
[n]	+	o	−	o	o	−
simple palatals	+	o	+	o	o	−
grooved fricatives	o	o	−	o	o	−
[l]	o	+	o	o	o	o
[r]	o	+	o	o	+	+

Vowels were analysed in the same way as consonants. The results were less rich, but showed related effects. Two viseme classes were worth identifying: vowels with lip spreading, and vowels with lip rounding. These, together with the neutral vowel schwa, made up the great majority of cases.

As in consonants, the stablest overall pattern was that omissions rose in errors which fitted the context and CV errors fell. Table 12.4 summarises.

Table 12.4 Context and the main types of vowel error: percentage of elements of a given type which elicited a given type of response

		Lip spread	Lip rounded	Schwa
Contextually apt errors	correct	25	47	50
	viseme correct	53	17	n/a
	viseme wrong	9	24	n/a
	omissions	13	12	25
Contextually inappropriate errors	correct	23	55	50
	viseme correct	58	23	n/a
	viseme wrong	14	22	n/a
	omissions	5	0	8

This summary conceals a curious pattern involving both context and phonetic closeness in relation to the two main viseme classes. It is summarised in table 12.5. In the first quadrant, both vowel classes show similar close balances between correct identifications and misidentifications which are nevertheless in the right viseme class. In the other quadrants, there is a consistent and quite different pattern. For the lip-spread group, correct identifications are much rarer than misidentifications in the right class, whereas exactly the opposite is true in the lip rounded class. The pattern has a natural reading – when almost everything fits, even fairly strong default rules can be over-ridden. However one would like a more precise understanding.

Table 12.5 Viseme classes, context and phonetic closeness in relation to the percentage of responses to a given element type which are correct or in the correct viseme class

		Phonetic relationship of source to response:			
		close		less close	
		lip spread	lip rounded	lip spread	lip rounded
contextually	correct	36	43	21	50
apt	viseme correct	37	43	58	0
contextually	correct	28	75	13	40
inappropriate	viseme correct	58	25	61	20

As with consonants, there is a relationship between the relative frequencies of vowels in the source and error types. Table 12.6 summarises. The general pattern is that subjects are most successful both at attaching an appropriate meaning and at approximating the phonetic structure when the representation of less common vowel types is highest. The first relationship is clearly reminiscent of the finding that distinctive consonants – semivowels and bilabials – tend to invite the use of context.

Table 12.6 Error type and percentage of elements in the source which belong in particular categories

classification of error	lip spread	schwa	lip rounded	other
phonetically less close	50	26	18	6
phonetically close	46	20	20	13
contextually inappropriate	49	27	20	4
contextually apt	48	22	19	11

12.2.3. Conclusion

This study was prompted by concern to develop accounts of lipreading which acknowledge the role of higher order knowledge, and indicate why lipreading is difficult even when that knowledge is available.

It is important to start with the observation that significant errors are rare. That is inexplicable unless lipreaders make heavy use of linguistic and contextual knowledge.

The data support the assumption that considerations derived from context are inextricably involved throughout the process of lipreading. In particular context-related considerations seem to be involved in controlling basic decisions about segmentation and phoneme identity. Higher order processes do not appear to be forced to use the output of processes which take these decisions without reference to meaning.

Once context is taken into account, very few errors seem to involve irreducible ambiguity. Instead the key problem appears to be deploying information which is in principle available. That problem often seems to hinge on the fact that the components which are involved are not intended to function together (at least not as a self-contained system), and so do not complement each other. There are respects in which processes which are sensitive to meaning seem to allow more precise use of visual information than meaning-free processes. The main examples involve discriminations within the commonest class of vowels, those which involve lip spreading; and within the commonest class of consonants, the "simple alveolars". However invoking meaning tends to conflict with the use of information about structure: it promotes omissions and intrusions, which tend to have particular phonetic properties. It can also lead people to consider some misinterpretations which they would be unlikely to make otherwise. Meaning-based processes also seem to be overly concerned with particular kinds of cue, which are not necessarily particularly informative. On a more general level, there do not seem to be good arrangements for storing visual sequences which were missed initially so that they can be revisited in the light of subsequent information.

All of this needs to be understood as a statement of hypotheses. However the hypotheses are well enough founded to provide useful guidance for research on lipreading as a meaning-based process. What is important from the present point of view is that they portray lipreading as a process which is eminently likely to make heavy demands on the central resources which are involved in reasoning, memorisation, and the control of other activities.

12.3. The impact of lipreading on other cognitive processes

The theme of this part is the way lipreading impinges on mental activities which hearing allows us to carry out smoothly and without conscious effort as we listen. The work was prompted by the experience of a practising lipreader, summed up in the previous chapter by saying "it is impossible to lipread and think at the same time."

Once the point has been stated, it is clear that it makes theoretical sense. Cognitive psychology recognises that a wide range of mental processes depend on access to a central resource which has a limited capacity. It is most often referred to as working memory (Baddeley 1986). Perceptual processes do not normally require space in working memory. Their operations may be complex, but they are carried out by self-contained "modules" (Fodor 1983) whose only communication with central processes is to pass them processed information. However it appears that lipreading depends on high level knowledge in a way that contrasts with straightforward forms of perception. It is eminently reasonable to suppose that accessing that knowledge, and manipulating it to reach conclusions, will call for space in working memory. As a result, it will deny other processes the space they need to operate.

This point is interesting theoretically. Evidence that lipreading makes heavy demands on space in working memory would be strong support for the view that lipreading is critically dependent on high level knowledge and inference. However at least as important are the practical consequences. If Rice's intuitive judgement (see chapter 11) is correct, then lipreading imposes a double barrier. It obstructs the immediate recovery of the words a speaker says. But it also means that once they have been recovered, there is a barrier to remembering and using them in the normal way. If this second barrier exists, then clearly it ought to be recognised.

12.3.1. Experiment 1

It is an axiom of modern linguistic research that "the language user has to go beyond the literal meanings of utterances in order to understand the intentions of the speaker and the likely meaning of an utterance in a particular context" (Greene 1986: 24). The hypothesis behind this study is that lipreading will impair the inferencing which is needed for full comprehension because the working memory which it requires is occupied by extracting the literal meaning.

12.3.1.1. Method

Three groups of subjects were used in the experiment; deafened lipreaders, hearing lipreaders and control subjects. The first two groups received only visual input, while the control group had both visual and auditory input. In all there were six deafened lipreaders, eight hearing lipreaders and eight control subjects. The deafened lipreaders were selected because they were considered to be among the best in the Belfast area. They were the three deafened subjects considered above (i.e. nos. 4, 5 and 17 in table 3.1) plus three others (nos. 7, 9 and 12 in table 3.1). The hearing subjects were selected because they had achieved high scores on a prior test of lipreading ability which was given to all first and second year psychology students.

Five short passages were used. They were designed to be approximately equal in length and difficulty. After each passage eight questions were asked. Four of these questions required recall of information which was stated overtly in the passage: the other four required the subject to draw inferences from the passage. The questions were presented in a random order so that the subject was unaware of the type of question he/she was being asked. However the passages were always presented to the subjects in the same order.

During presentation of the passages subjects were instructed that each sentence in the passage could be repeated up to a maximum of three times. A repetition could be signalled by the subject raising his/her hand. Immediately after hearing each passage subjects were asked to summarise it. The questions were then asked in the subject's normal mode of communication.

12.3.1.2. Results

Subjects were scored on the number of correct reponses made to each passage. The results were subjected to a three way analysis of variance, distinguishing responses to the two question types but pooling the two groups of lipreaders (hearing and deafened).

The key finding is an interaction beween mode of presentation and question type (F 1, 20 = 4.55, p = 0.046). Table 12.7 presents the means. They confirm that the lipreaders suffered a specific disadvantage on the questions which depend on inference.

Table 12.7 Number of correct answers as a function of question type and presentation

mode of presentation	directly available	inference required
auditory	2.75	2.48
lipreading	2.54	1.71

There was also a strong interaction between mode of presentation and passage number (F 4, 80 = 3.99, p = 0.005). Table 12.8 presents the means.

Table 12.8 Number of correct answers as a function of passage number and presentation

mode of presentation	passage number				
	1	2	3	4	5
auditory	3.13	2.00	2.44	2.38	3.13
lipreading	1.57	2.11	2.25	2.32	2.40

The natural interpretation of the trend is that the lipreaders improved with practice over the session. When experienced and novice lipreaders were compared, the only difference which approached significance involved this trend: it was less marked among the experienced lipreaders, though not significantly so (F 4, 48 = 2.23, p = 0.08). The obvious assumption is that these patterns simply involve the need to get used to the task.

Subjects' summaries of the passages showed another contrast between modes of presentation. The summaries were scored on the number of points from the passage that they incorporated. These scores in themselves did not depend on mode of presentation. However it was noticed that the lipreaders' summaries appeared to be closer to the wording of the original passage than the listeners. To check this an analysis of variance was carried out on the ratio of words drawn directly from the passage to points contained in the summary. A significant difference between the modes of presentation was found (F 1,

20 = 6.80, p = 0.017). There were no other significant effects or interactions. However when the two groups of lipreaders were compared, a significant interaction emerged (F 3, 36 = 3.02, p = 0.042). Once again, the novice lipreaders changed more over time. Rather surprisingly, the change was in the direction of more verbatim recall. The natural conclusion is that verbatim recall is an adaptive strategy for dealing with the constraints that lipreading imposes on memorisation.

12.3.1.3. Discussion

This experiment tested the prediction that lipreading would make it difficult to draw inferences during comprehension. The prediction was confirmed. The second main finding was unexpected, but closely allied. The lipreaders' spontaneous recall was closer to the original wording than that of the listeners. This finding probably should have been predicted given the strong evidence that elaborating material results in better recall (e.g. Anderson 1990: 178–218). Our view of lipreading implies that each word is the subject of considerable cognitive processing, and so it should not be surprising that lipreaders tend to recall individual words.

Most comparisons between novice and experienced lipreaders confirm the widespread finding that the groups are remarkably similar. The one exception is the finding that initially novices show less verbatim recall than experienced lipreaders. The natural interpretation is that it takes time to learn that the peculiar mode of processing which is enforced by lipreading has its own distinct advantages. However, the exception proves the rule in the sense that the lesson appears to be learnt within the span of an hour. The truly remarkable fact is that there is so little difference between people who have depended on lipreading as their main mode of communication for decades and people whose previous experience of lipreading consists of a five-minute test.

12.3.2. Experiment 2

The previous study used relatively natural materials. This is useful because it establishes that the limitations imposed by lipreading are practically relevant. However the material does not allow us to probe the details of the limitation in any depth. This experiment examined the interaction between lipreading and memory using a task which is less natural, but which has been used extensively to probe memory processes. The task is free recall of a list.

Two main characteristics of list recall were of interest.

First, we were concerned with the process of categorisation in list recall.

When a list contains items which fall into a few categories, items which belong in the same category tend to be reported together at recall even when they are presented in a random scatter through the list. We hypothesised that lipreaders would not show that effect. The reasoning was that working memory would be needed to carry out the process of categorisation, and lipreading the actual words would use too much space in working memory to allow categorisation.

Second, we were concerned with serial-order effects. List recall generally shows three components. Items presented early in the list are recalled particularly well. This is called a primacy effect, and it reflects the way items are encoded from short-term stores (which are associated with working memory) into long-term storage. Items in mid-list are recalled if they have been transferred to long term memory, but this is not as achieved as often as it is at the start of the list. Items at the end of the list are recalled particularly well because some of them remain in short term store. This is called the recency effect. Since we were interested in central aspects of processing rather than simple residence in short term store, we followed list presentation with an interference task which eliminates the recency effect.

12.3.2.1. Method

Sixteen subjects participated in this experiment. Eight were allocated to the lipreading group. All subjects in the lipreading group were hearing lipreaders who had been involved in the previous experiment.

All subjects were required to recall two lists, each containing twenty-one words. In the first list the words were unrelated: in the second they fell into six categories. The categorised list was constructed in two stages. First, local category norms (Brown 1978) were used to identify words which were strongly associated with categories. A preliminary experiment was then run to select words which were truly lipreadable from this pool. Categories which had at least three highly lipreadable members were used in the main experiment. The words in the uncategorised list were taken from other tests of lipreading and had all been shown to be highly lipreadable.

An explicitly unblocked design was used. The order of words was randomised within each list, with the constraint that no two words from the same category appeared beside each other. Different randomised lists were used for each subject. The order of presentation of the lists from subject to subject was also counterbalanced so that half the subjects received the uncategorised list first and half the categorised one first.

Subjects were warned that they would have to try and remember as many of the words as possible and that they would have to complete a distractor task before commencing to recall the words. The distractor task was to count backwards from a given number for about thirty seconds. Subjects were not cued that any of the words in the list were related or that they could be remembered more easily by categorising the list.

All subjects were told that each word would have to be repeated twice but that if they felt unsure of the word that they had either heard or lipread they should indicate this by raising their hand. A further four repetitions could then be given. If subjects still could not make sense of the word they indicated this by shaking their head. If subjects did not raise their hand it was assumed that they had lipread the word and the experimenter continued with the next word. This limited the amount of rehearsal control subjects could perform.

Responses were given on written answer sheets. The experimenter also recorded which words the subject had been unable to lipread, which words had required repetitions, the number of repetitions needed and finally the time taken to recall the lists.

12.3.2.2. Results

Contrary to expectation, analysis of the categorisation scores showed no difference between the two groups. Categorisation was measured by first counting the number of words which appeared beside at least one other word of the same category, and then dividing these scores by the number of words recalled. Both groups gave scores close to 55%, which indicates that categorisation did occur. Lipreaders scored slightly lower, but a t-test shows that the difference was far from significance (df = 14, t = 0.27, p = 0.79).

Conversely, the two groups differed unexpectedly in recall. Recall was measured as a percentage of the total number of words which had been registered correctly during presentation. This was because despite the precautions which had been taken the lipreaders were unable to lipread all the words in the lists. Analysis of variance showed significant main effects of mode of presentation (F 1, 12 = 21.0, p = 0.0006) and of list (F 1, 12 = 18.6, p = 0.001). Table 12.9 summarises the relevant means. There was no significant effect associated with which list was presented first (categorised or uncategorised) and there were no significant interactions.

Table 12.9 Recall as a function of mode of presentation and list type

presentation	categorised	uncategorised
lipreading	41.90	21.73
listening	64.29	49.40

Table 12.9 suggests that the categorised list may have given lipreaders a greater proportional gain than it gave listeners. This was checked by taking the ratio of score on the categorised list to score on the uncategorised list for each subject. When the two groups are compared with respect to these ratios, the difference is almost significant (t = 1.85, df = 14, p = 0.086 (2 tailed)).

Inspection indicates that the groups did differ with respect to serial position effects. Figure 12.1 illustrates this fact. The controls' scores showed a marked downward trend against serial position, reflecting the expected primacy effect. The trend was absent in the lipreaders. Regression was used to confirm the statistical robustness of the effect. Three predictors were considered: a constant advantage for the listeners; a linear change with list position for both groups; and an "interaction" term which is zero for the lipreaders but changes linearly with position for the listeners. The first and the third were highly significant predictors (p = 0.0001) and the second was far from significance, confirming that list position does affect the two groups differentially.

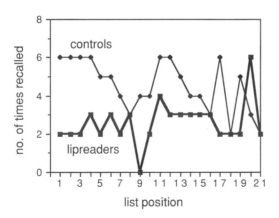

Figure 12.1 Serial position effects on list recall

12.3.2.3. Discussion

Because the serial position effect found here was totally unforeseen, we replicated the study with a variety of modifications. The absence of a primacy effect was confirmed (Sweeney 1991: 28–60). The finding reinforces the view that lipreading places a special burden on working memory. There is debate over the nature of the primacy effect, but it is generally taken to reflect the space which is available in working memory early in the task, so that items which come in early have a good chance of being maintained long enough to be transferred into long term storage. What the evidence suggests is that lipreaders do not have that window of opportunity. Their working memory is heavily occupied from the outset, rather in the way the listeners' memory is occupied in the middle of a list-memorisation exercise. If that analogy is accurate, then it provides a useful way of conveying the kind of overload that lipreaders experience.

However two unexpected findings call for explanation. First, categorisation was as apparent among lipreaders as it was among the controls, despite the evidence from serial position that lipreading restricted the space available to them in working memory. If anything, lipreaders benefitted more from the opportunity to categorise than listeners did. Second, the fact that lipreaders performed worse than controls in this experiment appears to conflict with their performance in the previous experiment, where they answered literal questions as well as controls did. The difficulty is heightened by the fact that in that context the lipreaders were more likely than controls to recall information in words close to the original. This experiment seems on the surface to favour a strategy that leads to verbatim recall.

The simplest explanation is that categorisation is a relatively simple form of organisation – probably simpler than the organisation involved in near-verbatim recall of prose. It does not require a great deal of working memory, but it does facilitate long-term storage. What does demand space is the construction of associations which make it possible to recall material with little intrinsic organisation. That is a natural extrapolation from modern research which views list learning as a process of constructing arbitrary associations so that items can be embedded in a network of long term knowledge (e.g. Anderson 1990: 198–209). The practical implication is that superficially simple memory tasks may be as difficult for lipreaders as superficially complex ones if they mean that working memory is needed to impose order on inputs which have little of their own.

12.3.3. Experiment 3

This experiment takes up another standard method of probing memory, the use of a secondary task.

Once again the incentive came from a co-author's practical experience. FR commented that even tasks which do not depend critically on vision seem to be impaired by lipreading. This corresponds well to psychological theory. Working memory is involved in the control of activity as well as the manipulation of information, and so one would expect to find competition between the manipulation of information which is involved in lipreading and the execution of a secondary task.

It is not easy to find secondary task which allows this expectation to be tested. The main difficulty is that lipreading depends on visual attention, and so there is an inevitable conflict between it and any task which involves visual control. To argue that there is a difficulty involving competition for working memory, one needs a task which does not present that more straightforward type of competition.

We devised a coin-sorting task to meet this problem. A box containing a mixture of (small) 1p coins and (large) 2p coins was placed on the table in front of the subject. A shield was placed around the box, which allowed the subjects to lift out the coins, but prevented them from seeing what they were doing. Subjects' task was to remove 1p coins as quickly as possible, while they were either lipreading or listening to a test passage.

12.3.3.1. Method

Twenty subjects took part. They were divided into two groups, hearing lip-readers and controls. The subjects used in the lipreading group had participated in some of the previous lipreading experiments, and all were high scorers in a previous lipreading test. The lipreading task involved six passages. They were recorded on video tape by an experienced lipspeaker. They were read slowly, and each sentence was repeated to help maximise comprehension. The lipreaders were given only visual input (i.e. the sound was turned off), while the controls received normal auditory and visual input. Subjects were asked to watch the video of the passage so that they could answer questions on it as well as possible, and to pick out as many 1p's as that allowed them to do.

After each passage subjects were asked eight questions. They were of the verbatim kind used in experiment two. None of the questions required inferences to be made.

12.3.3.2. Results

Table 12.10 summarises the mean scores for the two groups.

Table 12.10 Performance on the comprehension test and sorting

	listeners	lipreaders
number of questions correct (max = 8)	7.6	5.9
number of coins sorted	42.4	26.9

The most useful overall analysis comes from standardising scores both for coins sorted and for questions answered so that the listeners had a mean of 0 and a standard deviation of 1 on both tasks. An analysis of variance was carried out on data transformed in this way (averaging over passage to simplify standardisation). There was a significant main effect of mode of presentation (F 1, 18 = 38.0, p = 0.0001) and a significant interaction between mode of presentation and passage (F 1, 18 = 32.2, p = 0.0001). The lipreaders' score on the questions was 6.17 standard deviations below that of the listeners, and the number of coins they sorted was 1.17 standard deviations below the listeners' (in both cases, the standard deviations are those of the listeners).

The relationship between the individuals' comprehension and coin sorting was explored more fully in a regression. It used three variables to predict coins sorted – listeners' comprehension scores, lipreaders' comprehension scores, and group (listener or lipreader). There was a significant positive relationship between coins sorted and lipreaders' scores (t = 2.46, p = 0.026). The relationship between listeners' scores and coins sorted was not significant (t = 1.22, p = 0.24), but the trend was in the opposite direction. This is to say that listeners tend to show a trade-off between the two tasks, comprehension and sorting, whereas the lipreaders who were best at comprehension were also best at sorting.

There were order effects, but they were unremarkable. Both groups became better at coin sorting with time and the lipreaders became better at comprehension (the listeners began near maximum).

12.3.3.3. Discussion

In broad terms, the experiment demonstrates what it set out to. Lipreading not only makes for reduced comprehension, it impairs the ability to do other things at the same time – even when they do not demand visual attention.

There is a superficial problem in that this study found a difference between the lipreaders' and the listeners' comprehension, whereas experiment 1 found no such difference on the literal questions. The difference is probably straightforward, and has nothing to do do with the lipreaders. Their scores were remarkably close in the two studies. (They averaged 5.93/8 here and 2.54/4 in the literal questions in experiment 1). The listeners, however, scored better in this experiment. This probably reflects the fact that they heard every sentence repeated here, but did not get repetitions in experiment 1 unless they asked for them.

More interesting is the positive correlation between coin sorting and comprehension scores. The key observation is that the best lipreader performed close to the mean for the listeners in both respects. This was not the pattern that we anticipated. We had expected that even lipreaders who matched listeners on comprehension would have a hidden deficit which was made visible by the coin-sorting task. That is the natural expectation if good lipreading performance depends on heavy use of working memory.

The natural conclusion is that the very best lipreaders are good enough at extracting visual patterns to make relatively low demands on working memory. This re-emphasises two points made in part one: first, that irreducible ambiguity of the stimulus is probably less of a problem than tends to be assumed; and second, that there are "star" lipreaders who are well worth studying.

Nevertheless, it is unwise to focus too hard on issues which only affect stars. The basic fact remains that for most of the lipreaders in this experiment, whose performance compared well with the good deafened lipreaders in experiment 1, lipreading encroached very considerably on the working memory that they needed to perform another task while they were lipreading.

12.4. Conclusion

This chapter can be seen from three points of view.

From the theorist's point of view, it suggests ways of progressing towards an account of lipreading which gives central processes full recognition. In that context its main contribution is probably to identify hypotheses which can be pursued empirically and techniques which relate to them. Although we have not dwelt on them, there are many questions about our findings which an experimentalist would want to answer before accepting a particular theoretical interpretation. That is almost inevitable when research breaks new ground. It is also worth noting that the findings raise issues which may be relevant to more general problems, such as the role of working memory in linguistic comprehension, as well as the specific problem of lipreading.

From a pragmatic point of view, the findings in 12.2 have some significance. It seems likely that instruction in lipreading will be most effective when it is based most solidly on knowledge of the difficulties that practising lipreaders encounter. Our study may be able to contribute in that respect. In particular it seems useful to be able to describe the general balance between errors in segmentation, errors in simple recognition, and errors in contextual inference; and it is possible that describing the errors which tend to accompany the use of context may allow people to compensate for them. We also suspect that instruction may benefit from summarising lipreading not in terms of ambiguity, but in terms of linking three types of information, all partial: information about likely meanings, information about rhythmic structure, and information about individual sounds. These points can only be tested through practice.

The findings of 12.3 are much more directly relevant, though. In a broad sense, there seems to be no doubt that lipreading does disrupt other mental processes which would run smoothly alongside listening – memorising what has been said, organising it, drawing inferences from it, and controlling other activities. It is important for people who rely on lipreading to organise their communication in a way that acknowledges this – that includes people who talk to lipreaders as well as the lipreaders themselves. It is important to understand that when breakdowns occur because of these malinteractions, they reflect the nature of lipreading and not ill will or mental disorder on the part of the lipreader. There is also a good case for bringing tests concerned with central side effects into the evaluation of lipreading. It is important to know whether devices which improve lipreading do so at the cost of still further depressing users' prospects of remembering what they lipread. Conversely, devices which do not appear to improve performance (e.g. because it is at ceiling) may actually produce large benefits if they make it likelier that what was detected will be understood and recalled.

From the viewpoint of the book as a whole, the chapter reaffirms the point that acquired deafness brings with it a striking number of non-obvious ramifications. Deafened people are effectively faced with memory limitations as well as limitations of immediate comprehension, and with limitations in the ability to "time share" mental resources which are usually taken for granted. These problems have yet another level of ramification, at which point they converge with the problems of speech production which are the central focus of the book. If people are unable to draw obvious inferences from simple statements, or to remember what they are known to have understood at the time, or to do more than one thing at a time, then other people are likely to draw their own conclusions, and they are not likely to promote satisfying interaction.

Chapter 13
Understanding the quality of deafened people's lives

13.1. Introduction

This chapter summarises a study which has run parallel to the communication-oriented research reported so far. In broad terms it is concerned with deafened people's quality of life. Its focus is not on deriving an overall measure for their quality of life, but on understanding the factors that go to make their lives satisfying or unsatisfying in their own judgement. Without that kind of understanding it is difficult to assess the significance or insignificance of the findings in the previous chapters.

The research was prompted by the sense that investigations which were emerging at the time left an important gap unbridged.

On one side of the gap, Thomas and his co-workers showed in the early 1980's (Thomas – Gilholme Herbst 1980: 78) that acquired deafness had a strong tendency to result in clinical depression (see chapter 1). On the other side, a number of projects looked at the impact of acquired deafness in highly functional terms. Again, chapter 1 summarises the main findings. Several groups considered relationships between employment and acquired deafness. The frequency of marital breakdown was studied. Wood – Kyle (1983: 179) produced their table of the difficulty experienced when communicating in various situations. With these findings came models which described adjustment to acquired deafness in terms of accepting limitations which the authors appear to assume are reasonably well defined (Rice 1984: 16; Kyle – Jones – Wood 1985).

The gap that we perceived involved psychological consequences of acquired deafness other than outright depression. The fact that depression is so prevalent strongly suggests that such consequences do exist: that in addition to its external and observable consequences, acquired deafness regularly generates effects which are internal and psychological. Clinical depression seems likely to be the extreme, measurable sign of these effects, rather than a self-contained event. It is a sign of upheavals which change the landscape of people's subjective worlds.

The logical conclusion that this must be so was reinforced both by talking to our own deafened informants and by reading published self accounts (e.g.

Abrahams 1972; Anderson 1980; MacCartney 1980). They pointed to strong internal emotions and philosophical tensions as things that one used to value cease to be an issue, things that one has always taken for granted are threatened, and the social framework which used to underpin one's sense of identity contracts. At the very least, we felt it was unsafe to assume that someone in that position would have the same preoccupations and values as a typical middle class researcher.

Despite the compelling quality of observations which we read in self-accounts and heard from individual informants, we were acutely aware of the need to establish how representative they were. Individual observations can always be written off as eccentric. We were also aware of the need to establish that the psychological concomitants of acquired deafness were not curiosities, without any real bearing on the real quality of people's lives. These considerations led us to develop a two-phase approach in which interviews were integrated with a questionnaire designed to provide information about the prevalence of experiences and to provide multiple ways of examining the impact of various experiences on people's lives.

13.2. Method

The informants who took part are described in detail in chapter 3 (see sections 3.3.1. and 3.3.2.) and summarised in table 13.1. They are a substantial sample, covering a wide range in terms of both level of loss and age at onset.

Table 13.1 Summary of the sample who completed questionnaires/interviews

level of loss	age at onset of deafness				
	< 5	5–18	19–30	31–60	> 60
< 60 dB	4	3	3	9	5
60–79 dB	5	3	0	6	3
80–99 dB	3	1	3	4	2
100–119 dB	1	7	6	5	1
120 dB	3	7	3	0	0

Informants provided two kinds of information: they filled in a questionnaire, and they participated in an interview with the first author. The interview was semi-structured. Informants were asked to describe a day in their life, and the interview aimed to cover a number of specific topics: when they lost their hearing, their initial reaction, methods of communication, sources of help, perceived attitudes of hearing people, and any experience of depression. They were also encouraged to follow up any topic that they felt was important. In practice it is difficult to exert close control over interviews with people whose hearing is seriously impaired. As a result informants set their own agenda to a considerable extent – particularly when they were eager to talk, as many were. This was accepted.

Work on the first twenty interviews has been reported by Cowie – Stewart (1986). They were used together with sources from the formal research literature and published self-accounts to identify recurrent concerns which appeared to be worth pursuing in the questionnaire. The basic format of the questionnaire was intended not only to document experiences, but also to examine their impact on people's lives. Most questions had two parts. The first, part A, dealt with quasi-objective assessments of the frequency or the extent of particular situations. The second, part B, was concerned with the impact that the relevant experience had on the informant's life. For each part, informants were asked to circle the most appropriate alternative on a scale. Examples of the two main formats which were used are as follows.

Format 1:
You go to a social event or an outing with other people
who have hearing problems.

A. Does this happen to you?   Yes-often   Yes-sometimes   Yes-rarely   No

B. What effect do events   Very good   Good   Little/no   Bad   V. Bad
   like this have on your life ?   effect   effect   effect   effect   effect

Format 2:
A. Hearing people don't know what it's like to be deaf.

| Strongly agree | Agree | Unsure | Disagree | Strongly disagree |

B How is your life affected by hearing people's knowledge
(or lack of knowledge) about deafness?

| Made much better | Made better | Little or no effect | Made worse | Made much worse |

The questionnaire contained 41 two-part questions of this kind. In addition it included preliminary questions about biographical and medical issues and a final question which asked informants to choose one of six categories describing the overall impact of deafness on their lives (from "on balance improved" to "almost completely destroyed"). Full details of the questionnaire will be available in Stewart-Kerr (forthcoming).

13.3. Results

The interview transcripts were subjected to a formal content analysis, but that will not be reported in depth. The main use of the interviews will be to convey what the abstract quantitative findings mean.

It is useful to begin with three questionnaire items which we refer to as indicator variables. One of these is the final question which considers the overall impact of deafness. The others are two paired questions which consider depression (part A deals with its frequency, part B with the severity of its impact on the informants' lives). The significance of these items is that they all reflect the global effect of acquired deafness, though in at least partly different ways.

Table 13.2 summarises the informants' assessments of the overall effect of deafness on their lives. It reaffirms the gravity of the problem: over a third of the informants report that their lives were badly restricted or destroyed by their hearing loss.

Table 13.2   Assessments of the overall impact of deafness

assessment of overall effect of deafness	number of respondents	percentage of respondents
almost completely destroyed	8	11%
badly restricted	19	26%
restricted	22	30%
some inconvenience	21	29%
little / no effect	2	3%
on balance improved	1	1%

Both questions on depression confirm its prevalence in deafened people. Table 13.3 shows that over 50% of the questionnaire respondents encountered feelings of depression more than rarely. Table 13.4 shows that almost two thirds of the respondents felt badly or very badly affected by feelings of depression. (It may seem paradoxical that some respondents reported good or very good effects: the point is that they rarely or never experienced feelings of depression.) It is interesting that this last item, which represents the least direct approach to assessing the impact of deafness, suggests the worst assessment of the problem.

Table 13.3 Reported frequency of depression

	yes-often	yes-sometimes	yes-rarely	never
umber of respondents	16	23	17	17
percentage of respondents	22%	31%	23%	23%

Table 13.4 Reported impact of depression

	very good effect	good effect	little/no effect	bad effect	very bad effect
number of respondents	1	4	22	29	17
percentage of respondents	1%	6%	30%	40%	23%

It is revealing that these measures of impact are not simply related to audiological or social variables. Multiple regression analyses were carried out on each one, using the ten variables which seemed most likely to be useful predictors. None of the regressions gave a significant overall result. In the process only three individual predictors showed significant or near-significant associations with an indicator variable. They were level of loss (just significantly associated with overall effect); tinnitus which caused annoyance (a near-significant association with frequency of depression); and employment status, i.e. employed/unemployed (significantly associated with overall effect and almost significantly associated with depression frequency).

For the remaining questionnaire variables, the first task is to identify a manageable number of central themes round which the data cohere. Factor analyses provide a formal tool for doing this. Two factor analyses were run, one for the part A items and one for part B. Variables with low sampling adequacy were deleted after initial tests, leaving 34 items in each analysis. Total sampling adequacy was 0.76 for the part A questions and 0.71 for part B questions. Bartlett tests of sphericity were highly significant ($p < 0.0001$), indicating that both sets of data were suitable for factor analysis.

Both analyses generate about ten factors. Not much should be made of the smaller factors: they are not particularly stable, in the sense that modest changes in the sample can shift the pattern considerably, and interpretation tends to be awkward because not many items have high loadings on the factor. We dealt with this problem by considering only factors which accounted for more than 10% of the variance. A reasonably clear set of themes emerges when that is done.

In each analysis there were four factors which met our criterion of accounting for 10% of the variance. They are summarised in table 13.5. Two themes come through both analyses: the corresponding factors load highly on similar sets of items, and there is a substantial correlation between the factor scores. The other two factors in each analysis draw together themes which are divided over several smaller factors in the other analysis. One of the values of the part-A / part-B structure is that different parts of a question encourage people to look at the same issue from somewhat different angles, and so it is not unexpected that themes are balanced and grouped slightly differently in the two analyses. There is no serious reason to doubt that both groupings are valid and informative. It is worth noting that if only one of the types of question had been asked, themes which come through strongly on the other analysis would not have emerged.

Table 13.5   Themes associated with factors which account for 10% of variance in at least one analysis, and the percentage of variance that each accounts for

	part A	part B	correlation
benefit from positive experiences	10.1%	14.5%	.481
distress over failures in interaction	16.1%	14.0%	.594
abandonment		13.3%	
restriction		10.1%	
malinteraction by hearing people	16.6%		
communicative deprivation	12.3%		

The names used in table 13.5 give a rough sense of the themes which come through the analysis. Fuller descriptions of the factors are given below, but before doing that it is useful to address an obvious question: do these themes have any real relevance to the quality of people's lives, or do they simply reflect psychological accompaniments to acquired deafness which are of no great practical significance? Our procedure allows us to tackle this question in four ways.

(1). For themes which come through the part-B analysis, the nature of the questions indicates an overall impact on people's lives. A part-B factor is defined by the presence of a consistent pattern in people's answers to questions which ask how their lives are affected by experiences or tendencies related to the theme. This generally means that a substantial group of people feel their lives are made worse (or better) by the relevant set of experiences or tendencies, whereas another group feel relatively unaffected by them.

(2). Closely related, but by no means equivalent, we can look at the frequencies of different types of answer to the relevant part-B questions. This is done below for some of the key themes.

(3). We can examine comments in the interviews which are relevant to the themes. Again, this is done below for some of the key themes.

(4). Regression can be used to establish whether scores on the factors which have been identified contribute to predicting the indicator variables. Since these reflect the global impact of deafness, a variable which is relevant to predicting them has a claim on relevance to the overall quality of life. That approach is developed now.

A regression analyis was carried out for each of the three indicator variables. Each used six independent variables corresponding to the six themes in table 13.5. Where a factor was found in both part A and part B the variant which accounted for more variance was used (hence there were two variables derived from part A and four from part B). All of the regressions yielded highly significant predictions. It will be recalled that the indicator variables were not well predicted by audiological data, and so the overall success of the regressions is informative in itself. It suggests that the overall quality of deafened people's life becomes intelligible if, but only if, attention is paid to experiential issues of the general kind we have been considering. For completeness we examined the effect of extending the regressions to include the three socio/audiological variables which had some predictive value. In the context of the factor scores none of the extra variables made anything approaching a significant contribution to prediction.

Table 13.6 summarises the contributions of individual factor scores. It gives the probability associated with each factor's contribution to the model. It can be seen that three of the factors make a significant contribution to predicting all three of the index variables, and all of them make a significant contribution to predicting at least one. This is particularly important in the case of the factors based on part A, where we have no guarantee from the nature of the items that the factor has a bearing on the quality of life.

Table 13.6 Significance of major factors as predictors of index variables in regression analysis

	Factor	Depression		Overall
	from part	frequency	impact	effect
benefit from positive experiences	B	.093	.044	.137
distress over failures in interaction	B	.001	.001	.012
abandonment	B	.173	.002	.012
restriction	B	.007	.003	.003
malinteraction by hearing people	A	.246	.260	.036
communicative deprivation	A	.001	.001	.001

Of the six themes which emerge from our analysis, three are represented to at least some extent in the literature. These will be discussed briefly. The others have received very little attention, but on the evidence of the part-B questions they involve the items which evoke by far the strongest effects on people's lives, for good or ill. They will be discussed at more length, and the informants' comments in the interviews will be used to convey what these themes mean in reality.

The communicative deprivation factor is the one which most simply reflects impaired speech reception. Extreme scorers on the factor report that they frequently experience situations where people speak to them through someone else; where a family member or friend takes over things they used to do; where people repeat to help them understand; and where someone accompanies them on official appointments in case of difficulty. They often feel lost in conversation, and they report longing to hear particular sounds.

At first sight, these items might be interpreted in terms of reversion to a dependent role. Writers with a background in social work have seen that role as a bigger problem than the actual communicative handicap. Beattie (1981: 311) raised the issue memorably when she described how "relatives can deprive a person of his or her rights as a family member and 'exclude him from the joys and sorrows of everyday life' so that he becomes an onlooker, with his dependency and uselessness magnified." This case would be bolstered if a factor whose essence was communicative dependence were a strong predictor of the overall impact of deafness. However additional evidence suggests otherwise.

Within the factor analysis, the factor has an appreciable loading on time spent at home because of deafness. It is people who do not spend much time at home for this reason who tend to score badly on this factor. The implication of this finding is that the essence of the factor, with its powerful bearing on over-all quality of life, is being deprived of communication rather than taking on a dependent role. The support of a family seems to be a partial remedy for the problem, not a part of it.

Looking outside the factor analysis, we find that the factor is strongly re-lated to audiological variables. For each of the major factors we carried out a regression to establish how well it could be predicted by the most promising social and audiological variables. The strongest relationship ($r^2 = 0.384$) was found in the case of communicative deprivation. The variables which made significant contributions to the prediction were level of loss, annoyance from tinnitus, and reliance on lipreading, suggesting that the factor is very closely tied to the basic communicative handicap. Two social variables also made contributions which came close to significance, viz., sex and marital status. Communicative deprivation is less likely to occur among informants who are female or married, suggesting again that social support tends if anything to al-leviate the problem.

The theme of restriction is implicit in the literature which was discussed in the introduction, dealing with issues such as employment and mobility. High scorers on the restriction factor report that they are particularly affected in their lives by feeling held back from what they want to do, spending more time at home, and not having a job. This fits the literature's pragmatic out-look. The link is reinforced by the regression using social and audiological variables, which is highly significant (with $r^2 = 0.366$): the only individual variable which contributes significantly is employment status. However there are other elements in the factor which are less straightforward. High scorers also feel affected by longing to hear particular sounds, and by the sense that deafness is like a glass case separating them from the world. The phrasing of the last item came from a deafened informant who put a distinctive experience vividly:

> When I waken up in the morning I cannot hear water, I cannot hear the kettle, I cannot hear anything … I have to get up and dress without hear-ing anything whatsoever. I don't think I shall ever be able to overcome that feeling. … You're just in a glass case looking out at the world mov-ing around but you don't know anything about …

The quotation conveys a sense of confinement which is not simply socio-economic, though the speaker was also very much concerned with lost social and career opportunities. The factor analysis suggests that this combination is not at all eccentric. The quality which the quotation captures is perhaps most easily summed up as existential. Wood (1987) has pointed out that existentialist concepts have a good deal of relevance to the experience of deafness, and our evidence reinforces his case. It is worth noting that the "glass case" experience is described as having a bad or very bad effect on life far more often than other, more concrete items.

Extreme scorers on the next factor are badly affected by the feeling that people don't know what it's like to be deaf; by the feeling that people can't be bothered with them; and by fear of missing important information. The distinctive theme which comes through is a combination of need, loss and isolation which is best summed up as a sense of having been abandoned. It is coupled with items which are linked to the previous factor too, longing to hearing particular sounds and feeling that deafness is like a glass case separating them from the world: these clearly fit the theme. It is natural to link this theme to the view put forward by social scientists that becoming deaf leads to responses of alienation and mourning (e.g. Meadow-Orlans 1985: 43).

The first theme to be considered in more depth is the one which comes through the questionnaire most strongly, accounting for large factors in both part A and part B. It has been described as distress over failures in interaction. Table 13.7 summarises the items which have strong associations with the factor. The predominant theme is the negative feelings which surround communication for deafened people. It is clear from the numbers of people reporting very bad effects on their lives that these feelings correspond to a major source of difficulty. In fact of the twelve questions which receive "very bad" responses most often, five are associated with this theme; five more are associated with the theme of malinteraction, which is considered next; and the others are depression and the "glass case" experience mentioned above.

The interviews give some sense of the intensity of these feelings. One informant says: "Embarrassment ... I can feel the hairs on my neck stand on edge when I have misheard". Another conveys her struggle with the feeling of stupidity: "People say something ... you don't know what they say. You feel a right mutt ... I'm continually saying to myself it doesn't really matter, if it's anything of great importance you'd be made to understand it, but it's a mighty tough job". Still another admits that: "I just clam up ... I'm always afraid of making mistakes and then I don't say anything". A very similar point is made by another man: "I find it hard to contribute because I don't know what the general line of conversation is at any particular point. You wouldn't say anything because it may be out of context ... you would stand back rather than as-

Table 13.7   Percentage of informants giving each response type to part B questions
associated with the factor "distress over failures in interaction"

effect on life of feeling ...	very good	good	little/ none	bad	very bad
embarrassed at misunderstanding	0	1	14	56	29
stupid at misunderstanding	0	1	19	56	23
afraid of missing information	0	1	23	56	19
afraid of saying the wrong thing	0	4	27	51	18
left out in a conversation	0	3	30	48	19
lost in a conversation	0	0	34	49	16
afraid of missing warning sounds	0	3	45	36	16

sert yourself. You feel inadequate". A very practical fear is that "you might say yes to something and get yourself into trouble."

Many of the comments on these themes link them to destructive consequences. People are often aware that their behaviour is likely to be viewed unfavourably, but that is better than the distress of trying to participate. The mildest consequence is withdrawal from a particular encounter. One informant comments: "There are many occasions when I would like to ask questions but in case I don't hear the answer I just don't do it. I think that probably gives the impression that I'm not interested which isn't the case, it's just to save embarrassment". More often, informants describe long term withdrawal. In some cases the withdrawal is partial. For example a man admits that "as soon as the meeting's over I come out so that they'll not talk to me." Another lady reports that she "avoids long conversations with people ... I can just speak a wee bit, the time of day and then I let it go." However in other cases the results are more drastic. One lady reports: "I used to answer people wrong and I could see them laughing at me and it just put me I didn't want to mix with company or friends". Another explains "You feel an absolute mutt, with the consequence that you tend to retire out of social life". An opposite strategy, which may not be more acceptable in the long run, is to take over. This is a perfectly conscious decision for at least some: "I have to dominate the meeting, I make myself the artificial centre of attention so that people will just speak to me ... instead of speaking to the chairman they would be speaking to me".

These feelings can also have internal consequences. They constitute a source of strain, and can apparently have a physical impact on people's health. Informants report being "tensed up." One reports: "I develop a headache with worrying about whether or not I'm going to pick it up". Another says that "if someone's talking and I can't hear them I know it's going to annoy me terribly."

Inability to hear warning sounds is reported less often in the interviews, which corresponds to the questionnaire data. Nonetheless it is a problem for some. Informants report being "nervous at night" and "unable to sleep." One voices concern that "When I'm asleep, I can't hear a thing, they could be knocking the house down and I wouldn't even know". Insecurity when crossing roads is reported by another who recalls "that when I was on the road, the traffic is coming, and comes round the corner. I'm trying to watch them coming up the road but I can't see them coming round the corner and I can't hear them".

The key point to make about this theme is that flawed interaction is surrounded by intense psychological effects. The distress tends to infect even interactions which succeed, because the deafened person often does not know that they do. These internal effects are no less real than the practical limitations that are more obvious to an outside observer. A person with normal hearing may tend to think of communication as a means to pragmatic ends – promotion, shopping, travel, or whatever. But it is a profound misunderstanding to gauge the effect of acquired deafness by its impact on those ends. The ability to communicate is crucial for self-esteem and the esteem of others in its own right, not just as an aid to achieving the various things by which people usually measure their success or satisfaction. Our everyday ways of measuring success or satisfaction depend on the assumption that fundamental abilities, such as basic communication, can be taken for granted. When the assumption fails, new issues arise which can dwarf the ones we usually stress. As the song says, "You don't know what you've got till it's gone".

The second of the themes to be considered in some depth has been labelled malinteraction by hearing people. It is emphatically "by" hearing people, not "with" hearing people. The point is that people who score high on this factor report that hearing people behave in ways that at best lack insight. Concretely, their questionnaire responses indicate that hearing people ignore them in conversation; don't repeat things to help them understand; speak to them through a third party; and use exaggerated gestures and mouth movements instead of speaking normally. More globally, they report feeling that hearing people underestimate them, and can't be bothered with them. It is of special interest for us that they also report hearing people don't understand what they say.

The factor scores for this theme are predicted by the regression using social and audiological variables, though not particularly well ($r^2 = 0.292$, $p = 0.012$). The only individual variable whose contribution comes close to significance is marital status (t = 1.98, p = 0.052). Those who are married tend to report this kind of malinteraction more than those who are not. This is consistent with the earlier point that marriage tends to decrease communicative deprivation. It points towards the reasonable conclusion that marriage has a mixture of positive and negative consequences.

Table 13.8 shows scores on part-B items associated with the factor. They are generally comparable with the scores for the previous factor, and between them the two incorporate the great majority of the items which a substantial proportion of informants report have a very bad effect on their lives.

Table 13.8 Percentage of informants giving each response type to part B questions associated with the factor "malinteraction by hearing people"

effect on life if hearing people...	very good	good	little/ none	bad	very bad
can't be bothered with them	0	0	32	45	23
ignore them in conversation	0	0	33	44	23
don't repeat things	1	3	36	40	21
do/don't underestimate them	1	0	37	42	19
use exaggerated gestures etc.	0	7	45	33	15
speak through a third party	0	4	53	23	19
do /don't understand what they say	5	4	60	23	7

Malinteraction by hearing people is a theme which comes through the interviews as well as the questionnaire. It is often voiced in very general terms: "You meet people that don't have time for you"; they "will not give you a conversation"; when "people think you're deaf, they don't want to talk to you." There are also recurring judgements about the way hearing people regard those who have hearing problems. The most frequently mentioned belief is that "Hearing people think you're stupid" or as one person put it "They think you're brainless".

Several specific forms of problem are mentioned. People forget that lip-reading depends on being seen, so as one lipreader points out: "Whenever they turn their face away, words are a jumble". When they fail to understand, informants report that people laugh at their mistakes, are impatient with them, shout at them, and tell them to "forget it." Having to repeat conversation is a particular source of difficulty. As put by one informant: "You get tired of asking people to repeat themselves ... they get annoyed when you keep asking them". There are also subtler kinds of problem. One informant points out that even when there is no overtly negative behaviour, hearing people tend not to make positive moves that could facilitate interaction: "Deaf people have to take a first step towards making conversation with hearing people ... I have found that myself ... it's more or less up to me to project myself than for them to project towards me". On a similar level, support which is critical may not be given. An informant explains that "The deaf person has to come out of his shell". He continues "I don't think I'm out of mine yet, but I'm trying to get out of it. Having gone out, you've made the effort, give him (the deaf person) encouragement".

In keeping with the formal data, a relatively high proportion of malinteractions are reported within the circles of family and friends. For example informants comment that "My son, he gets fed up repeating" and "when my husband had been talking to me, I would have had to ask him what he said, he lost his temper and he would say 'Never Bother'!"

Several comments make explicit links between this kind of experience and more general consequences. One lady comments on the sense of isolation: "They don't seem to bring you into the conversation. You're more or less isolated, it hurts". Another outcome is withdrawal. As one informant comments: "I avoid company like the plague, it embarrasses me, it embarrasses them". Several informants describe a direct connection between malinteraction and depression. As explained by one man : "You get a wee bit depressed, especially if you're in company, and they're talking, you're left out. They don't mean to do it but they have to stop and tell you what the conversation is about".

Some informants condemn hearing people for what they see as rudeness and impatience. However at least as many are very aware of the other person's point of view. As explained by one informant:

> They would deny this but they do avoid you, because it is a trouble to have someone like me in the company. They have to stop to explain what's being said ... even your best friends get weary of it and they do tend not to bother ... People I've known all my life ... you see after a while that they are tired in so much as they are responsible to keep you in touch with the proceedings and it spoils their enjoyment.

Another says:

> I would imagine that it takes a bit of effort on their part to repeat things to someone who can't hear too well, to go out of their way to face that person ... .it's very hard for them to get a response, because when you

can't hear something perhaps you might pretend that you do hear and give the wrong response signal and then people don't think you're getting the message ... eventually you will drop out or they will drift away.

Another is of the opinion that "You can't expect people to tell you everything that's going on for people have to concentrate themselves". Several informants comment that hearing people are embarrassed because they don't know what to do.

There is a temptation to write off negative comments about hearing people as embittered misperceptions, attempts to blame other people instead of accepting one's own disability. That kind of interpretation may well underlie the claim that deafness leads to paranoia, which is often made but not borne out by formal research (see e.g. Thomas 1981: 226–227). That is not the picture which emerges from the interviews, particularly not from the kinds of comment that were cited in the previous paragraph. The picture which emerges is of a genuine problem: hearing people need to make special efforts to interact successfully with deafened people, and they often do not.

Undoubtedly this evidence highlights moral questions: What are the obligations of a person who does not have disabilities to a person who does? How honest is our society's claim to care for the disadvantaged, and what does dishonesty in this respect mean for people who discover it when they become disadvantaged? It would be self-deception to pretend that these questions did not arise. However the questions need to be faced properly, not used as rhetorical devices. In particular it would be utterly wrong to pass casual judgement on people who are in daily contact with a deafened person and share the burden of the disability.

There is, however, another, less intractable implication of the evidence. Hearing people are participants in the phenomenon of deafness, and it should be a serious concern for research to consider measures which make them more likely to react positively and appropriately to a deafened person. If speech abnormalities increase the likelihood of negative reactions which we know have a major bearing on deafened people's well-being, then they should be taken very seriously.

Table 13.9 shows the items with substantial loadings on the last factor, which we have called benefit from positive experiences. The point which stands out immediately is that in almost every case the majority of responses are positive. Hence our basic interpretation of the factor is that it singles out at one extreme those who are able to derive benefit and encouragement from at least some experiences; and at the other, those for whom very little is outright positive.

Table 13.9 Percentage of informants giving each response type to part B questions
associated with the factor "benefit from positive experiences"

effect on life of ...	very good	good	little/ none	bad	very bad
having an enjoyable conversation	52	34	10	3	1
people repeating to help understand	22	38	23	14	3
people not noticing they are deaf	18	29	37	8	8
old friends including them in activity	7	11	64	14	4
religious feelings	27	14	49	5	4
understanding human nature better	8	40	40	11	1
feeling people do (or don't) make as much allowance as can be expected	5	29	36	26	4
feeling people do (or do"t) behave better when they know you are deaf	1	27	41	21	10
people understanding speech	5	4	60	23	7

The literature is curiously silent on things that give deafened people happiness, but perhaps the first two in the table are taken for granted. The third is related to themes which are discussed at length, "passing" as hearing and disclosing hearing loss (e.g. Jones 1987: 131–139; Orlans 1987: 97–99), but it does not seem to be considered that "passing" may be a source of enjoyment. Keeping contact with old friends might be foreseen as a major source of pleasure, and for some it is. However it is distinctly double edged. Interviews indicate that for some it is a bitter reminder, and for some it is a painful obligation which involves pretending to enjoy social events which are completely inappropriate for a deafened person.

The next group of items raises a theme which is scarcely contemplated in the academic literature on deafness, though it comes through in self-accounts with some regularity. It hinges on attention to moral and religious issues. It makes perfect sense that these issues should become more important, particularly as a source of uplift, when people are denied fulfilment by routes that are more conventional in contemporary Western society. The evidence strongly suggests that that does happen.

The importance of religious life is absolutely clear from the questionnaire. Over a quarter of the informants report that their religion makes their lives much better, making religion the second greatest source of very positive experience. The theme also comes through in the interviews. One man describes how "I more or less pushed the depression out of the way, I had religious faith and it helped me". Several of our informants have very deep commitments to the church – for instance, at the time of writing one of them is in India working voluntarily (and without pay) on a church project. Our figures presumably reflect the fact that Northern Ireland remains a strongly religious community anyway, but informal experience suggests that strong religious commitment is a feature of deafened people's lives elsewhere too.

A related source of support is philosophical. Informants see their handicap as an incentive to achieve a kind of moral balance and insight that ordinary life does not demand. So one informant describes himself as having become "a caring person" and is ashamed of neglecting other hearing-impaired people he met earlier in life. Others say that deafness has made them more "observant, patient and understanding of other people." Informants also describe voluntary work, some making a considerable committment to helping people with hearing losses which are more disabling than their own.

A somewhat different philosophical theme also comes through, that is coming to terms intellectually and emotionally with the problems that one faces. A major issue in this area is coming to terms with the way hearing people behave. It has already been mentioned that informants regularly express understanding of behaviour which causes them distress. The questionnaire responses indicate directly that informants feel they benefit from achieving a sympathetic view of hearing people, and a similar feeling is implicit in the fact that a considerable number of respondents claim to have gained by achieving a better understanding of human nature. Some informants go further. One restates a classical response to the problem of pain: "One single light with this handicap is to show others how things can be overcome and what a horrible world it would be if everybody was normal. People would become harder if they didn't see deafness and blindness about."

Several other sources of reinforcement which are not reflected in the questionnaire come through in the interviews. A few, strikingly few, mentioned "seeing the funny side." Another, more widespread strategy is comparison with other disabilities. As explained by one informant "Thinking of the agony of those people and never a word of them, it lifts my gloom". For another, comparison with blind people is a reminder that "it would be worse if you lost your sight." Two informants recall with obvious emotion the vivid, transforming effect that a hearing aid had on their lives.

It would be misleading not to say that many of these positive notes have negative counterparts. Moral change was not always felt to be for the better. Several informants described becoming less confident and having a lower self esteem. Two people describe "losing part of themselves" in that they are no longer the kind of people they used to be. Some informants describe themselves as being "irritable", "bad tempered" and "nervous" since their deafness onset. Others describe themselves in relation to other people: "I'm a damn' nuisance to them", or "Maybe I'm a selfish person". Some comparisons with other disabled groups have a positive effect, but others focus on the frustration that deafened people "have every other faculty and cannot hear, it does lead to isolation." Others groups are seen as better off: "You can see their ailment and they get a bit of compassion", and they get "more sympathy" from hearing people. The prelingually deaf are felt to suffer less because "what you've never had you never miss." What these points emphasise is the reality of the problems that deafened people face in the philosophical and moral sphere. It is easy to be undermined or embittered by hearing loss, and nobody should belittle adjustments which allow people to transcend that.

The final item in Table 13.9 returns us to the particular theme of this book. About ten per cent of the informants reported that their life was improved by feeling that at least people could understand their speech.

13.4. Discussion

There are some necessary cautions about the methods of this chapter. The construction of the questionnaire affects the factors that can emerge and their relative magnitudes. For instance, the factor of distress over failures in interaction is large partly because the questionnaire contained several items on the theme. Our methodology provides protection against any accusation that the factor's prominence is a self-fulfilling prophecy, since the factor makes a substantial contribution to predicting the indicator variables, and its ability to do that has nothing to do with the number of questions on the theme. However it may be that other factors would have come through had we included more questions which were relevant to them. It is also fair to note that there is some unfairness in the comparison between our factors and socio/audiological variables as predictors of the indicator variables. Our factors and the indicator variables came from the same questionnaire. One would expect a subject's cast of mind as he or she completed the questionnaire to influence answers on both the indicator variables and the items which went to make up the factors. This common element should strengthen the prospects of predicting some questionnaire-based scores from others. This is a real qualification, though it is weakened by the fact that socio/audiological variables did predict some factor scores. That being so, their limited ability to predict overall measures has to be taken seriously.

All this has to be said, but it does not seem to undermine the basic thrust of the argument. The strongest defence is the coherence between the various sources – the interviews, conclusions based on plain percentage responses to the part B questions, and conclusions based on more abstract statistics. Given that, doubts about any one aspect of the method cannot invalidate the general picture.

The focus of the chapter has been on the things that deafened people feel affect their quality of life, for better or worse. The central theme is that it is wrong to impose criteria which are essentially concerned with differentiating among reasonably typical members of society with their full faculties. There are whole dimensions of experience where those individuals lie clustered almost indistinguishably at one end of a continuum. One of the obstacles to understanding deafness is that it can be difficult to see that it might be possible to occupy a very different position on those dimensions, let alone what it might mean.

It is important to stress the need to shift perspective, but it is equally important not to overdo it. Deafened people are not incomprehensible aliens, and it is possible with some guidance and imagination to visualise what their position is like. Deafness does not, as some early accounts tend to suggest, throw a mysterious switch which directly and inescapably distorts the mind. It creates situations of which most people have some experience – humiliating ineptitude at basic tasks, failure by other people to appreciate one's needs, a sense of both emotional and practical confinement, a sense of irreversible loss, and plain lack of communication with other people. Most people experience such situations occasionally and singly. Deafened people do not necessarily experience all of them, but many of them experience more than one to a considerable extent, and they continue without prospect of release. This is a position which it is possible to understand at least intellectually, and the understanding provides some basis for response at least on a personal level.

The focus of the book in general is on speech. The general point above applies to speech: it is wrong to judge what disordered speech means to deafened people as if it were a purely functional device for transmitting lexical items. Speech is an integral part of the communication process, and that process has a psychological significance for deafened people which is far removed from its significance to those who can almost always take effortless communication for granted.

On a specific level, the evidence shows a distinctive place for speech. It is one of the few items that is associated with responses at both extremes, positive and negative. The sense that people can at least understand their speech makes some informants' lives very much better: the impression that people can not makes other informants' lives very much worse. On that basis, and in the overall context of deafened people's experience, it is worth considering what can be done for their speech.

References

Abberton, Evelyn – Adrian Fourcin – Stuart Rosen – J. Walliker – David Howard – Brian
Moore – Ellis Douek – S. Frampton
  1985 "Speech perceptual and productive rehabilitation in electro-cochlear stimulation", in: Robert Schindler – Michael Merzenich (eds.), 527–537.
Abberton, Evelyn – Ann Parker – Adrian Fourcin
  1983 "Speech improvement in deaf adults using laryngograph displays", in: J. Pickett (ed.), 171–188.
Abrahams, Pat
  1972 "The effects of deafness", *Hearing* 27, 9: 260–263.
Ainsworth, Bill – David Lindsay
  1984 "Identification and discrimination of Halliday's primary tones", *Proceedings of the Institute of Acoustics* 6: 379–383.
Anderson, Bo
  1980 "On becoming and being a deafened adult", *Proceedings of The 1st International Congress of the Hard of Hearing*. Hamburg: 70–73.
Anderson, John
  1990 *Cognitive psychology and its implications*. (3rd edition.) New York: W. H. Freeman.
Ashley, Jack
  1985 "A personal account", in: H. Orlans (ed.), 59–70.
Baddeley, Alan
  1986 *Working memory*. Oxford: Oxford University Press.
Bailey, Peter
  1983 "Hearing for speech: the information transmitted in normal and impaired speech", in: Mark Lutman – Mark Haggard (eds.), 1–34.
Ball, Virginia – Andrew Faulkner
  1989 "Speech production of postlingually deafened adults using electrical and acoustic speech pattern prostheses", *Speech, Hearing and Language: Work in Progress*, University College London, 3: 13–32.
Ball, Virginia – Andrew Faulkner – Adrian Fourcin
  1990 "Effects of fundamental frequency and speech feedback on voice production in postlingually profoundly deafened adults", *British Journal of Audiology* 24: 393–409.
Ball, Virginia – K. Ison
  1984 "Speech production with electro-cochlear stimulation", *British Journal of Audiology* 18: 251.
Banfai, P. – A. Carczag – Sr. Petra Luers
  1984 "Clinical results: the rehabilitation", *Acta Otolaryngology,* supplement 411: 183–194.

Beagon, Frances
   1989   The role of speech variables in the assessment of the linguistic competence of the hearing-impaired. [Undergraduate thesis, School of Psychology, The Queen's University Belfast.]
Beattie, J.
   1981   Social aspects of acquired hearing loss in adults. [Unpublished Ph.D. dissertation, University of Bradford, UK.]
Bedford, A. – G. Foulds
   1978   *The personal distress inventory and scales.* Windsor, Berks: NFER (National Foundation for Educational Research).
Bergman, Moe
   1952   "Special Methods of Audiological Training of Adults", *Acta Otolaryngology* 40: 336–345.
Berry, G.
   1933   "The psychology of progressive deafness", *Journal of The American Medical Association* 101: 1599–1603.
Bilger, R.
   1977   "Psychoacoustic evaluation of present prostheses", *Annals Otology Rhinology and Laryngology* 86, supplement 38: 92–140.
Binnie, Carl – Raymond Daniloff – Hugh Buckingham
   1982   "Phonetic disintegration in a five-year-old following sudden hearing loss", *Journal of Speech and Hearing Disorders* 47: 181–189.
Bishop, Milo – Robert Ringel
   1973   "Orosensory perception, speech production and deafness", *Journal of Speech and Hearing Research* 16: 257–266.
Blood, Gordon – Ingrid Blood – J. Danhauer
   1974   "Listeners' impressions of speakers with and without hearing losses", *Journal of the Acoustic Society of America* 61: S 58.
Blood, Gordon – Blair Mahan – Melvin Hyman
   1979   "Judging personality and appearance from voice disorders", *Journal of Communication Disorders* 12: 63–68.
Boothroyd, Arthur – Laurie Hanin – Larry Medwetsky
   1988   Speech production changes in cochlear implantees. [unpublished ms.]
Bower, Tom
   1979   *Human development.* San Francisco: W. H. Freeman.
Brandt, John – Kenneth Ruder – Thomas Shipp Jr.
   1969   "Vocal loudness and effort in continuous speech", *Journal of the Acoustical Society of America* 46: 1543–1548.
Brankin, Adrienne
   1985   Attitudes towards the adolescent hearing-impaired based on their speech and video presentation. [Undergraduate thesis, School of Psychology, Queen's University Belfast.]
Braud, C. – E. Braud – C. Boudreaux – N.Steger – D. Mecklenburg – E. Tobey
   1987   Influence of cochlear prosthesis upon vowels produced in context. Paper presented at the annual convention of the American Speech-Language-Hearing Association, New Orleans, LA.

Breed, P. – T. Mous
n.d.   Sudden loss of hearing: a specific problem. [Unpublished manuscript.]
Breed, P. – A. van den Horst – T. Mous
1980   "Psychosocial problems in suddenly deafened adolescents and adults", *Proceedings of The First International Congress of Hard of Hearing*, Hamburg: 313–319.
Brown, Gillian – Karen Currie – Joanne Kenworthy
1980   *Questions of intonation*. London: Croom Helm.
Brown, William
1978   *Belfast category norms 1971–1977*. Belfast: Department of Psychology.
Bunting, C.
1981   *Public attitudes to deafness: a survey carried out on behalf of the Department of Health and Social Security*. London: HMSO.
Butterworth, Brian (ed.)
1980   *Language production; speech and talk.* (volume 1) London: Academic Press.
Carney, Arlene – Jack Gandour – Soranee Petty – Amy Robbins – Wendy Myres – Richard Miyamoto
1988   "The effects of adventitious deafness on the perception and production of the voice onset time in Thai; a case study", *Language and Speech* 31, 3: 273–282.
Carterette, Edward – Morton Friedman (eds.)
1976   *Handbook of perception VII: Language and speech.* New York: Academic Press.
Colley, Ann
1989   "Cognitive motor skills", in: Dennis Holding (ed.), (second edition.), 229–248.
Collins, M.
1979   "Fundamental frequency and formant structure in deaf speech: influence of a hearing aid in a case study", *Journal of The Acoustical Society of America* 65, supplement 1: 569.
Cooper, H. – L. Carpenter – W. Alesky – C. Booth – T. Read – J. Graham – J. Fraser
1989   "UCH/RNID Single channel extra cochlear implant: results in thirty profoundly deafened adults", *Journal of Laryngology and Othology*, supplement 18: 22–38.
Cowie, Roddy
1985   "Reading errors as clues to the nature of reading", in: Andrew Ellis (ed.), 73–107.
1987a   "The new orthodoxy in visual perception I: reassessing what makes environments perceivable", *Irish Journal of Psychology* 8: 50–60.
1987b   "The new orthodoxy in visual perception II: conjectures and doubts about internal processes", *Irish Journal of Psychology* 8: 99–110.
1988b   "The dimensions of acquired hearing loss", in: Roddy Cowie (ed.), 1–12.
Cowie, Roddy (ed.)
1988a   *Coping with acquired hearing loss*. Belfast: Department of Health and Social Services.
Cowie, Roddy – Ellen Douglas-Cowie
1983   "Speech production in profound postlingual deafness", in: Mark Lutman – Mark Haggard (eds.), 183–231.

Cowie, Roddy – Ellen Douglas-Cowie – Joan Rahilly
  1988   "The intonation of adults with postlingually acquired profound deafness: anomalous frequency and distribution of elements", in Bill Ainsworth – John Holmes (eds.), *Proceedings of SPEECH '88, 7th FASE Symposium*, Edinburgh, vol. 2: 481–487.
Cowie, Roddy – Ellen Douglas-Cowie – Patricia Stewart
  1986   "A response to Goehl and Kaufman (1984)", *Journal of Speech and Hearing Disorders* 51: 183–185.
Cowie, Roddy – Lorraine Gailey – Marie-Louise McCorry – Rosie Burns
  1982   "Speechreading: structure and variation in a skill", *Journal of the Northern Ireland Speech and Language Forum* 8: 57–69.
Cowie, Roddy – Patricia Stewart
  1986   "What deafened people say about coping with deafness", *Bulletin of the British Psychological Society* 39, 1986: A37.
  1987   "Acquired deafness and the family: a problem for psychologists", *Irish Journal of Psychology* 8: 138–154.
Creegan, Dennis
  1966   "Adapt or succcumb", in: Paul Hunt (ed.), *Stigma: the experience of disability.* London: Geoffrey Chapman.
Crystal, David
  1969   *Prosodic systems and intonation in English*. Cambridge: Cambridge University Press.
Currie, Karen
  1980   "An initial 'search for tonics'", *Language and Speech* 23: 329–350.
Cutler, Ann (ed.)
  1981   "Slips of the tongue and language production", *Linguistics*, special issue 19, 7 and 8: 561–847.
Darwin, Christopher
  1976   "The perception of speech", in: Edward Carterette – Morton Friedman (eds.), 175–226.
Davis, Adrian
  1983   "Hearing disorders in the population: first phase findings of the National Survey of Hearing", in: Mark Lutman – Mark Haggard (eds.), 35–60.
  1989   "The prevalence of hearing impairment and reported hearing disability among adults in Great Britain", *International Journal of Epidemiology* 18: 911–917.
Davis, Hallowell – Richard Silverman
  1978   *Hearing and Deafness*. (4th edition.) New York: Holt, Rinehart and Winston.
Davison, Collette
  1979   Attitudes towards the hearing-impaired based on their speech. [Thesis for the degree of M. Sc. Developmental and Educational Psychology, Department of Psychology, Queen's University Belfast.]
Denmark, John
  1969   "The psychiatrist's contribution", *Proceedings of the Royal Society of Medicine* 62: 965–967.

Denes, Peter – Elliot Pinson
  1973 *The Speech Chain: The Physics and Biology of Spoken Language.* New York: Anchor Books, Anchor Press/Doubleday.
Dodd, Barbara
  1976 "The phonological systems of deaf children", *Journal of Speech and Hearing Disorders* 41: 185–198.
Dodd, Barbara – Ruth Campbell (eds.)
  1987 *Hearing by eye: The psychology of lip-reading.* London: Lawrence Erlbaum.
Doster, Leslie
  n.d. Speech after profound hearing loss. [Unpublished manuscript, Department of Communicative Disorders, University of Central Florida]
Douglas-Cowie, Ellen
  1978 "Linguistic code-switching in a Northern Irish village: social interaction and social ambition", in: Peter Trudgill (ed.), 37–51.
  1984 "The sociolinguistic situation in Northern Ireland", in: Peter Trudgill (ed.), 533–545.
Douglas-Cowie, Ellen – Roddy Cowie
  1979 "Speaking without hearing", *Journal of the Northern Ireland Speech and Language Forum* 4: 54–70.
  1984 "Sociolinguistics: a frame of reference", *Journal of the Northern Ireland Speech and Language Forum* 10: 89–104.
Douglas-Cowie, Ellen – Roddy Cowie – Patricia Stewart
  1987 "Understanding Speech Deterioration in Acquired Deafness", in Jim Kyle (ed.), 65–79.
Dowell, Richard – Peter Seligman – Lesley Whitford
  1990 Speech perception with the 22-channel cochlear prosthesis: A summary of ten years development. Oral Paper to Conference on Tactile Aids, Hearing Aids and Cochlear Implants, National Acoustics Laboratory, Sydney, Australia (Proceedings forthcoming).
Drew, G. C. – W. P. Colquhoun – Hazel Long
  1958 "Effects of small doses of alcohol on a skill resembling driving", *British Medical Journal* 5103: 993–999.
East, C. – H. Cooper
  1986 "Extra-cochlear implants: the patients' viewpoint", *British Journal of Audiology* 20: 55–59.
Edwards, John
  1979 "Judgements and confidence reactions to disadvantaged speech", in: Howard Giles – Robert St. Clair (eds.), 22–43.
Ellis, Andrew (ed.)
  1985 *Progress in the psychology of Language 1.* London: Lawrence Erlbaum.
Ellis, Andrew – Geoff Beattie
  1986 *The psychology of language and communication.* New York: Guildford Press.
Engelmann, Larry – Kathleen Waterfall – J. Hough
  1981 "Results following cochlear implantation and rehabilitation", *Laryngscope* 91, 2: 1821–1833.

Erber, Norman
    1987   "Electronic simulation of hearing loss: developing speech communication skills in family and friends", in: Jim Kyle (ed.), 55–64.
Espir, Michael – Clifford Rose
    1976   *The basic neurology of speech.* (2nd edition.) Oxford: Blackwell.
Finney, J.
    1977   Progressive hearing loss in adulthood: implications for the family. [Unpublished MSc thesis, University of York, UK.]
Fodor, Jerry
    1983   *The Modularity of Mind.* Cambridge, Mass: MIT/Batsford.
Fourcin, Adrian – Ellis Douek – Brian Moore – Stuart Rosen – John Walliker – David Howard – Evelyn Abberton – S. Frampton
    1983   "Speech perception with promontory stimulation", *Annals of the New York Academy of Sciences* 405: 209–294.
Frick, R.
    1985   "Communicating emotion: the role of prosodic features", *Psychological Review* 97: 412–419.
Gailey, Lorraine
    1981   The speechreading process in normal hearing adults: Indications from consistency and variability in performance across verbal materials. [Unpublished Ph.D. dissertation, School of Psychology, Queen's University Belfast.]
    1987   "Psychological parameters of lip-reading skill", in: Barbara Dodd – Ruth Campbell (eds.), 115–141.
Garber, Sharon – Karlind Moller
    1979   "The effects of feedback filtering on nasalisation in normal and hypernasal speakers", *Journal of Speech and Hearing Research* 22: 321–333.
Gathercole, Susan
    1987   "Lip-reading: Implications for theories of short-term memory", in: Barbara Dodd – Ruth Campbell (eds.), 227–241.
Giles, Howard
    1979   "Sociolinguistics and social psychology: an introductory essay", in: Howard Giles – Robert St. Clair (eds.), 1–20.
Giles, Howard – Peter Powesland
    1975   *Speech style and social evaluation.* London: Academic Press.
Giles, Howard – Robert St. Clair (eds.)
    1979   *Language and social psychology.* Oxford: Blackwell.
Giles, Howard – C. Sassoon
    1983   "The effect of speakers' accent, social class background and message style on British listeners' social judgements", *Language and Communication* 3: 305–313.
Glendinning, Frank
    1982   *Acquired hearing loss and elderly people.* University of Keele: Beth Johnson Foundation and the Department of Adult Education
Gobl, Christopher
    1989   "A preliminary study of acoustic voice quality correlates", *Speech Transmission Laboratory Stockhlom, Quarterly Progress and Status Report* 4: 9–22.

Goehl, Henry – Diana Kaufman
    1984   "Do the effects of adventitious deafness include disordered speech?", *Journal of Speech and Hearing Disorders* 49: 58–64.
    1986   "The Real Thing: A reply to Cowie, Douglas-Cowie and Stewart", *Journal of Speech and Hearing Disorders* 51: 185–187.
Goffman, Erving
    1968   *Stigma: notes on the management of spoiled identity.* Harmondsworth: Penguin.
Goodman, Kenneth
    1976   "Reading: a psycholinguistic guessing game", in: Harry Singer – Robert Ruddell (eds.), 259–271.
Gracco, Vincent – James Abbs
    1985   "Dynamic control of the perioral system: kinematic analyses of autogenic and non-autogenic sensorimotor processes", *Journal of Neurophysiology* 54: 418–432.
Greene, Judith
    1986   *Language understanding: a cognitive approach.* Milton Keynes: Open University.
Haggard, Mark
    1983   "New and old concepts of hearing aids", in: Mark Lutman – Mark Haggard (eds.), 232–277.
Hallam, Richard – S. Rachman – Ronald Hinchliffe
    1984   "Psychological aspects of tinnitus", in: S. Rachman (ed.), 31–53.
Halliday, Michael
    1967   *Intonation and grammar in British English.* The Hague: Mouton.
Hammarberg, Britta – B. Fritzell – J. Gauffin – J. Sundberg – L. Wedin
    1980   "Perceptual and acoustic correlates of abnormal voice qualities", *Acta Otolaryngologica* 90: 441–451.
Hardick, Edward
    1976   "Aural rehabilitation programs for the aged can be successful", *Journal of The Aural Rehabilitation Association* 10: 51–67.
Harris, Charles
    1965   "Perceptual adaptation to inverted, reversed and displaced vision", *Psychological Review* 72: 419–444.
Harris, Kathleen
    1970   "Physiological aspects of articulatory behaviour", *Haskins Laboratory Status Reports on Special Research* 23: 49–67.
Hazell, Jonathan – S. Wood – H. Cooper – Dafydd Stephens – A. Corcoran – Robert Coles – J. Baskill – J.Sheldrake
    1985   "A clinical study of tinnitus maskers", *British Journal of Audiology* 19: 65–146.
Heath, Alison
    1987   "The deafened: a special group", in: Jim Kyle (ed.), 163–168.
Hinchliffe, Ronald
    1983   *Hearing and balance in the elderly.* London: Churchill Livingstone.
Holding, Dennis (ed.),
    1981   *Human skills.* (1st edition.) Chichester: John Wiley and Sons.

Holding, Dennis (ed.),
  1989   *Human skills.* (2nd edition.) Chichester: John Wiley and Sons.
Holding, Dennis
  1989   "Final survey", in: Dennis Holding (ed.), 281–292.
Hood, R. – R. Dixon
  1969   "Physical characteristics of speech rhythm of deaf and normal hearing speakers", *Journal of Communication Disorders* 2: 20–28.
Horii, Yoshiyuki
  1982   "Some voice fundamental frequency characteristics of oral reading and spontaneous speech by hard of hearing young women", *Journal of Speech and Hearing Research* 25: 608–610.
House, William
  1978   "The clinical value of single-electrode systems in auditory prosthesis", *Otolaryngology Clinic of North America* 11: 201–208.
Hull, Raymond
  1977   *Hearing impairment among aging persons.* Lincoln, Nebraska: Cliffs Notes, Inc.
Hurst, Melanie – Eugene Cooper
  1982   "Employer attitudes towards stuttering", *Journal of Fluency Disorders* 8: 1–12.
Izdebski, Krzysztof
  1980   "Long-term-average spectra (LTAS) applied to analysis of spastic dysphonia", in: V. Lawrence – B. Weinberg (eds.), 89–94.
James, William
  1890   *The Principles of Psychology.* New York: Holt.
John, J. – J. Howarth
  1965   "The effect of time distortions on the intelligibility of deaf children's speech", *Language and Speech* 8: 127–134.
Jones, Austin
  1969   "Stimulus-seeking behaviour", in: John Zubek (ed.), 167–206.
Jones, Lesley
  1987   "Living with hearing loss", in: Jim Kyle (ed.), 126–139.
Jones, Lesley – Jim Kyle
  1984   In or out of the circle? Family relationships and loss of hearing in early adult life. Paper presented at the 2nd International Congress of The Hard of Hearing, Stockholm.
Kalin, R. – D. Rayko
  1980   "The social significance of speech in the Job Interview", in: Robert St. Clair – Howard Giles (eds.), 39–50.
Kaplan, Harriet
  1985   "Benefits and limitations of amplification and speechreading for the elderly", in: Harold Orlans (ed.), 85–98.
Kaufman, Diana – Henry Goehl
  1985   " Belief and evidence: a reply to Zimmermann and Collins", *Journal of Speech and Hearing Disorders* 50: 221–223.

Kelso, Scott – Betty Tuller – E.Vatikoitis -Bateson – Carol Fowler
  1984   "Functionally specific articulatory cooperation following jaw perturbations during speech: evidence for coordinative structures", *Journal of Experimental Psychology: Human Perception and Performance* 10: 812–832.

Kinney, Charles
  1948   "Loss of speech due to meningitic deafness", *Archives of Otolaryngology* 47: 303–309.

Kirchner, John – Masafumi Susuki
  1968   "Laryngeal reflexes and voice production", *Annals of New York Academy of Science* 155: 98–129.

Kirk, Karen – Bradly Edgerton
  1983   "Effects of cochlear implant use on voice parameters comment", *Otolaryngologic Clinics of North America* 16: 281–292.

Kishon-Rabin, Liat – Laurie Hanin – Arthur Boothroyd
  1990   Lipreading enhancement by a spatial tactile display of fundamental frequency. Oral Paper to Conference on Tactile Aids, Hearing Aids and Cochlear Implants, National Acoustics Laboratory, Sydney, Australia (Proceedings forthcoming).

Knapp, Mark
  1978   *Nonverbal communication in human interaction.* (2nd edition.) New York: Holt, Rinehart and Winston.

Knapp, P.
  1948   "Emotional aspects of hearing loss", *Psychosomatic Medicine* 10: 203–222.

Kolers, Paul
  1970   "Three stages of reading", in: H. Levin and J. Williams (eds.), 90–118.

Krebs, John – Nicholas Davies (eds.)
  1984   *Behavioural ecology: An evolutionary approach.* Oxford: Blackwell.

Krebs, John – Robin McCleery
  1984   "Optimization in behavioural ecology", in: John Krebs – Nicholas Davies (eds.), 91–121.

Kyle, Jim
  1985   "Deaf people: Assessing the community or the handicap?", *Bulletin of The British Psychological Society* 38: 137–141.

Kyle, Jim – Lesley Jones – Peter Wood
  1985   "Adjustment to acquired hearing loss: a working model", in: Harold Orlans (ed.), 119–138.

Kyle, Jim (ed.)
  1987   *Adjustment to acquired hearing loss.* Bristol: Centre for Deaf Studies.

Lambert, Wallace
  1979   "Language as a factor in intergroup relations", in: Howard Giles – Robert St. Clair (eds.), 186–192.

Lane, Harlan – Bernard Tranel
  1971   "The Lombard sign and the role of hearing in speech", *Journal of Speech and Hearing Research* 14: 677–709.

Lane, Harlan – Jane Webster
  1991   "Speech deterioration in postlingually deafened adults", *Journal of The Acoustical Society of America* 89, 2: 859–866.

Lane, Harlan – Joe Perkell – Mario Svirsky – Jane Webster
    1991   "Changes in speech breathing following cochlear implant in postlingually deaf-
            ened adults", *Journal of Speech and Hearing Research* 34: 526–533.
Laver, John
    1980   *The phonetic description of voice quality.* Cambridge: Cambridge University
            Press.
Lawrence, V. – B. Weinberg (eds.)
    1980   *Transcripts of the ninth symposium: Care of the professional voice.* part 1.
            New York: The Voice Foundation.
Leder, Steven – Jaclyn Spitzer
    1990   "A perceptual evaluation of the speech of adventitiously deaf adult males", *Ear
            and Hearing* 11, 3: 169–175.
Leder, Steven – Jaclyn Spitzer – Cameron Kirchner
    1987   "Speaking fundamental frequency of postlingually profoundly deaf men", *An-
            nals of Otology, Rhinology and Laryngology* 96: 322–324.
Leder, Steven – Jaclyn Spitzer – Cameron Kirchner – Carole Flevaris-Phillips –
Paul Milner – Frederick Richardson
    1987b   "Speaking rate of adventitiously deaf male cochlear implant candidates and nor-
            mal-hearing adult males", *Journal of The Acoustical Society of America* 82:
            843–846.
Leder, Steven – Jaclyn Spitzer – Paul Milner – Carole Flevaris-Phillips – Cameron
Kirchner – Frederick Richardson
    1987a   "Voice intensity of prospective cochlear-implant candidates and normal-hearing
            adult males", *Laryngoscope* 97: 224–227.
Leder, Steven – Jaclyn Spitzer – Paul Milner – Carole Flevaris-Phillips –
Frederick Richardson – Cameron Kirchner
    1986   "Reacquisition of contrastive stress in an adventitiously deaf speaker using a sin-
            gle-channel cochlear implant", *Journal of The Acoustical Society of America* 79:
            1967–1974.
Lee, David – Rowleigh Lishman – James Thomson
    1982   "Regulation of gait in long jumping", *Journal of Experimental Psychology: Hu-
            man Perception and Performance* 8: 448–459.
Levelt, Willem – Giovanni Flores D'Arcais (eds.)
    1978   *Studies in the perception of language.* Chichester: John Wiley.
Levin, Harry – Joanna Williams (eds.)
    1970   *Basic studies on reading.* New York: Basic Books Inc..
Lieberman, Philip
    1967   *Intonation, perception and language.* Harvard, Massachusetts: MIT Press.
Lind, E. – W. O'Barr
    1979   "The social significance of speech in the courtroom", in: Howard Giles – Robert
            St. Clair, 66–87.
Ling, Daniel
    1976   *Speech and the hearing impaired child: Therapy and practice.* Washington, DC:
            The Alexander Graham Bell Association for the Deaf Inc.

Littlejohns, Peter – A. John
1987 "Auditory rehabiliatation in an elderly population", in: Jim Kyle (ed.), 28–36.
Luchsinger, Richard – Godfrey Arnold
1965 *Voice, speech, language*. London: Constable.
Lutman, Mark – Mark Haggard (eds.)
1983 *Hearing science and hearing disorders*. London: Academic Press.
Lyxell, Bjorn – Jerker Ronnberg
1987a "Guessing and speechreading", *British Journal of Audiology* 21: 13–20.
1987b "Cognitive determinants for speechreading skills", in: Jim Kyle (ed.), 48–54.
MacNeilage, Peter – J. de Clerk
1964 "Typing errors as clues to serial ordering mechanisms in language behaviour", *Language and Speech* 7: 144–159.
MacNeilage, Peter – Peter Ladefoged
1976 "The Production of Speech and Language", in: Edward Carterette – Morton Friedman (ed.), 75–120.
Massaro, Dominic
1987 "Speech perception by ear and eye", in: Barbara Dodd – Ruth Campbell (eds.), 53–83.
Maurer, James – Ralph Rupp
1979 *Hearing and aging: tactics for intervention*. New York: Grune and Stratton.
McCall, Rosemary
1984 *Speechreading and listening tactics: a guide for self help*. London: Robert Hale.
McCartney, Brian
1980 "The psychology of the hard of hearing – which world do I belong in?", in: *Proceedings of the 1st International Congress of the Hard of Hearing*, Hamburg: 12–26. McClelland, James – David Rummelhart
1981 "An interactive activation model of context effects in letter perception: part 1. An account of basic findings", *Psychological Review* 88: 375–407.
McDaid, Michaela
1987 Attitudes towards the hearing impaired, based on a naturalistic interpersonal situation.[B.A. Thesis, Department of Psychology, Queen's University Belfast.]
McGurk, Harry – John McDonald
1976 "Hearing lips and seeing voices", *Nature* 264: 746–748.
McKay, Donald
1970 "Spoonerisms: the structure of errors in the serial ordering of speech", *Neuropsychologia* 8: 323–350.
Meadow-Orlans, Kathryn
1985 "Social and psychological effects of hearing loss in adulthood: a literature review", in: Harold Orlans (ed.), 35–57.
Millar, Sharon
1987 Accent in the classroom, sociolinguistic perspectives on the teaching of elocution in some Belfast secondary-level schools. [Ph.D thesis, Queen's University Belfast.]
Milroy, Jim
1981 *Regional accents of English: Belfast*. Belfast: Blackstaff Press.

Mogford, Kay
    1987   "Lip-reading in the prelingually deaf", in: Barbara Dodd – Ruth Campbell (eds.), 191–211.
Monsen, Randall
    1981   "Speech of the adventitiously deafened", *Progress Report 24, Central Institute for the Deaf Research Department*, 818 South Euclid, St. Louis, U.S.A.
Monsen, Randall
    1983   "The oral speech intelligibility of hearing impaired adults", *Journal of Speech and Hearing Disorders* 48: 286–296.
Morgan-Jones, Ruth
    1987   "Deafness and marriage: aspects of their interaction", in: Jim Kyle (ed.), 182– 195.
Morgon, A. – C. Berger-Vachon – J. Chanel – G. Kalfoun – C. Dubreuil
    1984   "Cochlear implant: experience of the Lyon team", *Acta Otolaryngology,* supplement 411: 195–203.
Myers, Thomas
    1969   "Tolerance for sensory and perceptual deprivation" in: John Zubek (ed.), 289– 331.
Newell, Karl
    1981   "Skill learning", in: Dennis Holding (ed.), 203–225.
Nicholl, Pat
    1981   The social implications of speech deterioration in the post-lingually deaf. [B. A. thesis, Department of Psychology, Queen's University Belfast.]
Norman, Donald
    1981   "Categorisation of action slips", *Psychological Review* 88: 1–15.
Norton, Norma
    1975   "Cochlear implants: initial experience with 15 patients", *Hearing Speech Action* 1975: 16–21.
Noteboom, Sibout – Johannes Brokx – Jacobus de Rooij
    1978   "Contributions of Prosody to Speech Perception", in: W. Levelt – G. Flores D'Arcais (eds.), 75–107.
Oller, Kimbrough – Charleen Kelly
    1974   "Phonological substitution processes of a hard-of-hearing child", *Journal of Speech and Hearing Disorders* 39: 65–74.
Orlans, Harold (ed.)
    1985   *Adjustment to Adult Hearing Loss.* London: Taylor and Francis.
Orlans, Harold
    1987   "Sociable and solitary responses to adult hearing loss", in: Jim Kyle (ed.), 95– 112.
Orlans, Harold – Kathryn Meadow-Orlans
    1985   "Responses to hearing loss: effects on social life, leisure and work", *SHHH Newsletter*, January-February: 5–7.
Osberger, Mary Joe – Harry Levitt
    1977   "The effect of timing errors on the intelligibility of deaf children's speech", *Journal of The Acoustical Society of America* 66, 5: 1316–1324

Osberger, Mary Joe
   1988   "The speech of implanted children", in: Elmer Owens – D. Kessler (eds.), 257–
          281.
Oster, Ann-Marie
   1987   "Some effects of cochlear implantation on speech production", *Speech Trans-
          mission Laboratory Stockholm, Quarterly Progress and Status Report* 1/ 1987:
          81–89.
Owens, Elmer
   1989   "Present status of adults with cochlear implants", in: Elmer Owens – D. Kessler
          (eds.), 25–52.
Owens, Elmer – D. Kessler (eds.),
   1989   *Cochlear Implants in Young Deaf Children*. Boston: Little Brown.
Oyer, E. Jane – B. Paolucci
   1970   "Homemakers' hearing losses and family integration", *Journal of Home
          Economics* 62: 257–262.
Oyer, Herbert – E. Jane Oyer (eds.)
   1976   *Aging and Communication*. Baltimore, London: University Park Press.
Oyer, Herbert – E. Jane Oyer
   1985   " Adult hearing loss and the family", in: Harold Orlans (ed.), 139–154.
Parker, Ann
   1983   "Speech conservation", in: William Watts (ed.), 234–250.
Penn, Jacques
   1955   "Voice and speech patterns in the hard of hearing", *Acta. Otolaryngology*,
          supplement 124.
Perkell, Joe
   1980   "Phonetic features and the physiology of speech production", in: Brian But-
          terworth (ed.), 337–372.
Picheny, M.A. – N.I. Durlach – L.D. Braida
   1986   "Speaking clearly for the hard of hearing II: Acoustic characteristics of clear and
          conversational speech", *Journal of Speech and Hearing Research* 29: 434–446.
Pickett, J. (ed.)
   1983   *Papers from the Research Conference on Speech-Processing Aids for the Deaf*
          Washington DC: Gallaudet College.
Plant, Geoff
   1983   "The effects of a long-term hearing loss on speech production", *Speech Trans-
          mission Laboratory Stockholm, Quarterly Status and Progress Report* 1/ 1983:
          18–35.
Plant, Geoff
   1984   "The effects of an acquired profound hearing loss on speech production", *British
          Journal of Audiology* 18: 39–48.
Plant, Geoff
   1990   Training with single-dual-and multichannel tactile aids. Oral paper to Tactile
          Aids, Hearing Aids and Cochlear Implants Conference, Sydney, Australia. (Pro-
          ceedings forthcoming).

292   *References*

Plant, Geoff – Britta Hammarberg
1983   "Acoustic and perceptual analysis of the speech of the deafened", *Speech Transmission Laboratory Stockholm, Quarterly Progress and Status Report* 2–3/ 1983: 85–107.
Plant, Geoff – Ann-Marie Oster
1986   "The effects of cochlear implanation on speech production", Speech Transmission Laboratory Stockholm, Quarterly Progress and Status Report 1: 65–84.
Quirk, Randolph – Ann Duckworth – Jan Svartvik – Jan Rusiecjki – A. Colin
1964   "Studies in the correspondence of prosodic to grammatical features in English", in: *Proceedings of the Ninth International Congress of Linguistics*. Mouton: The Hague, 679–691.
Rachman, S. (ed.)
1984   *Contributions to medical psychology*, vol. 3. Oxford: Pergamon Press.
Rahilly, Joan
1991   Intonation patterns in postlingually deafened and normal hearing people in Belfast. [Ph.D. dissertation, Queen's University Belfast.]
Ramsdell, Donald
1978   "The psychology of the deafened and hard of hearing adult", in: Hallowell Davis – Richard Silverman, 499–510.
Ramsden, Richard
1981   "Rehabilitation of the suddenly deafened adult", *Ear, Nose and Throat Journal* 60: 49–54.
Read, Theo
1989   "Improvement in speech production following use of the UCH/RNID cochlear implant", *Journal of Laryngology and Otology* supplement 18: 45–49.
Rice, Frank
1984   *Deafness: The social work task*. Social Work Advisory Service. Northern Ireland: Department of Health and Social Services.
Rice, Frank
1988   "The experience of being deaf", in: Roddy Cowie (ed.), 23–28.
Ries, Peter
1985   "The demography of hearing loss", in: Harold Orlans (ed.), 3–22.
Riordan, Carol
1977   "Control of vocal-tract length in speech", *Journal of the Acoustic Society of America* 64: 998–1002.
Rothwell, J. – M. Traub – B. Day – J. Obeso – P. Thomas – C. Marsden
1982   "Manual performance in a deafferented man", *Brain* 105: 515–542.
Salmoni, Alan
1989   "Motor skill learning" in Dennis Holding (ed.) (2nd edition.), 197–228.
Schank, Roger – Robert Abelson
1977   *Scripts, plans, goals, and understanding*. Hillsdale, N.J.: Lawrence Erlbaum.
Scherer, Klaus – Howard Giles
1979   *Social markers in speech*. Cambridge: Cambridge University Press.
Scherer, Klaus
1986   "Vocal affect expression: a review and a model for future research", *Psychological Bulletin* 99: 143–165.

Schindler, Robert – Michael Merzenich (eds.)
  1985   *Cochlear implants.* New York: Raven Press.
Schlesinger, Hilde
  1985   "The Psychology of hearing loss", in: Harold Orlans (ed.), 99–118.
Schmidt, Richard
  1988   *Motor control and learning* (2nd edition.) Champaign, Illinois: Human Kinetics
          Publishers.
Schow, Ronald – John Christensen – John Hutchinson – Michael Nerbonne
  1978   *Communication disorders of the aged: a guide for health professionals.* Bal-
          timore: University Park Press.
Sherrard, Carol – Arthur Still
  n.d.   Postingual deafness and speech production. [Unpublished manuscript]
Siegel, Gerald – Herbert Pick
  1974   "Auditory feedback in the regulation of voice", *Journal of The Acoustical So-
          ciety of America* 56, 5: 1618–1624.
Silverman, E.
  1976   "Listeners' impressions of speakers with lateral lisps", *Journal of Speech and
          Hearing Disorders* 41: 547–552.
Silverman, Richard – Donald Calvert
  1978   "Conservation and development of speech", in: Hallowell Davis – Richard Sil-
          verman, 388–397.
Simon, Claude
  1979   "Suprasegmentals of deaf speech: influence of hearing aid in a case study",
          Journal of The Acoustical Society of America 65: S569.
Singer, Harry – Robert Ruddell (eds.)
  1976   *Theoretical models and processes of reading.* Delaware: International Reading
          Association.
Smith, Clarissa
  1972   Residual hearing and speech production in deaf children. [Ph.D dissertation, The
          City University of New York.] University Microfilms International, Ann Arbor,
          Michigan.
  1975   "Interjected sounds in deaf children's speech", *Journal of Communication Dis-
          orders* 8: 123–128.
St. Clair, Robert – Howard Giles (eds.)
  1980   *The social and psychological contexts of language.* Cambridge: Cambridge Uni-
          versity Press.
Stewart-Kerr, Patricia
  n.d.   The experience of acquired deafness: a psychological perspective. [Ph.D. dis-
          sertation in preparation, Queen's University Belfast.]
Summerfield, Quentin
  1983   "Audio-visual speech perception, lipreading, and artificial stimulation", in:
          Mark Lutman – Mark Haggard (eds.), 132–182.
  1987   "Some preliminaries to a comprehensive account of audio-visual speech per-
          ception", in: Barbara Dodd – Ruth Campbell (eds.), 3–51.

Summers, Jeffrey
    1975   "The role of timing in motor program representation", *Journal of Motor Behavior* 7: 229–241.
Sweeney, Claire
    1991   The cognitive problems posed by lipreading, particularly in regard to the recency effect. [BSc thesis, School of Psychology, Queen's University Belfast.]
Tartter, Vivien – Patricia Chute – Sharon Hellman
    1989   "The speech of a postlingually deafened teenager during the first year of use of a multichannel cochlear implant", *Journal of The Acoustical Society of America* 86: 2113–2121.
Thomas, Alan
    1984   *Acquired hearing loss: psychological and psychosocial implications*. London: Academic Press.
Thomas, Alan – Katia Gilholme-Herbst
    1980   "Social and psychological implications of acquired deafness for adults of employment age", *British Journal of Audiology* 14: 76–85.
Thomas, Alan – Margaret Lamont – Margaret Harris
    1982   "Problems encountered at work by people with severe acquired hearing loss", *British Journal of Audiology* 16: 39–43.
Thomas, Julie
            (personal communication) Speech in recently implanted patients at Queen's Hospital Birmingham: informal observations.
Thornton, A.
    1986   "Estimates of the numbers of patients who might be suitable for cochlear implant procedures", *British Journal of Audiology* 20: 221–229.
Trudgill, Peter (ed.)
    1978   *Sociolinguistic Patterns in British English*. London: Edward Arnold.
    1984   *Language in the British Isles*. Cambridge: Cambridge University Press.
Turnbaugh, Karen – Barry Guitar – Paul Hoffman
    1981   "The attribution of personality traits: the stutterer and the nonstutterer", *Journal of Speech and Hearing Research* 24: 288–299.
Van der Lieth, L.
    1972   "Experimental social deafness", *Scandinavian Audiology* 1: 81–87.
Walden, Brian – Robert Prosek – Allen Montgomery – Charlene Scherr – Carla Jones
    1977   "Effects of training on the visual recognition of consonants", *Journal of Speech and Hearing Research* 20: 130–145.
Waldstein, Robin
    1989   Acoustic characteristics of the speech of the postlingually deafened: implications for the role of auditory feedback during speech production. [Unpublished Ph.D. dissertation, Brown University.]
Waters, Tracey
    1986   "Speech therapy with cochlear implant wearers", *British Journal of Audiology* 20: 35–43.
Watts, William (ed.)
    1983   *Rehabilitation and acquired deafness*. London: Croom Helm.

Welch, R. B.
1978   *Perceptual Modification: Adapting to Altered Sensory Environments*. London: Academic Press.

Wholwill, Joachim – Jack Nasar – David DeJoy – Hossein Foruzani
1976   "Behavioural effects of a noisy environment: task involvement versus passive exposure", *Journal of Applied Psychology* 61: 67–74.

Wilson, Frank – M.Welbank – M.Ussher
1990   "Including customer requirements in the design and development of telecommunications services: the case of videotelephony for people with special needs", *Proceedings of the 13th International Symposium on Human Factors in Telecommunication*, Torino 1990: 171–176.

Wood, Peter – Jim Kyle
1983   "Hospital referral and family adjustment in acquired deafness", *British Journal of Audiology* 17: 175–181.

Wood, Peter – Anthony Turner – Ron Pearl
1986   "The National Association of Deafened People: a survey of membership characteristics." London: The National Association of Deafened People.

Zimmerman, Gerald – Patricia Rettaliata
1981   "Articulatory patterns of an adventitiously deaf speaker: implications for the role of auditory information in speech production", *Journal of Speech and Hearing Research* 24: 169–178.

Zimmerman, Gerald – M. Collins
1985   "The speech of the adventitiously deaf and auditory information: a reply to Goehl and Kaufman (1984)", *Journal of Speech and Hearing Disorders* 50: 220.

Zubek, John (ed.)
1969   *Sensory deprivation: Fifteen years of research*. New York: Appleton-Century-Crofts.

Author Index

Subject Index

Eija Ventola (Editor)

Functional and Systemic Linguistics
Approaches and Uses

1991. XIV, 499 pages. Cloth.
ISBN 3 11 012740 7
(Trends in Linguistics.   Studies and Monographs 55)

Systemic linguistics, which has developed from Firthian linguistics, and such functional approaches to language as, for
example, the Prague School, have always shared common
ground. This collection of 21 original articles captures some of
the newest developments in functional linguistics.

Part I deals with theoretical considerations (dynamic vs.
synoptic/static option, probabilities of systems, the notions of
register, transitivity, and rank).

Part II presents analyses of spoken conversational data,
both from a theoretical and from an applied point of view.
Topics include recoverability, minimal exchanges, evaluative assessments, and discourse skills in patient interactions
and in educational contexts.

Part III centers around analyses of written data and covers
functional theories in teaching writing, various ideologies in
writing and their realization, intertextuality, cohesion and
coherence in texts, and foreign learners' difficulties in academic writing.

Contributors are M. A. K. Halliday, Nils Erik Enkvist,
Frantisek Daneš, John A. Bateman and Cécile L. Paris,
William McGregor, Ronald Geluykens, Amy B. M. Tsui, Jay L.
Lemke, Elke Teich, Eirian Davies, Jonathan Fine, Francis
Christie, Barbara Couture, James R. Martin, Paul J. Thibault,
Gill Francis and Anneliese Kramer-Dahl, Kevin Nwogy and
Thomas Bloor, Michael Hoey, Gerald Parsons, Helen Drury,
Anna Mauranen and Eija Ventola.

mouton de gruyter

Berlin · New York

Richard J. Watts, Sachiko Ide, Konrad Ehlich (Editors)

Politeness in Language
Studies in its History, Theory and Practice

1992. 23 x 15.5 cm. x, 381 pages. Cloth.
ISBN 3-11-013184-6
(Trends in Linguistics. Studies and Monographs 59)

This collection of 13 original papers focusses on the phenomenon of politeness in language.

It presents the most important problems in developing a theory of linguistic politeness, which must deal with the crucial differences between lay notions of politeness in different cultures and the term "politeness" as a concept within a theory of linguistic politeness.

The universal validity of the term itself is called into question, as are models such as those developed by Brown and Levinson, Lakoff, and Leech. New approaches are suggested.

In addition to this theoretical discussion, an empirical section presents a number of case studies and research projects in linguistic politeness. These show what has been achieved within current models and what still remains to be done, in particular with reference to cross-cultural studies in politeness and differences between a Western and a non-Western approach to the subject.

mouton de gruyter

Berlin · New York